TONY ASPLER'S CELLAR BOOK

HOW TO DESIGN,
BUILD, STOCK AND MANAGE
YOUR WINE CELLAR **WHEREVER** YOU LIVE

TONY ASPLER'S
CELLAR BOOK

 Random House Canada

www.randomhouse.ca

Random House Canada and colophon are trademarks.

Library and Archives Canada Cataloguing in Publication

Aspler, Tony, 1939–
    Tony Aspler's cellar book : how to design, build, stock and manage
your wine cellar wherever you live / Tony Aspler.

ISBN 978-0-307-35711-3

    1. Wine cellars. I. Title. II. Title: Cellar book.

TP548.5.A6A86 2009   641.2'2   C2009-901832-2

Page 324 constitutes an extension of this copyright page.

Text design by Andrew Roberts

Printed in the United States of America

10 9 8 7 6 5 4 3 2 1

TO DEBORAH, who can spot a corked wine faster than I can. My constant companion in the wine cellar and everywhere else.

CONTENTS

ACKNOWLEDGMENTS

I had a lot of fun writing this book—and a lot of help from the wine community around the world. I blitzed friends and colleagues with e-mails, shamelessly asking for their advice as well as their wine cellar stories. Such is the generosity of those who love wine that no one refused my requests for information and they willingly shared their own experiences. My thanks to them all. Some are recognized in the body of this book; others I will mention here: John Szabo, M.S., for his insights into restaurant cellar management, wine writer Dean Tudor for his incisive editorial input, Greg Zeisman and Laird Kay at the Wine Establishment for their cellar design expertise, Gary Larose of Rosehill Wine Cellars for his advice on wine cabinets, Marc Russell for his expertise in off-site wine storage and Jacques Marie for his encyclopedic knowledge of wine and food. But most of all, I must thank Michael Drobot and his team at KoolR Products Inc., who came up with an offer I could not refuse: they would build my new wine cellar in the condo basement if they could film the construction process. The answer was yes, in a heartbeat.

During the year and a half it took me to write this book I would lie awake at night thinking of the perfect cellar and what to put into it. This led to the concept of "Tony's Dream Cellar"—a selection of ten or so wines from all the regions I have covered here. It's a very personal choice from what I consider to be the world's best wines. After forty-odd years of chasing the grape around the globe I am still learning about wine and am constantly amazed by the alchemy of great winemakers. Their arcane rituals turn perishable berries into a delicious beverage that can elevate the soul.

In a few years' time my Dream Cellar candidates might be different, but that's the beauty of wine. No doubt you will have your own list, which is only as it should be, since we all taste wine through our own cultural filter. My car licence plate is CLARET, which perhaps tells you that I was brought up in England on red Bordeaux (although some of my best wine experiences have been with Burgundy). But these days I find myself drinking more New World wine. When I moved house in October 2008 I discovered that more than half my cellar was stocked with New World wines. So I would like to thank winemakers everywhere for making life tolerable in bad times and a celebration in good ones.

Finally, I raise a glass to those who guided me on this cellar quest: my literary agent, Dean Cooke, who helped shape the original concept for this book; Anne Collins at Random House Canada, who was intrigued enough to publish it; and my editor, Sarah Brohman, who took an unruly manuscript and moulded it into coherence—which is also the art of the winemaker. Further thanks to Craig Pyette who transformed the manuscript to a book and Gillian Watts who did the heavy lifting with my prose. The photos were taken, for the most part, by my friend Steve Elphick, whose shots also grace the pages of *The Wine Atlas of Canada*. And, finally, a special thank-you to Pinot the Wonder Dog, the wheaten terrier who slept at my feet during those endless hours in front of the computer screen.

"The key to aging is cellaring."

François Labet, the proprietor of Burgundy's Château de La Tour, a property within the walled vineyard of the Clos de Vougeot, whose family owns the largest portion of the vineyard: 15 of the 124 acres.

INTRODUCTION

Anyone who has ever lifted a glass of wine, studied its colour, sniffed its bouquet and savoured the first sip either has a wine cellar or dreams of having one. Call it the oenological imperative.

A wine cellar is not necessarily a damp cave with cobwebs in the bowels of some drafty English country house or a hermetically sealed, temperature-controlled room in a New York condo with five thousand bottles individually racked. A cellar is any collection of wines that you lay down for future drinking—be it a dozen or so bottles in a cardboard carton under the stairs or the contents of a wine fridge in the kitchen. And by *future* I don't necessarily mean ten or fifteen years. I mean a week, a month, a year; it all depends on how you structure your wine drinking.

A wine cellar can be many things: a sanctuary, a museum, a larder, an ego trip. It all depends on how it is perceived and how it is used. This book will tell you everything you want to know about cellaring wine, whether you are a novice with a dozen bottles in the bedroom closet or a dedicated collector with twenty thousand bottles.

There is, of course, a large community of wine drinkers who have yet to learn the delights of owning their own wine cellar. Consider how much time elapses from the point of purchase of a bottle of wine to the pulling of the cork. The average, according to highly anecdotal evidence (eyewitness accounts by store managers), is fifty-four minutes. Most consumers pick up wine on their way home to dinner. They buy it; they drink it. Since a goodly number of forward-thinking wine enthusiasts actually acquire wine to lay down, this average time would suggest that some bottles are opened in parking lots and consumed al fresco from brown paper decanters. This book, I hope, will encourage the fifty-four-minute constituency to consider the benefits of laying wine down; in other words, to create a cellar.

Indulge me by letting me begin with my own experiences in cellaring wines and my relationship with a variety of cellar situations in forty years of wine appreciation. I pose the ultimate existential question—"Why cellar wines?"—which leads into a history of wine storage and a very personal (and non-erotic) account of my lifelong love affair with wine cellars. Then we move into the practical advice: the do's and don'ts of wine storage in a domestic situation, and how to build and manage your own cellar (selecting the site, determining the size and the ultimate design, using software programs designed to catalogue and keep consumption records up to date). I will also tackle the question of alternatives to building a cellar.

But the most important question, of course, is how to stock a cellar. This book provides guidelines for anyone, whether their regular tipple is a $15 Australian or a $500 Grand Cru Classé Bordeaux, who wants to keep on hand a supply of wines that will age with grace and dignity and be there ready to consume for a mid-week dinner or a spontaneous special celebration. The bulk of this book is devoted to my suggestions for general approaches to establishing a cellar. I outline basic techniques for evaluating the right cellar for your needs. But I avoid considering price and, to a certain degree, specific bottles, suggesting instead a themed approach. Are you just getting into the wine game? Do you want an investment cellar that will appreciate in value or an inheritance cellar to hand down to your children? Is it a New World or an Old World cellar for you? Are you more interested in building a collection for sustained consumption over many years, or are most of your favourites from New World vineyards—wines that will likely be consumed in just two to three years?

For example, every cellar should have a bottle of bubbly—a sparkling wine, to use the correct terminology—but are you game for the hundreds of dollars it will take to cellar a Dom Pérignon or a Roederer Cristal? Perhaps a Veuve Clicquot or Pol Roger, more moderately priced, will suit your needs. Or maybe champagne is too rich for your budget. How long will these wines keep? Can you cellar an Italian prosecco or a cava (sparkling wine) from Spain, a German Sekt or even a California sparkler? Will they last as long in your cellar as a true champagne?

These and other crucial questions for the novice or the true wine lover are answered in the course of encouraging and assisting in the establishment of the home cellar, small or grand, for all those (now in the millions and growing each year) who have fallen under the spell of the glorious grape. And there are sections on how to taste and serve wines, as well as a glossary of wine terminology and grape and wine definitions.

In suggesting wine for different types of cellars, I have made lists of recommended producers in specific wine regions who have a track record of making good wines even in dodgy vintages. I have also listed for each region the wines I would love to have in my Dream Cellar. And I have dispensed with vintage charts, since these are only a rough guide to the quality of wine produced in a stated year; like the weather report, they are right about 50 percent of the time.

WHY WINE NEEDS CELLARING

Wine is a difficult and finicky house guest. We're lucky that wine doesn't have its own voice; otherwise, it would spend most of the time complaining and we would have to send it for professional counselling. It would always be going on about something or other. Wine gets "bottle shock" when first introduced to the container in which it will spend its life, rather like an unsuccessful first date that turns into a lock-down arranged marriage. Wine doesn't like to travel and has to rest several weeks on arrival at its destination before it gets back its mojo (balance). It has no desire to go to Florida for the winter; it doesn't like fluctuations of temperature or being jostled by vibrations from machines (clothes dryers, compressors, dishwashers, elevators, trains, subways or passing traffic, etc.). It abhors bright light and heat and does not like the smell of paint, solvents, detergents or household refuse (strong odours can, over time, seep through the cork and affect the flavour of the wine). Given its finicky disposition, wine, if truth be told, probably suffers from agoraphobia: if those bottles in your basement had their way they would rather be slumbering in the dark, damp cellar where they were born and would not have to travel at all. But life is hard, and wines, like pets, are there for our enjoyment. And, like pets, wine responds best to kindly treatment rather than benign neglect or abuse.

My heart bleeds when I see where some people store their wines. I have been in kitchens that have wine racks installed over refrigerators, with bottles slowly cooking from the rising heat and being massaged into old age by the vibrations of the compressor. I have seen wines stored in terra cotta tubular tiles set into stone walls beside a fireplace in the den. I have seen wines stored in unheated attics that bake in summer and freeze in winter—rather like Madeira lodges, which encourage the oxidation of their wines this way. And I have to confess that my own parents used to keep the single ceremonial bottle of Manischewitz in the linen closet, at a temperature above the thermostat setting in the living room. So be kind to your wine. It will reward you for your concern.

Wine, like human beings, begins to die the moment it's first exposed to air. Sad but true. It's all a matter of time, and some of us live longer than others. Like us, all wines do not age at the same rate; some, because of their grape variety and their conditions of growth (soil, heat, length of time on the vine, extract, balance of sugar and acidity, winemaking technique and storage), will live longer than others. I have tasted wines that were over a hundred years old and still gave pleasure. On the other hand, I have tasted young wines that had become old before their time, dried out, lost colour, yet were still corseted with tannins.

In white wines it is the acid that gives wine its structure and its ability to age; think of acid as the skeleton of the wine, the frame that supports the fruit. In reds it's the phenolics—colouring matter in the skins and tannins from the skins, pits and stalks—that preserve the wine. Tannins are that bitter compound you experience when you bite into a grape pit or stalk or chew on a grape skin. In the leather industry they use tannic acid to preserve hides. There is tannic acid in wine that has the same preservative effect. When a wine ages, the tannins soften and will ultimately, after several years, precipitate as a sediment with colouring matter. The bouquet becomes more complex and the fruit begins to dry out. Red wines lose their colour as they age, while white wines, ironically, become deeper in colour.

The good news is that most red wines will get better with some bottle age—except Beaujolais Nouveau and rosés, which are made to be consumed within a year of their vintage date. I wish there were a mathematical formula that could tell you when a wine had reached its peak of maturity, but there isn't, and so we have to go by rough guesses. In my experience red Bordeaux is the most difficult wine to predict when to open. At three years after the vintage date it can taste lively and fruity behind its gripping tannins; a year or two later it can close down and go "dumb" before it opens up again after another three or so years' cellaring. That's why it's worth buying a case of a Bordeaux château you like and opening a bottle every year to try and catch it at its pleasure peak.

The quality growth of a wine is not a bell curve; it's more a jagged line that rises to a point, then plateaus for a year or two before going into decline as the fruit begins to dry out. As red wines age their acidity softens and the tannins and colouring matter begin to precipitate. That's why you see sediment in bottles of mature wines. The bouquet also changes, becoming more pronounced, losing its fruity fragrance and developing more organic nuances of chocolate, coffee beans or leather. Really old wines develop tertiary bouquets of soy, balsamic vinegar and stewed fruits. That's why grapes that are high in tannin produce cellar-worthy wines. The major varieties are

- Cabernet Sauvignon (especially from cooler regions like Bordeaux)
- Cabernet-Merlot blends (Meritage)
- Nebbiolo-based wines (Barolo/Barbaresco)
- Syrah/Shiraz (Rhône, Australia)
- Tempranillo (Spain)
- Sangiovese (Italy).

Aging Potential

The eminent British wine writer Jancis Robinson has compiled a list of major grape varieties and their potential lifespan as wine. The spread she gives speaks to the different styles of wine the grape can produce as well as the effect of regional differences and winemaking techniques. For instance, a Cabernet Sauvignon made in California as an inexpensive simple red will have a life of four years, whereas a top-flight Napa Valley Cabernet Sauvignon Reserve from a great vintage can live for twenty years. Similarly, the Hungarian variety Furmint, when vinified as a dry white wine, should be consumed within three years of its harvest date, but when made as a sweet wine, it can live for a quarter of a century.

- Chardonnay (2–6 years)
- Riesling (2–30 years)
- Hungarian Furmint (3–25 years)
- Loire Valley Chenin Blanc
  (4–30 years)
- Hunter Valley Sémillon
  (6–15 years)
- Cabernet Sauvignon (4–20 years)
- Merlot (2–10 years)
- Nebbiolo (4–20 years)
- Pinot Noir (2–8 years)
- Sangiovese (2–8 years)
- Syrah (4–16 years)
- Zinfandel (2–6 years)

- classified Bordeaux (8–25 years)
- Grand Cru Burgundy
  (8–25 years)
- Aglianico from Taurasi
  (4–15 years)
- Baga from Bairrada (4–8 years)
- Hungarian Kadarka (3–7 years)
- Bulgarian Melnik (3–7 years)
- Croatian Plavac Mali (4–8 years)
- Russian Saperavi (3–10 years)
- Madiran Tannat (4–12 years)
- Spanish Tempranillo (2–8 years)
- Greek Xinomavro (4–10 years)
- botrytized wines (5–25 years)

Cabernet Sauvignon is king when it comes to tannins, because of its small berry size. This means that the ratio of skin to pulp is high, and since tannins are concentrated in the skins as well as in the pits and stalks, the resulting wine will be higher in tannin than, say, Merlot, which has a larger berry size.

While some white wines can benefit from cellaring for up to a decade, most should be consumed within a year of their vintage date. The exceptions are domaine-bottled white Burgundy (never inexpensive); Chenin Blanc from the Loire Valley; Rieslings from cool-climate regions such as Germany, Austria and Ontario; some Rioja whites and sweet dessert wines (sugar is a great preservative) with good acidity (for example, Sauternes, Tokaji, icewine); and vintage-dated champagne.

Fortified wines such as port, sherry, Madeira and Marsala are the "no-brainer" cellar choices. They have inherent longevity because of their higher alcohol content (20 to 22 percent by volume), which acts as a preservative along with the residual sugar and acidity.

Generally—though I hate to admit it—the more you pay for a wine the more likely it will age well.

THE ORIGINS OF THE WINE CELLAR

Winemaking is the world's second-oldest profession, and no doubt it helped relieve the burdens of the world's oldest. But before wine could be stored, it had to be "invented." We have no record of how wine was first made but, like most beneficent inventions, it was probably accidental. And perhaps we owe our gratitude to a woman. According to a Persian legend the unnamed heroine was a concubine in the harem of King Jamsheed. The king was very fond of grapes, and in order to enjoy them year-round he had them stored sealed in jars. When he sent for one of the jars several months later, he found that the contents were fermenting. Believing the liquid to be poisonous, he had the jar labelled as such and placed in a far corner of the royal storeroom, out of harm's way.

A member of the harem who suffered from migraine had heard of this jar of "poison," and she decided to put an end to her misery by swallowing it. She broke into the storeroom and took a healthy swig. Instead of killing her, the liquid made her fall asleep, and when she awoke her headache was gone. She returned to the jar and polished it off. Summoned before the king to explain her odd euphoric behaviour, she confessed her transgression. Intrigued, he ordered a quantity of wine to be made for the delectation of his entire court. The fabled King Jamsheed is said to have lived for a thousand years—the earliest testimonial to the salutary effects of wine.

Whether there is any truth to this story or not, there is archaeological evidence in the remains of grape seeds, skins and stalks in clay potsherds that suggests wine was being made nearly seven thousand years ago in the area now known as the Fertile Crescent. Some of the earliest concrete evidence of the existence of wine was six nine-litre jars found in the floor of a mud-brick building dating from 5400 to 5000 B.C., in Hajji Firuz Tepe, a Neolithic village in the Zagros Mountains of northern Iran.

While the Old Testament does not actually state that Noah built a wine cellar in the ark, it's unthinkable that he would have undertaken such a long sea voyage without wine. According to Genesis 9:20–21, "Noah, the tiller of the soil, was the first to plant a vineyard. He drank of the wine and became drunk, and he uncovered himself within the tent." So obviously the old

Thomas Jefferson's Cellar

Of all the American presidents, the most wine-infatuated was Thomas Jefferson.

In his marvellous account of a 1787 bottle of Château Lafite auctioned in 1985 for the hammer price of US$156,000, Benjamin Wallace wrote: "Jefferson had been keen on wine for a long time. When he began building Monticello in 1769, at the age of twenty-six, the first part constructed was the wine cellar. As the second governor of Virginia, Jefferson gained access to the official stock of Bordeaux, Burgundy, German Rieslings and champagne. One story, passed down among Jefferson's slaves, held that his Virginia cellar had been emptied three years before he left for France, when British troops, commanded by the reviled Banastre 'The Butcher' Tarleto, destroyed Jefferson's casks and smashed his bottles with their swords, flooding the dirt floor." (From *The Billionaire's Vinegar*, New York: Crown Publishers, 2008, page 9.)

boy had a taste for wine. In his book *Noah's Ark: A Feasibility Study*, John Woodmorappe lists the number of paired-off animals he imagined to be on the ark: 7,428 mammals, 4,602 birds and 3,724 reptiles. Noah and his wife and the crew would have needed some refreshment after the long days of foddering and cleaning up after that lot.

Wine has an extensive history within Egyptian civilization too. Grapes were not native to the landscape of the country, so some scholars suggest that the vines may have been imported from Phoenicia, though the actual origins remain in dispute. What is known is that by the third millennium B.C., Egyptian kings had expansive wine cellars; one of the oldest in recorded history, dating back to Egypt's First Dynasty, was known as the Wine Store of the Hog.

The question remains: at what point in history did wine consumers discover that wine improves with age when stored under ideal conditions rather than just put away to be used when needed? Perhaps the answer lies in the size of the cellar and the amount of wine it could contain. The Mycenaean king Nestor (1400 B.C.) must have loved his wine. Excavations at Pylos uncovered the remains of a forty-foot-long room. According to William Younger, in *Gods, Men and Wine*, "down one wall was set a row of large jars; a double row down the middle of his cellar; and there may have been a fourth row of jars down the other long wall. . . . The capacity of the best preserved jars is somewhere about 200 litres so that the cellar could have held at least 6,000 litres of wine. This may mean that [if] 6,000 litres was being matured for two or three, or more years, then the annual intake of the cellar (and perhaps also the total size of the vintage) would of course have been less than 6,000 litres." So if the wine was aged for three years, the royal cellar must have held at least two thousand litres of wine, the equivalent of 222 cases of twelve bottles each. And that's the worst-case scenario.

In Persia an excavated cellar in the fortress in Nimrud, south of Nineveh, built by King Cyrus after he conquered Babylon in 539 B.c., was found to contain row upon row of huge terra cotta jars. Inscriptions suggest that the wines had been laid down for the king's male choir, who were served a quart a day. This daily ration of wine finds its echo during the Roman Empire, when centurions on the march were allocated a litre of wine a day; they used it to sterilize their water and disinfect their wounds, and they consumed it for pleasure. The longevity of Rome's dominance might well be ascribed to the health of its armies. While the troops of Gaul and Britannia were riddled with dysentery and cholera from tainted water, the Roman legions remained a healthy fighting force because of their daily ration of wine.

Certainly there is continuity in the use of wine cellars in Europe from Roman times to the present. The crypts of early churches would have been ideal spaces for storing wine in barrel and in bottle. The feeling you get when you visit ancient cellars in European wineries is that there is something ecclesiastical about the experience, particularly in the sherry bodegas of Jerez, whose above-ground cellars resemble cathedrals with their majestic vaulted ceilings.

But before I get into the nitty-gritty of wine cellars, storage systems, wine selection and wine management, a little personal history.

MY TIME IN THE CELLAR

The best cellar I never had was the air-raid shelter in the garden behind the garage of the family home in Herne Hill, South London. The house was built in 1934 or 1935, and with the threat of war my father, a doctor, had a bomb shelter built. It was a large tube of concrete about eight feet long (you had to crouch down to enter it by three steps and sit on a bench) and it was covered with earth, rocks and flowers to fool the Luftwaffe. I don't recall ever using it for its original purpose but my older sister remembers the family rushing down there at the sound of the air-raid siren. It would have made a superb natural wine cellar, but the only use I put it to when I was eleven years old was dragging on an illicit cigarette with the neighbour's son.

In 1956 I moved to Montreal and entered McGill University. As an English and philosophy major it was de rigueur to drink beer; then, as a graduate student in Dublin, it was Guinness. Only when I returned to England to work for the BBC did I have the vinous epiphany. Friday, March 25, 1966, was the day—or rather the evening—when I was Bitten by the Grape. The date is engraved on my heart.

My uncle Louis had invited me to dinner at his home in North London. He lived in a solid brick house on a street in Finchley with the delightful name Crooked Usage. Uncle Louis was a vegetarian until the sun went down, after which time he reverted to his carnivorous habits. Whenever he invited me to lunch it was invariably to an Italian trattoria (that served only fish) within walking distance of his office in Fitzroy Square, and unfailingly the wine he would order was a bottle of Soave Bolla. But at Friday night dinners—he at one end of the long polished table and Aunt Helen at the other— he always served the good stuff, and since he could afford it, he bought only First Growth Bordeaux and Château d'Yquem. Everyone should have an Uncle Louis.

The wine he served that night in 1966, the wine that set me on a path that would ultimately deflect me from a career in broadcasting, was 1959 Château Lafite. Uncle Louis, I would come to understand, always opened his clarets too young, and this brooding monster was weighed down with tannins and nervous acidity. But the nose was a revelation: it smelled like a humidor in which someone had stored rose petals alongside the cigars, and behind those fragrances lurked notes of wet earth and crushed black currants. This was my Proustian madeleine moment. I was hooked, and even if I could not afford Lafite, I determined that I would learn more about wine.

A couple of years earlier, I was living in a one-bedroom flat in Marylebone Street that used to belong to a hooker with a lurid sense of colour. In those days I used to frequent a pub chosen by Christine Keeler and the naval attaché at the Russian embassy, Eugene Ivanov, for their assignations. Their liaison would compromise the secretary of state for war, John Profumo, who was also involved with Keeler, and bring down the Conservative government. All this was happening in my neighbourhood and I was blissfully unaware of it as I sipped my pint of real ale.

I did have the rudiments of a cellar in those days: about a dozen bottles that I kept in a cardboard box on its side in the kitchen. I don't recall what those wines were but Mateus Rosé must have been amongst them, because that's what every red-blooded Englishman on the make ordered whenever he had to take a woman out to dinner. From the cardboard box I graduated to a coal hole in my lifelong friend's building on Gray's Inn Road in Kings Cross. Bernard Silver and I met in the

Boy Scouts when I was eleven, and we both agree that everything we need to know about life—except how to cellar wines correctly—we learned from Lord Baden-Powell. Bernie and his brother Clive owned a small advertising business, and below their offices was a cellar that was a ready-made set for a horror movie. The walls were running with water and the rats partied day and night.

Bernie had found some rusty old wine racks down there and suggested we invest in some wine. We had a mutual friend, Lionel Frumkin, whose family owned a wine store on Little Titchfield Street across the road from the CBC's London offices. (I began working for CBC Radio in 1965, first as a freelancer, then as a staff producer.) Lionel was a fourth-generation wine merchant who was writing a book titled *The Science and Technique of Wine*. At the time he was working for another wine importer in London called Southard's and had spent three years in Europe researching with renowned producers Delor in Bordeaux, Bouchard Père et Fils in Burgundy, Hugel in Riquewihr, Deinhard in Koblenz and Langenbach in Worms.

Lionel used to take me to the Christie's wine auctions, where together we would buy incredible Burgundies at knock-down prices. I still remember paying seventeen shillings and sixpence (around three dollars) for a bottle of 1964 Grivelet Vosne-Romanée and twenty-five shillings for that company's Grands Echézeaux. (In 1969 an American friend, Ray Smart, whom I introduced to the Christie's wine auctions, bought six bottles of 1885 Lafite, which auctioneer Michael Broadbent referred to as a five-star year, "the second half of the first great pre-phylloxera twin vintages." Ray sold me one of the precious bottles at the pro-rated price he had paid for the lot; it cost me £18. I could make a down payment on a house for what that bottle would cost today.)

Lionel suggested that the best way to learn about wine was to lay down a cellar. He was prepared to make a selection of red Bordeaux if Bernie and I were prepared to put up the cash. But we needed a third partner if we were going to have an interesting, wide-ranging selection of red Bordeaux, which were then enticingly inexpensive.

Among the other Canadians living in England during the 1960s was a beautiful young woman from Hamilton, Ontario. Cindy Bury also happened to be the Bunny Mother at the London Playboy Club. She was living with a dentist named John Riley, whose show-business practice included the Beatles and Roman Polanski (John made the fangs for Polanski's movie *Dance of the Vampires*). John Riley liked the good things in life and readily agreed to participate in the cellar adventure, so we all stumped up £200 each. I can't recall how many cases we purchased for our money but it was significant; the wall of claret certainly looked impressive in the racks of Bernie's office cellar. Lionel had given us each a list of the wines and recommendations as to when to open them. I don't think even he realized just how long the 1960s would last.

Suffice it to say, my third of the cellar was consumed long before it should have been (in homage to Uncle Louis, no doubt). But seeing those labels slide off the bottles in the Niagara Falls–like atmosphere and the rats' penchant for licking the glue accelerated my desire to open the bottles. Bernie was more circumspect about pulling corks, while John Riley seemed to have forgotten that he owned four bottles from each case. When Bernie reminded him, he said he was content to let the wines age and increase in value. Well, Dionysus is a perverse god. Bernie and I eyed John's portion of the claret with envy as we saw his portion of the cellar rising in value while our now-minuscule stock diminished.

In 1973, a year before the wine bubble burst and prices plummeted (the Arab oil embargo against the United States and Israel caused economic decline in Britain), Bernie moved his business out of the Gray's Inn Road building. He called John repeatedly to come and get his wines. John, for reasons best known to him, did not come, but the removal men did, and they did their job so thoroughly that there wasn't a bottle left in the cellar. When confronted with the empty racks, the moving company swore up and down that they had not touched a bottle, and suggested that thieves had broken into the empty building.

My next cellar was less ambitious: a small rack in what used to be a larder in a room off the kitchen of a basement apartment on Abbey Road. The building was (and still is) directly opposite the Beatles' studio. If you look at the *Abbey Road* album cover you can see a red-brick building on the right; I had the basement apartment. The problem with living on Abbey Road was that the street signs were forever being stolen and groups of tourists were always getting knocked down by cars as they tried to replicate the iconic photograph on the zebra crossing. For three years this was where I kept the wines I bought at auction, vowing that the next place I lived in would have a dedicated cellar with climate control.

In 1976, as a staff member of CBC Radio working in London, I was summoned to Toronto, which meant moving my wife, two children, cat and entire household, including car and wines, to Canada. As a returning resident who had been out of the country for more than a year, I was entitled to bring back up to a hundred

The Smallest Cellar in the World

Queen Mary's dollhouse at Windsor Castle was created by one of England's foremost architects, Sir Edwin Lutyens, in the early 1920s. Lutyens, who had designed many of England's famous country homes, had it built on a scale of one inch to one foot. The dollhouse, constructed in the style of an Edwardian stately home, stands over two metres high. It was completed in 1924 and is a perfect replica in miniature of a fully furnished house of the period, including electric lights, full plumbing and a flush toilet. In the basement is a wine cellar that houses actual wines syringed into tiny bottles and corked. Even the champagne bottles have little straw sleeves. All the bottles, incidentally, were hand-blown to scale by a London glass company in Fleet Street. The correct labels were photographed and then scaled down. Mary Stewart-Wilson's pictorial book *Queen Mary's Dolls' House* (London: Ebury Press, 1955) lists the contents of the cellar, truly fit for a queen:

CHAMPAGNE	Veuve Clicquot 1906 (5 dozen)
	Pommery & Greno 1915 (5 dozen)
	Louis Roederer 1911 (5 dozen)
	G. H. Mumm & Co. 1911 (5 dozen)
	G. H. Mumm & Co. 1911 (2 magnums)
CLARET	Ch. Lafite, Grand Vin 1875 (2 dozen)
	Ch. Haut-Brion 1888 (2 dozen)
	Ch. Margaux 1899 (2 dozen)
	Ch. Le Prieuré (2 dozen)

PORT	Cockburn Smithes & Co. 1878 (2 dozen)
	Taylor Fladgate 1896 (2 dozen)
	Warre 1900 (2 dozen)
	Dow 1912 (2 magnums)
	Royal Tawny (2 dozen)
SHERRY	Amoroso Pale Golden (2 dozen)
	Oloroso Puro 1872 (2 dozen)
MADEIRA	Finest Bual (2 dozen)
WHITE BURGUNDY	Montrachet 1889 (2 dozen)
	Graves-Supérieur
	Chablis-Moutonne 1904 (2 dozen)
SAUTERNES	Ch. d'Yquem 1874 (2 dozen)
BURGUNDY	Romanée 1904 (2 dozen)
HOCK	Rudeshheimer (2 dozen)
BRANDY	Grande Fine Champagne 1854 (2 dozen)
	Hennessy's ★★★ (1 dozen)
GIN	London Dry Gin (2 dozen)
RUM	Fine Old Jamaican Rum (1 dozen)
SCOTCH WHISKY	G. J. G. Smith's Glenlivet 1910 (¼ cask—28 gallons)
IRISH WHISKEY	J. Jameson & Sons, Dublin 1907 (¼ cask—28 gallons)

cases of wine while paying minimal duties. Given the extortionate taxes levied by the Ontario government on wines you bring into Ontario after you've been on holiday in Europe for a couple of weeks, I saw this as a once-in-a-lifetime opportunity. It was only a lack of funds that prevented me from going to the limit. Through Lionel Frumkin I bought twenty cases of 1970 Bordeaux, the best of which was Cos d'Estournel.

The house we bought on Keewatin Avenue in north Toronto had an unfinished basement. Apart from decorating, the house needed a deck at the back, new windows, a new kitchen and ultimately an extension on the third floor. So plans for a spectacular cellar to house my twenty cases of claret were put on hold. They had to repose in the quietest corner of the basement, well away from the leviathan furnace and walled off from where the children played. I had the builders who were putting in the deck erect some plywood walls at the north end of the basement and I built shelves for the cases. The shelving was pretty basic, rather like a coffin stood up on its end. The only climate control was opening the door to the room in winter so the wines would not freeze and using a pail of water in the summer to ensure there was enough humidity so the corks would not dry out.

As we gradually accomplished the long list of house improvements a new cellar began to seem like a possibility. By this time I was the *Toronto Star*'s wine columnist, and if anyone should have had a showplace cellar it should have been me. The problem was that it would have to fit into plans for a finished basement, which meant the only place it could go was next to that fire-breathing dragon of a furnace. After much negotiation with my wife and the architect, I got them to move the furnace from the centre of the basement to the south end. I had envisaged a room lined with racking in which I could have a table and a couple of chairs for tasting purposes and maybe a small wash basin. This would have meant taking space away from the den, and that was apparently non-negotiable. The space I was left with—where the old furnace had stood—was six feet by five feet, not much larger than my stand-up coffin; I was going to get my Dream Cellar, but writ small.

I called in the Wine Establishment to design and build it. They did a magnificent job, maximizing the space with double racking (one bottle behind another) on one wall and single racking on the other, with a red tiled floor and a cooling/humidifier unit on the back wall. Around this unit I nailed up the box ends of Bordeaux cases printed with the château name and vintage. The most impressive thing about the cellar was its door: it was made of California redwood and was three inches thick. With its Gothic-arch curve and its massive iron hinges it looked like the entrance to a cathedral in a provincial town in France.

It was almost a religious experience to install the bottles in the racks. I had nearly finished sliding them into their slots when one of the bottles, a simple California Cabernet Sauvignon, slipped from my hands and fell to the tiled floor. Miraculously, it remained intact, but it bounced and struck the neck of a 1976 Pernand-Vergelesses shipped by Joseph Drouhin. The bottle of Burgundy exploded and the cellar floor was christened. This is one of life's indisputable rules: the bottle you drop will not break but it will destroy one of the most expensive wines in your collection.

I loved that cellar and experienced a tragic sense of loss when divorce meant we had to sell the house. The wine was first moved to an apartment I rented for a year in a house on Avenue Road and then to a more permanent home on Claxton Boulevard. There were four suites in a building that a lawyer and old friend of mine from McGill days, David Alexandor, had bought and turned into a co-op. David and I lived in the upper part of the building in mirror-image three-bedroom lofts, while the first-floor apartments were sold to two women. There was no room for a cellar in my unit; in fact there was no room to barbecue either, since there was no backyard, only a laneway for access to the garages at the back. So I bought a hundred-bottle wine cabinet that I kept in my study and stored the rest of the wines in a room in the basement. This was not ideal but I rationalized by saying that the wines stored there would be consumed within six months.

It was my present wife, Deborah, who convinced me we had to move. Deborah loves gardening and we had no garden. I am not good with moving. I had lived for six years on Claxton Boulevard and I liked the street and the neighbourhood. The cats, Nancy and Tanya (named inexactly after the skaters), liked the loft and I had gotten used to barbecuing in the garage with the door open. The only thing that could convince me to move was having my own wine cellar again.

Two years after we married, Deborah and I bought a house on Craighurst Avenue, with a Starbucks on the corner and a great butcher and cheese shop within a two-minute walk. The house had been built in 1918 (we learned this from an old newspaper we found in the wall when a pipe burst) and, although it had been renovated several times, there was a lot of work to be done: new deck, new porch, new windows, new door to the deck; levelling and laying interlocking brick the length of the driveway, changing the entrance to the master bathroom and constructing another bathroom on the third floor. My wine cellar was again placed low on the list of priorities.

But I stuck to my guns, and before the money ran out I called in the Wine Establishment again and had them design a cellar for the available space. It was about the same size as the previous one in terms of area, but instead of a virtual square it was longer and narrower. In order to get the space we had to steal a wardrobe-sized corner from what the previous owners had used as an office. And the cellar site was adjacent to the furnace—this meant heavy insulation. There was racking along three walls; in order to maximize the contents, I again had double racking installed along one wall, which I used for white wines. When filled it contained 1,100 bottles. I also had wines in long-term storage at an off-site secure facility on King Street at Spadina, called the Fine Wine Reserve (of which more later).

This was not to be the last wine cellar in my life. Deborah and I bought a condo on Mount Pleasant Road (by this time we had acquired a wheaten terrier called Pinot the Wonder Dog) and we moved lock, stock and barrel in October 2008 (except that I had no room for the "barrel," my wine collection). Condos are notoriously limited when it comes to wine storage, so I solved the problem by negotiating with the builders to buy space in the underground parking area to build my own wine cellar. This one, I promised myself, would be big enough to accommodate a collection I could afford only if I won the lottery. When I started writing this book, the new cellar was only a fantasy. Read the epilogue to discover the end of this tale.

INVESTING IN WINE

There is a subtle distinction between collecting wine and investing in wine. The two pursuits need not be mutually exclusive (you can sell off a case or two you've held for a few years and realize a healthy profit in order to buy more, thereby subsidizing your wine drinking). Collectors will usually have their wine in their own home or within easy access, while investors may never see their wine at all. They will have it stored off-site under secure ideal conditions and trade it like a commodity when the time is right.

If you envisage wine as something for buying and selling, then you should learn as much as you can about the product, just as you would research a company whose shares you intend to acquire. After all, wine is a commodity that can, under the right circumstances, increase in value, and quite handsomely too.

When the 1967 vintage of Château d'Yquem, the world's most sought-after dessert wine, was released in Ontario in 1972, it cost $17.95 a bottle. Today that wine, if you can find it, will set you back $2,500 a bottle. Last year a case of 1985 Domaine de la Romanée-Conti, arguably the best red Burgundy on the planet, sold at auction for US$237,000. A jeroboam of 1945 Château Mouton-Rothschild (the equivalent of six bottles) sold for US$310,700. Screaming Eagle, the California cult Cabernet Sauvignon, fetched US$130,900 for 42 bottles. And in 2007 a bottle of 1951 Grange, the first bottling of this iconic Australian Shiraz by Dr. Max Schubert, sold for A$53,900. And according to Peter Gago, the current Grange winemaker, it was not as good as the legendary 1953.

Not all wines appreciate as dramatically as these icon products, but the shrewd investor can outperform the stock market with a judicious selection of wines.

It is interesting to me that when people buy the most extravagant luxury items—rare cars, jewellery, yachts—most of the time these assets do not increase in price. . . . Wine is a rare asset as well. The same fundamental economic principles of supply and demand are at play. Just as they're not making any more Manhattan real estate, they're not making any more '61 Pétrus—or '05 Pétrus for that matter. Thus, even when investors pay up for a classic wine—that is, even when they pay what others see as insane prices—the market still generally goes higher over time because, again, these wines are diminishing assets, constantly being consumed, constantly shrinking in supply and constantly in demand.

From David Sokolin's book with Alexandra Bruce, *Investing in Liquid Assets: Uncorking Profits in Today's Global Wine Market*, New York: Simon & Schuster, 2008.

And you can have the added pleasure of restocking your cellar inexpensively when you sell off a case or two. But provenance is all, and investment-grade wines must be kept in ideal cellaring conditions.

Admittedly the current economic situation has stalled the fine wine market, but history has shown us that there are cycles in economic activity and eventually the market will rebound. If you are thinking of investing in wine there are some basic principles to follow. Buy only blue-chip wines, those that collectors or other investors covet. This means acquiring the big names: the First Growth Bordeaux, the top domaine-bottled Burgundies, super Tuscans and *garagiste* California Cabernet Sauvignon.

Like it or not, the wine market is driven by numbers. If Robert Parker or *Wine Spectator* gives a wine 98 points, it's going to sell out before you can spit. The wine becomes an instant collectible. On the rare occasion when a wine is given a perfect score of 100, it is elevated to the status of Holy Grail and no price is too much to pay for it. Why? Because there are growing legions of collectors around the world who want fine wines and only a finite supply of wines of each vintage. And for older wines, whenever a bottle is opened, the inherent value of the rest will rise.

But don't think about making a profit by "flipping"—buying one day and selling the next—unless you come across a Russian billionaire, a rock star or a dot-com whiz kid who desperately wants your five cases of 2003 Château Lafite for a dinner party on Saturday night. The experienced investor knows that you have to hold on to wine for at least five years to realize a decent profit. This means you have to buy wine when it is first released, preferably as "futures"—before the wine has been assessed by influential critics whose judgment will move the price. Like horse racing, the "form" of certain wineries is as important as the quality of the vintage.

You can follow the wine market just as you can the stock market, by tracking the London-based Liv-ex 100 Fine Wine Index (www.liv-ex.com), which follows the price movement of "100 of the most sought-after wines for which there is a strong secondary market."

Ten Best Investment Bets

Like classic cars and Impressionist paintings, icon wines are much coveted by collectors and hold their value, especially as a diminishing number of bottles are available as the years go by. These best investment bets, if well cellared, are

- First Growth Bordeaux
- Château d'Yquem
- Grands Crus Burgundies (red and white)
- Barolos and Barbarescos
- Vega Sicilia
- Super Tuscans (e.g., Sassicaia, Solaia, Tignanello)
- California superstars (Screaming Eagle, Colgin Family, Harlan Estate)
- Vintage Port
- German Riesling Beerenauslese and Trockenbeerenauslese
- Australia's Grange.

This is an electronic exchange serviced by about 150 wine merchants and professional traders. The wines they quote are mainly Bordeaux reds but the index also follows wines from Burgundy, the Rhône, Champagne and Italy. At the time of writing the year-to-date change was 9.54 percent, a much healthier return than the stock market.

Also keep in mind that there is more reward than simple return when it comes to investing in wine. Take note of what Howard Goldberg says in his book *All About Wine Cellars*: "Focused buyers can drink great wine free by judiciously acquiring two cases instead of one. As they consume the first, they watch prices rise for the second, and, at exactly the right time, dispose of the second case at a profit so substantial that it covers the cost of drinking the first. This is about as close to free lunch as it gets in the wine world, or anywhere else for that matter."

SO YOU WANT TO BUILD A WINE CELLAR

Cellars have always offered convenience, but it was likely the discovery of marked improvement in the quality of properly stored wines that accounts for their continued existence and growing popularity. While some wines are meant for immediate consumption, the impact of aging at the right temperature and under the right conditions can make what might have been an ordinary wine an extraordinary one. To paraphrase Monty Python, some wines are meant for laying down, and others for laying down and avoiding.

There are three basic kinds of cellars: the passive cellar, the aggressive cellar and the passive-aggressive cellar.

The quintessential passive cellar is something you probably won't see unless you visit the wineries of Europe or are invited to dine at the family seat of a British noble whose wine cellar is deep in the bowels of the ancestral home. This is a cobweb-hung dungeon of a place that could double as a torture chamber. It is so far below ground that it maintains a relatively constant temperature over the seasons without recourse to air conditioning. It is also invariably damp enough to remove the labels from bottles—which is why you will see unlabelled bottles stored in the subterranean cellars of Bordeaux and Burgundy and elsewhere on the European wine map.

The aggressive cellar can be above or below ground level, but it has to be climatically controlled by a device that will keep it at a constant year-round temperature of about 12–13° Celsius (55° Fahrenheit) as well as humidified to about 70 percent (more on this later). Examples of agressive cellars are found in commercial wineries of the New World, in domestic basements and in restaurants that respect the wines they offer on their lists.

A passive-aggressive cellar is one without any source of climate control other than opening the door on a very cold day so that warmth from the rest of the basement can keep the wines from freezing. It also lacks air conditioning to keep the bottles from roasting in high summer. Such cellars abound in cupboards under stairs and cubbyholes under porches. (You never get invited to see these cellars; they are the vinous equivalent of Norman Bates's mother who lives in the fruit cellar.) While this type of cellar is okay for the short haul—I'm talking weeks here, not months or years, if you have wines of distinction that you want to enjoy at their peak—I strongly advise that you consider some sort of climate control, be it a full-fledged wine room or simply a wine cabinet whose temperature you can adjust. But first you should decide in theory what kind of cellar you want.

Acquisition cellar: For those with the collector's gene who see wine as artifact. Think of this as more of a wine library than a temporary storage area. Nothing gives such collectors more pleasure than to have the same wine in several vintages.

Maturation cellar: For the wine lover who believes that all wines improve if left to age. This is not necessarily true, as we shall see in later chapters, but certain wines do require bottle age to soften their tannins and achieve the right balance of fruit, oak, alcohol and acidity for supreme drinking pleasure.

Consumption cellar: For most wine drinkers, a "revolving-door" cellar that is used a few times a week, if not daily. It's a place to keep wines at the right temperature and humidity until they are called up for service.

Serendipity cellar: For those who do not keep a record of what comes in and goes out of the cellar. Wines get lost in odd corners or behind other bottles in racks, then are suddenly rediscovered with delight or chagrin, depending on the condition of the bottle in question.

Inheritance cellar: For those who take the long view and want wines to hand down to their children, or at least to celebrate important occasions in the future such as weddings, first grandchild, etc. (These selfless folk do not subscribe to the sentiment expressed in a poster in a Toronto travel agency's window: *Fly First Class or Your Heirs Will.*)

Investment cellar: For the stockbroker mentality. Wine is a commodity that will, if wisely chosen, rise in value each year. The shrewd investor can drink for free by selling off a case here and there to finance new purchases. This game requires significant capital up front for acquisition of blue-chip wines that will increase in value.

Large-format cellar: For the dedicated aficionado who shares the philosophy behind the maturation, inheritance and investment cellars. These oenophiles want to have only magnums, double magnums and jeroboams in their cellars because they believe (quite rightly) that the larger the bottle, the more slowly and evenly the wine will mature (see page 72).

If you're like me you'll probably want the flexibility of all of these possibilities when you've acquired the cellaring space and stocked it with wine. Good thinking.

I have a cellar of about 800 wines in total. The bottles are on diamond shelving in a rather cool basement. I also have cardboard boxes on metal shelving; these boxes contain "in transit" wines or early drinking or library-type wines under $25. Plus, all of my white wines, sparklers and sweeties are in these boxes—maybe 200 wines in all. . . . One day we had the now-mayor of Toronto, David Miller, and his wife over for dinner. They had recently moved to Gothic Avenue, and they were both lawyers. This was some time before David ran for any kind of public office, maybe in the early 1990s. He asked to see my wine cellar, and so I showed him. Without thinking, to maximize my energy and time, I also took downstairs the obligatory host gift bottle of wine. I had temporarily forgotten that he had brought it. . . . When we went downstairs, I shoved it in the cardboard box labelled "Cheap Cab"—which is what it was. He stared at me, and said, "Yes it is! How might I be able to discriminate amongst wines?" Thus began a vinous relationship, and a good story he tells many times to others (to my embarrassment).

—Dean Tudor, owner of Gothic Epicures, www.deantudor.com

YOUR WINE PROGRAM

I will talk more about how and what to buy and what to stock later (see page 63), but there are some general factors to consider about the kind of wine you want to lay down and how much of it—before you begin to think about the physical envelope of your cellar. Think of this as your personal wine program.

There are many different types of wine cellars for different uses: commercial, institutional, retail and, of course, the focus of this book, private home cellars. But even home cellars can vary. When the urge to create a cellar happens, it's usually at the beginning of your wine-appreciation career. So we start with a beginner's cellar. As our tastes evolve and our knowledge increases, we move to a different plane, focusing on what we really like. Then we begin to consider the possibility of investing for the future, and maybe collecting with a view to selling off wines to finance future purchases or bequeathing your cellar to your children or grandchildren. It's not enough to know how many red wines you want to lay down. You have to understand what types of reds, in what format and when you intend to drink them, or, in a grander scenario, dispose of them at auction.

If you drink a bottle a night you'll need a thousand-bottle cellar. The math works like this: in one year you will consume at least 350 bottles if you and your partner drink a bottle of wine with dinner every night, and more if you entertain. And since you want to maintain a stock, you will purchase wine once or twice a month. A good rule of thumb is to buy two bottles for every bottle you consume. That way you can build your inventory more quickly.

Howard Goldberg, a colleague who writes on wine for the *New York Times*, offers the following mathematical guideline for the amount of wine you should keep in your cellar: calculate your family's annual wine consumption and multiply by 5. "If you and your wife finish 4 bottles during the business week (vacation aside) that would come to 50 weeks multiplied by 4, or 200 bottles a year: nearly 17 cases. Two wines each weekend would total 100 a year or nearly 9 cases. Add perhaps 48 bottles of super-premiums through the year (some of them given as gifts): 4 cases. In all, you would consume, share and give away nearly 30 cases—a total of 360 bottles."

If you're building a room that's going to have 7,000 bottles in it, try to imagine that cellar at full capacity. Now take a mental snapshot of what that room's going to look like fifteen years from now in terms of your acquisitions. Think about the wines you drink now and think about the wines you aspire to drink. Remember, a $20 or $30 bottle of wine now may be a $50 bottle of wine in five or six years, if properly stored. So today you may be a $20-bottle-of-wine drinker, but five years from now it could, and can, be a very different story.

The Well-Tempered Cellar

The great mistake I made with the first cellar I laid down (in London in the late 1960s) was that the entire collection was red Bordeaux. I have had the same breakfast for years, but I would not eat the same menu for dinner night after night. It's a good thing that I don't drink wine at breakfast.

The point is that you drink wine with food, and you will want a cellar from which you can draw a variety of wine styles to match the dishes that come out of your kitchen—and I don't mean the basic white-wine-with-fish, red-wine-with-meat formula. If you're cooking (or ordering in) Chinese or Thai, as a wine lover you'll want an appropriate bottle to accompany the meal. If you're barbecuing hamburgers or having pizza, you won't want to open an expensive bottle. A well-tempered cellar will allow you to have the right wine on hand for the occasion (see Food and Wine Matching, page 274).

Laying Down

In choosing wines to lay down, keep in mind that you will need wines for immediate consumption, for mid-term aging (one to two years) and for long-term aging (three years plus) and that they should be stored according to use. Wines that turn over quickly should be close at hand and readily accessible (don't forget, every time you open your cellar door the ambient climate will change, so you'll need to know the exact position of everyday house wines). Those for mid-term aging should be stocked deeper in the cellar and those for long-term aging belong in the farthest and coolest recesses of your space.

What Wines to Lay Down

There are wine enthusiasts who swear up and down that they will drink only French wines or Italian or German and would not be caught dead with a Chilean or New Zealand wine—or, God forbid, Canadian—on their table. That, of course, is their prerogative, though a cellar based narrowly on Bordeaux, Burgundy and the Rhône, Piedmont and Tuscany, or the Rhine, and Mosel precludes enjoying the fine wines now being produced on all continents between latitudes 30 to 50 degrees north and south of the equator. Such a classical approach to wine reminds me of art collectors who refuse to hang anything on their walls later than the French Impressionists. If your passion is for French wines I am not here to convince you to drink table wines from Portugal's Douro Valley. However, a majority of cellars will obviously be a mix of New World and Old.

The New World used to be a geographic concept, but now it's more philosophical as Old World producers emulate the techniques of their New World colleagues. Think of the New World as the former colonies of European nations, if you like. Regions such as California,

Wine and the Aging Factor

Why is it, you might ask, that one case of wine can give you different taste expressions, especially if the wine has some bottle age? Think of a case of wine as a dozen roses that you've brought home and put in a vase with water. After a day or two, one bloom may wilt, another might lose a petal or two. Wine, like roses, does not age uniformly. The position of the bottle in the cardboard or wooden case can affect its aging. If a wine is in the outside row and is stored exposed to sunshine or a heat source, that bottle could age faster than one that is protected by its neighbours. The position of a case of wine inside the hold of a ship transporting it from Europe can also be crucial to its future development. Then there's the problem of corks that can taint a wine.

Australia and Chile, although their commercial wine history goes back to the mid-nineteenth century, did not develop the kind of rigid traditional systems that grew over time in European wine regions, where the techniques of production were handed down through the generations from father to son and revered as holy writ. The brash New World was not bound by tradition, and its winemakers were eager to experiment with new methods in the vineyard and in the cellar. They were also readier to listen to what the consumers, the purchasers of their product, wanted.

New World winemakers, for the most part, make wines that are accessible and table-ready but will improve if cellared for two to three years. This means fruit-forward wines with lower acidity and softer tannins that you don't have to lay down for many years. Tannins are the bitter compounds in the skins, pits and stalks of grapes that give red wine its ability to age for a long time. When the wine is young, tannins can be coarse and have a drying effect, rather like drinking overly strong tea. As the wine ages the tannins soften and ultimately, if the bottle is left unopened, will precipitate out as sediment in the bottle. If you taste this sediment it's very bitter. If it gets stirred up it renders the wine cloudy, so it must be removed by decanting the wine and leaving the sediment (a mix of tannin and colouring matter) behind.

In order to produce softer red wines the winemaker has to convert short-chain tannins into long-chain tannins. This can be done by extending the ripening time of the grapes on the vine and by leaving the newly fermented wine in contact with the skins. Napa Valley winemaker Robert Sinskey summed up the New World approach in 2002:

Somehow the public consciousness has been brainwashed to believe that a good Cabernet Sauvignon should be a brawny, tannic and chewy monster. You know the kind, it's the one with so much tannin that it sucks the moisture from your mouth and causes your cheeks to cave in, making you look like you left your dentures sitting on the night stand. After which everyone stands around talking about how massive the wine is and how good it will be in a few years. Well, I'm sorry, but I don't get it. I am drinking the wine now. It should taste good today, tomorrow, next year and ten years after that. As it ages it should evolve, but it should taste good as it evolves.

When I first entered the wine business, I worked with a winemaker who confided that wine was like a person. "If you're surly when you're young," he said, "you'll be surly when you're old." Some big, bad tannic wines just never do open up as they age. The key is balance—rich yet elegant fruit, soft supple tannin and firm acidity.

CELLAR COMPONENTS

Choosing Your Cellar Site

Choosing your site is the most important decision you will make. In selecting the best site for your home cellar you have to eliminate the negative before you accentuate the positive, to coin a phrase. When considering a space, keep the following admonitions in mind before you begin to build.

- Don't site your cellar against an exterior wall if you can avoid it. Unless you have terrific insulation the walls will absorb and transmit heat. Remember that heat rises, so the lower the location in your house, the better for the wines.
- Don't site your cellar near the washer or dryer or where you use power tools. The vibrations will prematurely age your wines.
- Don't store wines near windows. The light will eventually cause them to oxidize and taste pruney (reds) or sherry-like (whites).
- Don't store wines where there is a lot of human traffic, such as in a corridor or along a kitchen wall. The wines will be constantly vibrating and exposed to light sources.

The Steps to Your Cellar

Once you know where your cellar will be sited and you have a general sense of your wine program, you will be able to balance the seven major components found in every good cellar.

Room Envelope: Establish total climate control to avoid condensation and drafts. This means making a perfect seal, not only at the entry point but also along the joins between the walls, ceiling and floor.

Finishes: Paints and sealants must be suitable for the environment created in the room and must not give off fumes.

Lighting: Light has an impact on wine: the darker the bottles are, the better for filtering out harmful spectrums of light. Hide the untinted glass bottles in the darkest corners of your cellar. Lights also give off heat. The goal is to have a crisp, cool white light to help you evaluate colour, so avoid fluorescent lighting or coloured bulbs.

Entry: Prepare a door that seals in the climate. It should be solid, at least one and three-quarter inches thick.

Racking System: Purchase ready-made rack systems or, if your budget permits, custom racking or lattice-frame racking made of glass or wrought iron. If you choose wood racking, the preferred species is Californian redwood, which is very stable and does not give off an odour. The slots may vary in depth from nine inches to thirteen inches. My advice is to go long rather than short to ensure stability.

Climate-Control System: A custom-designed climate-control system should cover all four climate protocols: heating, cooling, humidification and dehumidification. Whether custom-designed or cheap and cheerful, the best systems are capable of respecting all four of these protocols. Cheap and cheerful cooling boxes tend to be overworked; they should be replaced every three to five years.

Security Features: Do you need a retina scanner or just a good lock?

All of these seven components have to be in harmony with each other. As is so often the case in life, nature provides ideal examples. Throughout history, caves have been used as wine cellars. When we construct a home cellar, we should, if possible, take our cue from those caves. If you ensure that your cellar is to the greatest degree possible constructed from organic materials, it will be a success. Most cellars look like stone caves because they're organic rooms that will not harm the wines. Stained woods, bituminous caulking, oil-based paints, even a lacquered tasting table will eventually give off gases. Not only will this foul the environment and the climate you have so carefully created, it can and does pass through the cork and affect the flavour of the wine.

The mistake most do-it-yourself handymen make is to fail to enclose the cellar sufficiently with a vapour barrier. You end up getting warm air infiltrating the wine cellar or cold air under pressure passing through to a warmer location. When that happens, condensation

Innocent Intruders

Stories of kids who innocently take a Montrachet from the cellar to make wine spritzers at a barbecue or family members who reach for the Lafite when needing a wine to cook with are legion. To forestall such heart-stopping incidents, either lock the cellar door or designate one shelf or section of the cellar for family use, clearly labelled as such. Keep it well stocked with house wines: red, white and sparkling.

builds up in the walls, floor and ceiling. Wet building materials eventually fall apart and you wind up having to pull out the racking, move the wines and rebuild the room envelope. Greg Zeisman, who designs wine cellars for the Wine Establishment, says:

> We like to use wood studs, not metal studs. To fasten racks to the walls you need a sound structure. We typically use latex-adhesive plywoods to skin the room envelopes. The adhesives used in many ordinary plywoods contain formaldehyde. In a controlled environment the chemical agent in the adhesive will break down and has nowhere to go except into the room as formaldehyde gas. This will eventually penetrate the cork and get into the wine.
>
> For insulation we prefer mineral-fibre bats, fibreglass or inert rigid insulations that will not release their gases. All insulation shrinks over time and the cells contract and the cell walls break and the chemical inherent in the middle of the cell off-gases.
>
> Regardless of what insulating product we use, we always like to shrink-wrap the room in polyethylene plastic sheeting with a vapour barrier tape to tape the joints. We sometimes use more robust rubber membranes—but you have to be careful because of the adhesive used to bond the seams of these rubber sheets—we prefer to use the peel-and-stick.
>
> Most of the people who build under-the-porch cellars want to get their building materials quickly so they go to Home Depot and buy off-the-shelf general contractor products. They may be purchasing the wrong coatings and sealants—people who paint the walls with oil-based paint think it will hold up to the humidity better. This is a mistake.

If money were no object the perfect cellar would be an austere cave, without wine racking. Two pieces of aircraft cable would hold each bottle in suspension so the climate could reach all the sides of the bottle equally. If designers could figure out how to get wine bottles to float they would create the perfect ambiance for aging. The punt—the glass cone at the bottom of a wine bottle—gives thermal mass to the bottle and radiates coolness throughout the glass. So the goal of the cellar, in terms of air movement, is to continuously wash the perimeter walls with the climate so that you're chilling the bottom of the bottle, which will radiate coolness up to the cork. To get that air convection pattern you introduce cooling near the ceiling, since cold air falls and warm air rises. You should try to cycle the air horizontally like a tornado spiralling or washing down a vaulted ceiling like the tumbling action of a clothes dryer; that's the very best air movement pattern. Then you introduce humidity to mix with it.

Humidity is insidious: it expands to every corner of the room. Because of the high humidity in cellars you have to choose a wood for the racking and finishing that is resistant to mildew. The best woods to use in these circumstances are Californian redwood, red oak and untreated maple.

(For a hilarious account of what can go wrong when a wine cellar is poorly installed, read "The Wine Cellar from Hell" in Gordon Pape's book *The $50,000 Stove Handle and Other Perils of Home Improvement*.)

If You Don't Have the Funds to Build a Cellar
If you can't afford to build a wine cellar, be certain to keep wine away from light and in the coolest, darkest place you can find that is free of radical climate changes.

The lower third of your bedroom closet with the shoes on top is a better place than the kitchen—it's the most used room in the house and is rich in heat fluctuations, vibrations, light and odours.

If spending as little as possible yet keeping your wines in good shape is the goal, that unfinished room in the basement may not be the perfect solution. Remember, extreme cold will arrest development and extreme heat will accelerate maturation. Monitor the room every couple of days with a thermometer. You also might wish to consider a wine cabinet, but do plan to buy a good one, with a superior condenser. If you open the door of a wine cabinet (sometimes known as a wine refrigerator) six times during a Saturday night dinner party, it can take up to two days for the cabinet to bring its climate back to correct equilibrium, because its motor is so small. When selecting a wine cabinet, try to assess your consumption and collecting patterns. If you drink a bottle a night you'll need a thousand bottles' worth of cabinet capacity. Sub-Zero has one of the best wine cabinets on offer. See page 58 for what to look for in free-standing climate-controlled units.

If cellaring is not an option because of space restrictions, you might consider off-site wine storage (cellaring your wine in a secure environment). See page 56.

Ideal Cellar Temperature

The industry standard for cellaring wine is around 12°–13° Celsius (55° Fahrenheit), though it may not always be possible to keep to that rigorous standard. Your wines are not going to be at risk if you allow the temperature to rise to 15°C (59°F) or if the mercury drops to 10°C (50°F). But fluctuations must be as gradual as possible.

The yo-yo effect of sudden temperature changes will accelerate evaporation and prematurely age your wines. Dramatic fluctuations of temperature can damage your wine permanently. Lower temperatures will slow down chemical changes, while higher ones will speed them up (remember your high school chemistry).

The University of California at Davis conducted experiments to find out what effect heat has on wine. The researchers concluded that with each increase in

10 Rules for Wine Storage

1. Lay bottles down so that corks are always wet.
2. Maintain a constant temperature (10–13° Celsius). Don't place near heating ducts or pipes.
3. Choose a north wall to avoid summer heat.
4. Ensure some humidity and air circulation.
5. Avoid the kitchen (especially above a fridge): temperatures constantly rise and fall.
6. Avoid areas near vibrating machines (e.g., washers, dryers, power tools): the massaging action will prematurely age the wine.
7. Keep away from strong smells (e.g., paints, cleaning fluids) that could taint the wine.
8. Ensure the area is dark. Bright light will oxidize wine.
9. Store white wines and red wines for long aging nearest the floor, where a room is coolest.
10. Apartment dwellers, use your bedroom closet. It's dark and quiet.

temperature of 10°C (18°F) the rate of chemical change doubled. So if the ambient temperature of your kitchen is 22.8°C (73°F) while you're cooking (or in a restaurant dining room in winter), the wine stored there will age twice as fast as the bottles resting in your cellar at 12.8°C (55°F).

Ideal Cellar Humidity

If you have ever visited wine cellars in Europe, you'll know that you don't want to brush up against the walls; otherwise, your clothes will be marked with cobwebs, dust and the black fungus that grows on surfaces from the evaporation of alcohol—euphemistically called by the wine trade "the angels' share."

You will also notice that the bottles laid down to age do not have labels on them. The reason is, obviously, that the winery wants its labels to look pristine when they hit the market, but also because the cellar's dampness will not allow the labels to adhere to the bottles.

I have kept all my wine cellars at a relative humidity of approximately 70 percent. This level is sufficient to ensure that the corks will not dry out from the top and that the labels will not start to peel off. Above 80 percent humidity there is a danger of mould beginning to form.

You want to keep your wines at the right level of humidity and at a constant temperature to ensure that the corks will not dry out and that fluctuations of temperature will not cause the wine to expand and contract, causing evaporation. In extreme cases this concertina effect will lead to leaking corks.

Cellar Management

There is nothing more frustrating than visiting the cellar to select that 2003 Bouchard Père & Fils Vigne de l'Enfant Jesus and discovering that it has been consumed on some other occasion. To avoid this kind of mishap you will want

Does Wine Spoil?

One of the most asked questions in some form or other is "What can wine take before it begins to spoil?" Remember the guy who left a bottle of Lafite in the trunk of his car or the woman who left a bottle of champagne in the fridge for an occasion when she might need it?

This is a hard question to answer. Marc Russell, director of the Fine Wine Reserve in Toronto, calls it the "Chip Dip Phenomenon":

> If you leave some chip dip on the table for two hours and then you eat some it can be fine and nothing will happen to you. If you leave the chip dip on the table for five days in the summer you're going to get sick if you have some. You can keep eating it but at some point you're going to get sick. Clearly you'll get sick if you eat it after a week. Clearly you won't if you eat it after two hours. Is it possible to define the exact point when the chip dip goes off?
>
> We do know that if you leave your wine in a room that's 80°F for a year it's going to oxidize to prune juice. If you leave the same wine in a perfectly controlled cellar at 55°F it's going to be good. So like the chip dip manufacturer, when it comes to wine, we're going to say never leave your bottles out for more than two hours.

to create a library of data, whether it is as simple as keeping a cellar book or as sophisticated as software programs and wireless systems.

Some of the options now available for managing the inventory of your cellar are code readers, scanners and touch-screen computers that communicate with the wineries to tell you everything there is to know about a specific wine. These toys can be expensive and are really needed only by the dedicated wine enthusiast with an enviable stock of wine and the mindset of an accountant.

Over the past decade or so I have tested various types of cellar management software—some seventy-five programs—and I have come to the conclusion that the best one out there is free. It's called CellarTracker, and you can get it from www.cellartracker.com. This is the program I use to manage my own cellar. You can use it free of charge, but do consider making an optional donation to the program developer. Given how helpful this program is, trust me, it's worth it. Not only does CellarTracker help you manage your cellar inventory but the website also has a huge database of wine reviews from other users. You can also track the value of your collection. But before you commit, check out the following sites for more information on cellar management:

Vinoté: www.vinote.com/soft_comparison.php
The Wine Cellar Book:
www.thewinecellarbook.com/en/index.html
Wine Rack: www.winerack.com
eSommelier: www.esommelier.net (the Rolls Royce of cellar tracking systems).

Off-Site Storage

Certain situations demand off-site wine storage. You're moving house or downsizing to a condo or your collection has outgrown the basement cellar and an expensive addition is not an option. If you're storing wine for investment purposes, for resale in a decade or so, you'll want to ensure that it is being kept in optimum cellar conditions. And out of sight means out of temptation's reach.

There are two styles of storage away from home. The first is a basic lock-up where you rent a set amount of space on a monthly basis; to be economical you have to fill that space. Then there is the full-service facility, which is more costly because they will catalogue your cellar, transport the cases to the storage unit and deliver them to you as required. Here the pricing is by the case. You can find the service nearest to you by going online and Googling "off-site wine storage."

When I moved recently, I used a full-service company called the Fine Wine Reserve, located in Toronto. Its director, Marc Russell, has created a 5,000-square-foot state-of-the-art storage facility conveniently located near high-density condo developments. He estimates that he has 25 million dollars' worth of wine stored there. I have cellared a lot of wine in his facility for the annual Ontario Wine Awards entries and for auctions for my charitable foundation, Grapes for Humanity.

My first question to Marc was what happens in his facility if there's a power failure. He explained to me that the space is so heavily insulated—it has four- to five-feet-thick walls, as well as being underground—that they are not affected by power failures of up to five days' duration. "We shut the heating off in winter for a twenty-seven-hour period when there was a forty-degree difference between the cellar and outside, and the cellar changed 0.6°F in that period," he said.

What advice would he give to people who are looking for off-site storage?

"There are three important factors. Absolutely number one is fire protection. The most likely disastrous event is a fire in terms of the safety of your wines. There must be sprinklers. And the system must be annually inspected. Number two is authenticity. Is it just a basic climate-controlled warehouse or is it a wine cellar? If you're storing wines for a short period it's not such a big deal, but if you're storing wines for years or decades you want a real wine cellar. A basic climate-controlled warehouse will not be able to withstand blackouts and will have temperature fluctuations and probably won't have the proper humidity level. There's no vapour barrier, no insulation—it's not a wine cellar.

"You have to check the insulation factor, what equipment they have to raise the humidity levels all winter long, what equipment they have to lower humidity levels all summer long. Are they controlling humidity at all? Temperature stability requires lots of money—$125 a square foot—to do it properly. It's very easy for someone just to throw up some condensers and evaporators; they're cheap, [but they] just cool the space down. The third thing is you've got to look at the ownership of the company. How many years have they been in business? The second most common cause of wine being lost is usually management/ownership issues, like bankruptcy."

I also wanted to know how secure his cellar is. "We like to think that it is very secure. Security is two things: it's internal and external. [With] perimeter security you're preventing burglars—the wine heist, which is so rare it's almost non-existent. No burglar wants to have to bring an eighteen-wheeler here and haul tens of thousands of pounds of wine. They'd much rather go to a jewellery store and just bring a pillow case. Just the same, you have to take it seriously. We have motion sensors and cameras, steel doors and hold-open alarms and biometric fingerprint readers. Where security is often underestimated is your internal security. That's stuff being pilfered by people who are in the facility, be it employees, meter readers, contractors, electricians, plumbers, landlords—all the people who are walking round the facility, which they always are. The only defence against this is vigilance—being on the property as much as possible."

My experience with off-site storage has, thankfully, always been a happy one, although I will be only too delighted to be reunited with my wines when my cellar is ready to receive them.

Choosing a Wine Cabinet

If you don't want to go to the expense of building your own wine cellar in your house or apartment or storing off-site, but you do want to treat your wines with the respect they deserve, you can buy a stand-up wine cabinet. To get the best advice on how to select the best model to suit your purposes, I asked Gary Larose, whose Toronto company, Rosehill Wine Cellars, markets these units. Here are the tips he gave me.

Consider Your Location: If the cabinet is going in a place where no one will generally see it, then typically you can use cabinets that are not finished on the exterior. If the cabinet is going in the dining room or family room or will be visible in a hallway, then Larose suggests choosing a cabinet with an exterior wood or stainless steel finish. A few manufacturers use solid wood that is available in different stain colours for matching other furniture in the room. The second important item relating to location is the noise that the cabinet makes. Some are quieter than others, and of course you would not want a noisy one in the wrong place. This is tricky, as sometimes the same manufacturer can produce cabinets that vary in the noise levels of their compressors.

How Big Does It Need to Be? Cabinets generally range in capacity from 9 bottles to 622 bottles. The smaller ones are usually not great for long-term storage, as they are mainly chillers. As the price increases you usually get better-insulated walls and doors and a few other features such as less vibration and better humidity control. Stylewise, cabinets come as upright models (the most common) and also in a credenza version, with options in terms of single or double doors.

What Kind of Racking Do You Prefer? Some cabinets have fixed racks, either single or double-deep. Higher-quality cabinets have double-deep shelves that pull out like drawers. Metal shelves are common in lower-end cabinets and wood shelves are preferred in higher-end models. Beware of cabinets that have their shelves too close together, with space to fit only a standard Burgundy bottle. If you decide on this type you need to dedicate a shelf for champagnes, larger-size Burgundies and perhaps magnums. This can be done by removing one shelf, although some models do have a bigger space at the top or bottom.

What Temperature Control Will You Need? Single-temperature cabinets are the most common. Double-zone cabinets are also available: one section is dedicated to long-term storage for red wine and the other section is colder, for whites that are ready to drink. One cabinet brand makes a multi-zone cabinet; the top is for red wine ready to drink, and then as you go down towards the bottom the temperature gradually decreases. This allows various wines to be placed at their optimal temperature.

What's Your Budget? In a perfect world, price would be fourth or fifth on the list of criteria, but for many customers it's the number-one priority. Cabinets range from $800 for a 220-bottle unit right up to $10,000 for a custom wood cabinet, with perhaps large mouldings or even burl walnut inlays, that can hold 500 bottles.

Reliability: Gary Larose's last piece of advice is a warning. Do your homework to find out which manufacturers support their products in terms of honouring the warranty and offering speedy after-sales service.

A Final Word Before You Take the Plunge

For six years, while I was living in a loft in Toronto, I had a wine cabinet that could hold 100 bottles. I kept it in a closet in my office, removing the closet door so air could circulate around the unit. It worked perfectly, but as my wine collection grew I knew I had to move—

especially since my wife, Deborah, wanted a garden. So she got her garden and I got my cellar.

By now you probably have a pretty good idea as to what kind of wine storage will best suit your needs, whether it's a built-in cellar or a free-standing storage unit. Now comes the fun part: stocking your new wine cellar.

THE BEGINNER'S CELLAR

Think about the first wine you ever tasted. I will bet a dime to a doughnut it was either Mateus Rosé, Baby Duck or Manischewitz. Now I am not suggesting that wine-drinking novices should stock their cellars with cases of these wines. I am saying only that our tastes change, so keep that in mind when you draw up your list of wines that you'd like to have in sufficient quantity so that you don't have to drive to the liquor store every week.

The best way to discover what your palate responds to is to taste wines comparatively. That is, line up a few bottles of white wine from different regions and different grape varieties. Once you have opened the bottles, put them back in their brown paper bags so you can't see the labels, which might prejudice you. Then taste through them (you might want to use a paper cup so that you can spit the wine out if you need to—or you could just spit backwards). In order to cut down on the cost—and not have six or eight opened bottles in your fridge at the end of the session—invite a group of friends around, asking each to bring a bottle. To make sure you don't get duplicates, assign a specific wine for each member of your tasting group to purchase. You can pick from this generic list of readily available grape varieties and find examples costing between $10 and $20:

> Dry Riesling (Germany, Alsace or Ontario)
> Off-dry Riesling (Germany or Ontario)
> Unoaked Chardonnay (Chablis)
> Oaked Chardonnay (New World)
> Sauvignon Blanc (New World)
> Pinot Blanc (Alsace or New World)
> Pinot Gris (Alsace or New World)
> Gewürztraminer (Alsace or New World)

Chenin Blanc (Loire Valley)
Sémillon (New World)
Muscat (Alsace or New World)
Viognier (Pays d'Oc or New World).

Tasting each wine blind (without seeing the label) will help you refine your palate. Make a note of which wines you like or dislike and try to define what it is you like or dislike about them. If the party is a success you can repeat the experience with red wines, selecting varieties from this list:

Cabernet Sauvignon (New World)
Merlot (New World)
Cabernet Franc (New World)
Pinot Noir (New World)
Merlot (New World)
Gamay (Beaujolais)
Syrah (Rhône)
Shiraz (Australia)
Sangiovese (Chianti)
Nebbiolo (Barolo/Barbaresco)
Tempranillo (Spain)
Zinfandel (California).

Red wines, because of their tannin content (that bitter, woody taste you get if you bite into a grape pit or stalk or chew on a grape skin), may be difficult for the neophyte wine taster to enjoy. You may hear complaints that the wine tastes rough or bitter on the finish. Red wines, more than whites, really need food to accompany them. In a social setting with a large group, if the wines are not served with a meal, at least have some cubes of semi-soft or hard cheese available. The fat in cheese coats the tongue and ameliorates the mouth feel of tannin.

Liquor store managers tell me all the time that customers come in asking for a dry wine, but when they're presented with one in an in-store tasting, they find it too sharp or sour. Most wine novices don't enjoy really dry wines and prefer something with a little residual sweetness, such as an off-dry (or semi-dry) Riesling as opposed to a dry Riesling. You can determine your preference either way by tasting comparatively at home. But remember, a wine that you like by itself may not be the wine that goes best with the food you select to accompany it. A Muscadet from the Loire Valley in France might make you suck in your cheeks as if you were licking a lemon, but try that same wine with oysters and taste the transformation.

So when it comes to selecting wines for your cellar it helps to determine how you will be using them. Are they to be consumed as aperitifs, to be enjoyed before a meal on their own, or are they meant to accompany food? And if so, what dishes do you most enjoy? Let's take an extreme example. Say you have a vegetarian couple coming for dinner and you want to honour their food preferences. You won't be serving them meat or fish or poultry but you would like them to enjoy your ratatouille and nut cutlet with a bottle of wine. Such a menu cries out for Sauvignon Blanc from the Loire Valley, New Zealand or Ontario.

When it comes to food matching, I have found that the two most versatile wines are Sauvignon Blanc (among white wines), because of its acidity, and Beaujolais, because of its fruit character. Sauvignon Blanc from the Loire Valley is crisply dry and a perfect match for seafood and fish, as well as vegetable dishes such as asparagus and ratatouille. In New World style, particularly from New Zealand, it has a rounder, more tropical fruit flavour that is ideal for fish and white meats.

Beaujolais, made from the Gamay grape, is produced by a special technique the French call *maceration carbonique*. Other red wines are made by crushing the berries and allowing them to ferment in either a stainless steel tank or an open wood fermenter and then aging the wine in barrels. Beaujolais can be consumed as Beaujolais Nouveau some six weeks after it is fermented, because of the way it's made. Instead of crushing the berries, the clusters of Gamay grapes are piled, uncrushed, into a stainless steel vat under a blanket of carbon dioxide. The weight of the top mass presses down and eventually crushes the berries on the bottom. The yeast comes into contact with the sugar in the juice and the fermentation starts. But it has nowhere to go except inside the skins of the uncrushed berries above. After a week or so the clusters are pressed and the resulting wine is fruity and very low in tannin—a wine that you can drink as Beaujolais Nouveau.

What makes Beaujolais so versatile is the fact that you can consume it at room temperature with meat dishes or you can chill it for fifteen minutes in an ice bucket and serve it with fish dishes. The chilling lowers the perception of sweetness and heightens the perception of freshness, or acidity; you would not recognize it as the same wine. Try this experiment at home. Pour half a bottle of Beaujolais into a decanter and let it stand open for an hour while you chill the rest of the bottle in the fridge. Then pour yourself a glass of each and taste them side by side. It's like two different wines.

A 48-BOTTLE BEGINNER CELLAR

Keep it simple to start. Don't buy too many different types of wine until you have explored your palate preferences. Forty-eight bottles represents four cases that can fit in the bottom of a closet. For diversity I would purchase three bottles of each of the following wines, which will give you an interesting mix and a sufficient range of flavours and styles to meet most of your dining needs. You don't need to spend more than an average of $20 per bottle to acquire such a collection.

Whites

- **Sauvignon Blanc from New Zealand (or Sancerre or Pouilly-Fumé from the Loire):** a dry white with flavours of passion fruit, gooseberry and freshly cut grass, with lively acidity
- **Chardonnay from California (Sonoma):** a rich, full-bodied wine with buttery tropical fruit flavours and an evident spicy vanilla oak
- **Unoaked Chardonnay (Chablis):** a medium-bodied dry wine with a crisp apple and mineral flavour
- **Off-dry Riesling (Riesling Kabinett from Germany):** a light-bodied wine with a fine balance of fruit and acidity and apricot, honey and citrus flavours
- **Pinot Gris from Alsace:** a full-bodied wine with a sweet peach and citrus acidity
- **Viognier (Pays d'Oc or Chile):** another full-bodied wine with peach and orange-blossom notes and a touch of residual sweetness
- **Sparkling wine (Brut style):** Spanish cava or Australian sparkling—a medium-bodied dry bubbly with mineral, apple and citrus flavours

Reds

- **Beaujolais-Villages or one of the named village crus:** light- to medium-bodied, with fruity cherry and plum flavours and lively acidity
- **Shiraz from Australia or South Africa:** full-bodied, with blackberry and pepper flavours and a spicy oak finish
- **Cabernet Sauvignon (a petit château from Bordeaux):** medium-bodied, with cedar, blackcurrant and vanilla oak flavours
- **Carmenère from Chile:** full-bodied and fruit-forward, with black cherry/blackberry flavours and vanilla oak
- **Malbec from Argentina:** medium to full-bodied, with jammy blackberry and white pepper flavours and an oak component
- **Pinot Noir from New Zealand or Oregon:** medium-bodied, with black cherry, raspberry and violet flavours
- **Zinfandel from California (or Primitivo from Italy):** powerful and full-bodied, with plum, leather and oak flavours
- **Côtes-du-Rhône Villages:** full-bodied, with peppery blackberry flavour and balancing acidity
- **Rosé (dry) from Tavel or Ontario:** dry, with rhubarb and strawberry flavours—very refreshing. You'll find that a dry rosé is the perfect summer drink, especially out of doors.

BUYING WINE FOR CELLARING

Provenance is everything. Where did the wine live before you moved it into your cellar? You may have the most perfectly controlled space in which to store wine over the long haul, but if the bottle you buy has been subjected to prolonged heat or cold, temperature fluctuations or agitation before you acquire it, your cellar could become a rest home for the terminally ill. The shop where you bought that precious Bordeaux vintage may have treated the wine with all the respect that it deserves, but you know nothing of its journey. That Château Gruaud-Larose may have sat on a Halifax dock in the depths of winter or baked in a delivery van in July en route to the store from which you purchased it.

You can keep the odds in your favour with a little diligent eyeballing of your prospective purchase. First, be aware of how the store displays the wine. If the bottles are standing upright, this is not a good sign. It's simpler and cheaper to stock shelves with upright bottles and it takes up less space, but there is a distinct possibility that the corks will begin to dry out. The store proprietor might defend the practice: "These are fast-moving wines. The cork is not going to dry out in a few days." That's true, but is his stock control so good that he can guarantee no bottle stands upright for more than a few days?

Here is a checklist for considering the environment in which wine is displayed.

1. Check the lighting in the store. Is it bright and harsh? Not a good thing.

2. Check the temperature of the bottles. Are they warm? After hours, when the heat is turned off, the temperature will fluctuate dramatically.

3. Check the label. Has the colour faded from being exposed to sunlight? This could well mean that the wine is already oxidized. Also avoid labels that are scuffed or stained—unless it is a venerable bottle whose label is mottled with age like liver spots!

4. Check the capsule. Is it clean or does it show signs of leakage?

5. Check the ullage: the headspace between the cork and the wine. The fill should be as high as possible, leaving little room for air. If the level in a relatively recent vintage is down to the shoulder of the bottle, this is a warning sign that the wine has been subjected to abuse in its young life.

6. Check the colour of the wine. In colourless glass bottles this is easy; in green or brown bottles you can get a sense of the colour by holding the bottle up to the light and inspecting the neck. If a young white wine looks golden brown, the wine is maderized (oxidized to taste like Madeira).

7. Check the position of the wine on the shelf or rack. It is better to bend down and take the bottle nearest the floor than to reach for one at arm level. The lowest point is the coolest area.

Ullage is the empty air space between the meniscus of the wine and the business end of the cork. The measure of this space increases as the wine ages because of evaporation through the cork and between the cork and the glass neck. Very old wines can have a disconcerting amount of ullage, which is usually referred to in auction catalogues with terms such as "low neck" or "high shoulder." The term *ullage* comes from the Latin *oculus*, meaning "eye," and refers to the bunghole of a barrel. The French for eye is *oeil*, which gave rise to the verb *ouiller*: to fill the barrel up to the bunghole in order to exclude as much air as possible. The verb led to the noun *ouillage*, the measure of the amount of wine needed to fill a barrel to its bunghole. Its first recorded use in English was around 1300 A.D.

Vintners will leave a little headspace when they fill their bottles to ensure that the cork is not subject to pressure from oxygen in the wine at the time of bottling. This headspace is about half an inch. When you purchase wine, always check on the fill level. If the wine is from a recent vintage and has a low fill level, put it back on the shelf and find another bottle. Richard M. Gold, in his treatise *How and Why to Build a Wine Cellar*, writes about old wines with low fill levels: "Having tasted such wine, I'd avoid any bottle with more than 12 mm (½ inch) of ullage per decade of age."

CONSIDER LARGE-FORMAT BOTTLES

Most consumers buy wine in the 750-millilitre (mL) format, but the serious collector knows that wine matures more slowly and evenly in magnums (1500 mL) and larger-format bottles. If you are thinking of celebrating your daughter's birth by laying down wine for her wedding, you'll need to consider a Bordeaux, Burgundy or Super Tuscan of a great vintage in the 1500 mL size or larger. The wine matures more slowly because of its volume relative to the surface area of the glass bottle.

Unless you do an enormous amount of entertaining of large groups I would recommend that you keep only a limited number of magnums in your cellar, but you will always encounter occasions when you want to open a large-format bottle—there's nothing quite as impressive. But don't serve the wine directly from the 1500 mL (or larger) bottle; you'll want the wine to open up in a magnum decanter or a couple of 750 mL decanters. It's also devilishly hard to pour from a large bottle when you're standing over your guests at a dinner party.

One of the world's best wine cellars is located in the basement of a restaurant in the tiny village of Sainte-Marguerite-du-Lac in the Laurentian Mountains of Quebec. It's called Bistro à Champlain, and wine lovers fly in from all over to eat there. The proprietor, Champlain Charest, has a stock of some 28,000 bottles, and he buys only the finest wines. There are commercial cellars of this size and quality in the United States and Europe, but what makes this collection unique is the adjacent cellar where Charest keeps his large-format bottles. When I spoke with him, he had just purchased four three-litre bottles of 2001 Château d'Yquem and 2001 Pontet Canet.

"I used to buy more but now I choose what is available at the [Quebec] liquor board," he told me, "wines that will remain good for many, many years." I asked him why he had decided to collect large-format bottles. "First of all, I'm big, and I like big things. Secondly, I wanted to do something that people wouldn't see in any other restaurant that would attract people here. The third thing is that I can leave these bottles for a long time and leave them to my successors."

What is the range of sizes in Charest's cellar? "The smallest ones are magnums, about 450 of them. There are 150 three-litre bottles, 170 six-litre bottles and a few nine-litre bottles, and a large twenty-litre bottle of Jaboulet Hermitage La Chapelle 1995. Apart from over a hundred large bottles of Domaine de la Romanée-Conti, I have a lot of Château d'Yquem [and] many bottles from Burgundy, especially from Bruno Clair in Marsannay and Alain Burguet in Gevrey-Chambertin. And I have large bottles of Hermitage from Jean-Louis Chave, large bottles of Beaucastel Châteauneuf-du-Pape, large bottles of all the Grands Crus of Bordeaux, large bottles from many Pomerol châteaux, a few Pétrus, Pichon Lalande and L'Evangile."

How does he keep them secure? "I have a regular burglar alarm and also sprinklers and somebody who lives in the house all the time." What sort of cooling system does he have? "It's just a normal compressor and an evaporator. In the winter I store them at 14–15°C and in the summer mainly 13–14°C. I like to serve the wine cooler in the summer than in the winter."

BUYING WINE AT AUCTION

Auctions are a minefield, especially charity auctions. You never know what you're getting. Charitable foundations often badger their directors into reluctantly or dutifully donating bottles for the cause, and they choose wines of lesser vintages or bottles that have not met their expectations. I will bid at auction only if there is a pre-tasting of the wines before they come under the hammer or if I know in whose cellar they were stored.

The same principles apply as in selecting a prospective store purchase. You must see the bottle up close and personal. Check out the fill, the condition of the label and the capsule. And in the back of your mind remember that with icon wines such as Pétrus, Château d'Yquem and Romanée-Conti there are a lot of counterfeit wines in circulation. Wine fraud is as rampant as art fraud.

If you're buying vintage-dated wines that are at least five years old or older—be they from a wine merchant, a liquor board or a private individual—make sure you check them out first. When buying older wines from any source, be sure to inspect the bottle(s). Check the condition of the capsules and labels for deterioration, staining or mottling and, most of all, leakage. If the bottle has a screw cap, check the cap for dents or broken parts that could compromise the hermetic seal and allow air into the wine. Also look at the fill level; avoid any bottle that is below shoulder level unless you have a really old vintage and are desperate to sample it. Ask these questions of the vendor:

Where and how have the bottles been stored? If the wines have been stored for a long time in a basement or warehouse without climate control, be very wary.

What is the provenance of the bottle/case? How many owners and how many times has it been moved? If you are purchasing wine at auction, whether live or silent, it really is a case of *caveat emptor.* You have no idea how many times that bottle or case has been sold and resold; it may have been like an unwanted foster child, moving from home to home.

A Cautionary Tale about Shipping Wine in Winter

In 1999 I was called in by the food and beverage director of Fairmont's flagship property in Toronto, the Royal York Hotel, to assess the condition of a complete vertical "library" of Château Mouton-Rothschild. Since 1945 Mouton-Rothschild has commissioned an artist of international repute to design the top two inches of the label for every vintage. Such legends as Pablo Picasso, Marc Chagall and Andy Warhol, among others, have decorated this space.

Four years before, the hotel had purchased at auction a complete set of these bottles, dating from 1945 to 1994 (including the twin 1987 labels by the Canadian artist Jean-Paul Riopelle—the late Baron Guy de Rothschild liked both his designs—and Balthus's 1993 pencil sketch of a naked young girl, which was censored in the United States). The Fairmont chain paid $40,000 for the set, which was displayed in a glass-fronted wooden cabinet in its various properties across Canada.

In the winter of 1998 the wines were on display at Chateau Whistler, a ski resort in the Coast Mountain Range of British Columbia. Their next destination was Mont Tremblant, another ski resort, in Quebec, on the other side of the country. The hotel had made an inventory of the precious bottles, with a description of the fill level and condition of the label for each. As the collection left each property, notes were made if there had been any deterioration. Each inventory sheet was signed and witnessed by the hotel and the shipping company.

On January 8, 1999, the wines left Whistler in their polystyrene packing cases, a dozen wines standing upright in each container, set in wooden crates. They were transported in an unheated truck for three days of Canadian winter. When they arrived in Quebec, all the wines had frozen. Their corks had been forced out and most of the bottles had leaked. In some cases the corks were floating on the wine; in others, the corks had erupted through the lead capsules. Many fill levels were dramatically down, and even those bottles that had no evidence of leakage showed that the hermetic seal between the cork and the bottle neck had been broken. The possibility of oxidation was obvious.

Naturally the hotel sued the shipping company—the collection was ruined. The insurance company balked at paying $40,000 to replace the fifty-three bottles; they were prepared to pay only for bottles that were obviously ruined. According to my assessment, the integrity of the entire collection had been compromised. Not one of the wines had come through unaffected after being frozen. (Incidentally, the insurance company did ante up, but I never learned the ultimate fate of those ruined bottles.)

THE CLOSURE DEBATE

When it comes time to slide the bottles into the racks of your new cellar you'll probably find that several of the products—maybe many of them if your preference is for New World wines—are packaged under a screw cap. Traditionally wines have been stoppered with cork. But the bark of a tree is not a 100 percent guarantee that the wine will be sound when you open it. When was the last time you opened a cherished and long-cellared bottle of wine only to find that you couldn't drink it? It smelled like a flooded basement and down the sink it went. Pretty recently, I would imagine.

For my wedding in 1997 I ordered three cases of champagne. The importing agent who sold them to me said he would like to offer me, instead of one of the cases of twelve bottles, a Balthazar of the same champagne. A Balthazar contains sixteen bottles. He said it would be a great memento of the occasion—our families and friends could sign the bottle (although my wife said the empty bottle would only gather dust in the garage). When it came time for the champagne toast, the maître d' at the restaurant where the reception was held came up to me and whispered in my ear, "That large bottle of champagne, we can't serve it."

"What!" I exclaimed. "What's the matter? You can't lift it? You can't pour it?"

"No," he replied. "You would not want your guests to drink it. It's completely flat and oxidized." One bad cork had ruined sixteen bottles of champagne.

Wine spoilage can be due to a number of factors: a tainted cork, storage in an overheated area, oxidation through an ill-fitting cork or simply poor winemaking. But inevitably it's the cork that gets the blame. A compound called TCA (2,4,6-trichloroanisole)—which gives the stinky odour and flavour to "corked" wines—is one of the most powerful spoiling agents in the world. It is said that one teaspoonful could taint the entire annual wine production of the United States. Even a neophyte wine drinker can detect cork taint in as minute a quantity as five parts per trillion. The problem has been traced to the chlorine that is used to bleach and clean the corks punched out of the bark of cork trees. The chlorine lodges in the pores of the cork, and if any residual mould is left after the cleaning process the two components interact with the wine to create TCA.

If chlorine compounds have been used to wash down walls or clean hoses, TCA can affect the environment of an entire wine cellar—as happened at Gallo's Sonoma winery in 2003. It also occurred in the cellars of Hanzell Vineyards, Chateau Montelena and Beaulieu Vineyards in Napa. Those wineries had to undertake the great expense of thorough cleaning and purchasing new equipment to rid themselves of the problem. TCA can also permeate the wooden pallets on which wine boxes or sacks of cork are transported.

Anecdotal evidence suggests that about 5 percent of wines in a restaurant cellar are "corked." The problem is that many diners don't recognize a tainted wine because there are degrees of corkiness. Using something like the Richter scale for earthquakes, a wine that is, say, an 8 to 10 smells so bad that most people would turn their noses up at it. But a wine that is a 1 or 2 may not be detectable to any but the most trained tasters. The presence of TCA at levels that can barely be detected on the nose flattens out the bouquet and the flavour of a wine; it won't taste the same as a clean bottle. Wines with a lower concentration of alcohol, such as champagne, German Riesling and Portuguese Vinho Verde, tend to have a higher incidence of cork taint than sturdier wines. When I quizzed a group of wine professionals on the subject, their conclusion was that it is easier to detect cork taint in wines of low alcohol as opposed to those with higher alcohol, and it's more readily apparent in white wines than reds.

Winemakers and winery executives have been grappling with the problem for years and have tried many different remedies to combat the presence of TCA in their wines. Their immediate response: if cork—the material that has been used to stopper bottles since the first century A.D.—is the cause of wine turning, let's use another material. As early as the 1960s wineries began experimenting with the use of screw-cap closures. These bottles found their way onto airplanes for serving to economy class passengers, who immediately branded wine under screw caps as cheap. In the 1980s several companies began to manufacture plastic corks that came in a rainbow of colours. The large supermarkets in Britain, which sell 85 percent of the wines there, were fed up with customer complaints about corked bottles and demanded that their suppliers change over to the new stoppers. Plastic stoppers also cost less than natural cork, which appealed to the producers.

But soon problems with plastic corks began to surface. George Taber, in his excellent book *To Cork or Not to Cork*, explains that a cork contains 800 million cells that are filled with microscopic quantities of air. "Nearly 90 percent of cork's volume is made up of those tiny, trapped air pockets, and that gives the product its unique buoyancy and compressibility." Because plastic does not have the same elasticity as cork, it may not maintain the same hermetic seal and can allow air into the bottle. The result is an oxidized wine. Think of an apple that has been cut in two and left exposed to the air: it will turn brown and lose its fresh flavour. The same thing happens to wine if left exposed to air over time.

Since cork is made up of cells that contain minuscule amounts of air, it can feed oxygen to the wine and assist in its slow maturation. Screw caps, on the other hand, do not allow passage of air into the wine, and as a result wines under these closures will take longer to age and will appear fresher. But screw caps are not the perfect closure either. Because the seal is completely hermetic, any residual sulphur products from the winemaking process left in the wine will over time get bound in and produce a rubbery taste. Screw caps are fine for wines that you will open within a year or two of purchase, but I would think twice about cellaring red wines for five years or more under these closures.

The mark of winemakers who care about the condition of their wines is the length of the corks they buy. Long corks are expensive because they come from the bark of the oldest trees. Vintage port and Grand Cru red Bordeaux generally have the longest corks because they are cellared for decades. The longest corks are to be found in bottles of Angelo Gaja's single-vineyard Barbarescos—some 60 millimetres long. But sometimes corks can be too long, as Château Lafite discovered twenty years ago. The neck of the standard 750-millilitre wine bottle is about 50 millimetres long before it begins to flange out to create the shoulders. Lafite's corks in the 1980s were 54 millimetres long, which meant that the bottom of the cork extended beyond the neck; the extra length was compromising the hermetic seal and was exposed to the air space above the wine's meniscus. So Lafite's winemaker, Charles Chevallier, decided to shorten the cork to 49 millimetres to ensure a tight seal. For Angelo Gaja to use the longer corks he had to have special bottles produced, with giraffe-like necks.

I was living in a London flat with no cellar so stored my eclectic wine collection with a friend in the country whose eighteenth century house had a purpose-built cellar. All went well until the day that it began raining, and carried on raining until rivers broke their banks and people's homes filled with water. Hardly surprisingly in a house whose ground floor was flooded, the cellar filled to the brim. Some bottles came out from this experience with little aesthetic damage. Many were far less fortunate and some lost all notion of their origins and/or age. Which is why we do rather more involuntary blind tasting in our household than many other wine professionals. Interestingly, I have yet to find a bottle whose contents were evidently spoiled by their watery immersion so the corks seem to have performed their role pretty effectively. Even so, my affection for producers who print their wine's identity on corks has increased—what use are the words "mis en bouteilles dans nos caves"?—as has my fondness for screw caps and labels that are built to withstand a spell in an ice bucket.

—Robert Joseph, British wine writer

According to George Taber's research in *To Cork or Not to Cork*, "Some 20 billion wine bottle closures are used annually around the world . . . about 13 billion of those are still natural corks, and another 3 billion are technical corks (made from an agglomeration of cork particles with a disc of natural cork at both ends). . . . Plastic corks total some 2.5 billion. And screw caps, despite all the hoopla and recent success, are only about 1.5 billion."

New Zealand and Australia initiated the move to screw caps in the mid-1990s and many other New World producers have jumped on the bandwagon since. But the traditional wine-growing countries of Europe have not embraced the new technology to the same degree, fearing consumer resistance. After a couple of years in bottle, wines under screw cap began to show reductive notes— bound-in sulphur that smells like rubber.

Portugal, the world's largest supplier of cork, has belatedly tackled the problem of TCA. Cork cutters now harvest the bark higher up off the ground to avoid mould, and the curved planks are no longer left in the forests to dry. The boiling procedures have been cleaned up and high-pressure steam is applied to eradicate TCA. Whether these practices will finally eradicate the TCA problem remains to be seen.

This may not be the end of the story. In Germany and Austria several wineries are using a new closure called Vino-Lok, a glass stopper with a sealing ring made of ethylene vinyl acetate. Or maybe the wine industry should emulate the example of a small winery on Vancouver Island, Venturi-Schulze, which bottles its entire production under crown caps, like beer bottles. When I e-mailed Marilyn Schulze as to her company's experience with crown caps for red wines that require

Oh, the frustration of bad corks. I don't mean TCA-affected corks; I mean just plain bad ones—cheap ones, that should only have been allowed near wines for instant drinking, used for wines intended to age for a couple of decades and then some. I had two bottles of Savennières from a top estate—austere, steely wine, almost off-puttingly severe in youth, but rich, dry and honeyed in maturity.

Just the two bottles, a 1990 and a 1993. To tell the truth, I'd forgotten they were there. But I was cooking a mango and prawn curry—a fruity, spicy, fairly hot but potentially wine-friendly dish—and a rummage into the depths of the cellar produced these two. It might have been a match made in heaven, and at worst, I reasoned, it would be interesting.

The first cork crumbled. The wine inside was brown, oxidized, dead.

The second bottle, three years younger, came forward. That cork crumbled, as well. The wine was just as dead as the first bottle.

Coincidence? Maybe. Or just a combination of a lazy cork supplier and a producer keen to save a few centimes? A fraction more on the price I'd paid (and I'd happily have paid it) might have meant years more life for those wines. And I'd have been able to tell you if Savennières goes with prawn and mango curry.

—Margaret Rand, co-author of *Grapes and Wine* (with Oz Clarke) bottle aging, she replied: "The aging of red wines under cork versus airtight closure has been widely debated. . . . Our own very strong belief, based on our fourteen years' experience with crown capping, is that reds soften, round out and age beautifully in an anaerobic environment if they have been made well to begin with (with the right amount of air given during the winemaking process). It has been really rewarding to witness this and put the old myths to rest."

And so the debate continues. Ultimately it is up to you as a consumer whether you prefer the romantic ritual of pulling a cork or the technological hygiene of a metal closure. For my part, I'll take my chances with cork for red wines that need aging and turn to screw caps for white wines that I intend to consume within a year or two of the vintage date.

A WHO'S WHO OF MAJOR GRAPES

When confronted with a wall of labels in a wine store, it can be daunting to select the wine that is best suited to your taste. Before you head for the country or region that tickles your palate, it may be useful to have an idea what a particular grape variety might taste like. You'll soon discover your personal favourites.

Cabernet Sauvignon (red)

Produces long-lasting, deeply coloured red wines that are astringent when young but mellow with age. As red Bordeaux, particularly from the Médoc and Graves regions, the wines are leaner and more elegant than Cabernets grown in California, Australia or Chile. Often blended with Merlot.

Basic flavours: cedar and blackcurrant

Chardonnay (white)

Makes a dry wine whose range of flavours depends on where the grapes were grown and how long the wine stayed in oak (if at all). Chardonnay is labelled as such in most regions other than France, where it is named after the village where it was grown; examples include Chablis, Meursault, Montrachet and Pouilly-Fuissé. Champagne also uses Chardonnay in the blend and also exclusively as Blanc de Blancs champagne.

Basic flavours: cool climates—apple, pear, vanilla (if oaked), nutty; warm climates—tropical fruits, smoke, butter, spices

Chenin Blanc (white)

Wines can range from very dry to off-dry to sweet, as well as sparkling. Best known as Vouvray and Saumur (villages in the Loire Valley). Also grown in California, which makes a softer, less acidic wine, and in South Africa, where it is frequently called Steen.

Basic flavours: pear, quince, apple

Gamay (red)

The grape of Beaujolais. Makes a light, fruity wine that can be consumed young, especially chilled. When blended with Pinot Noir in Burgundy, the wine is called Passe-Tout-Grains.

Basic flavours: cherry, pepper

Gewürztraminer (white)

The most unforgettable of grapes. Grown in Alsace and Germany and throughout Europe as Traminer, the wines have an exotic perfume of lychees, rose petals and sometimes red peppers. They can suggest sweetness on the nose, but the best (from Alsace) are dry. Also produced in Oregon, California and Ontario. *Gewürz* is German for spicy and *Traminer* means from the town of Tramin in the former Austrian Tyrol (now Italian Termeno), where the vine was first propagated.

Basic flavours: lychee, rose petals

Grenache (red)

Widely planted in warm growing regions such as southern France and Spain. Makes a spicy, soft wine that is light in colour. Usually blended with other varieties such as Syrah, Mourvèdre, Carignan and Cinsault. Used extensively for rosé.

Basic flavours: raspberry

Grüner Veltliner (white)

The signature grape of Austria. Depending on the cropping of the vine, this variety can make a simple dry wine for immediate consumption. However, if yields are cut back, Grüner Veltliner can produce intensely flavoured, long-lasting wines of great quality.

Basic flavours: peach, grapefruit, white pepper

Merlot (red)

Very similar to Cabernet Sauvignon but softer, fruitier and faster maturing. In Bordeaux and many other regions, including California, it is blended with Cabernet to make the wine rounder. Merlot predominates in Saint-Émilion and Pomerol, producing dark, full-bodied wines.

Basic flavours: blackberry, blackcurrant

Muscat (white or, less commonly, black)

Although it is made as a dry wine in Alsace and sometimes in Australia, Muscat wines are generally sweet and rich. They are usually grown in warm climates; the hotter they are, the sweeter the wine will be, culminating in the Muscat of Samos (Greece). Black Muscat is invariably a sweet dessert wine.

Basic flavours: grape, honey, orange blossom

Nebbiolo (red)

Grown extensively in Piedmont and other northern Italian provinces, Nebbiolo produces the long-lived, somewhat austere Barolo and Barbaresco with their characteristic bitter finish.

Basic flavours: truffle, tar, roses

Pinot Blanc (white)

Similar in character to the Chardonnay, it is generally broader in flavours. Grown extensively in Alsace. The Italians call it Pinot Bianco and it is widely used in sparkling wines. In Germany it's the Weissburgunder. Generally low in acidity.

Basic flavours: apple, peach

Pinot Gris (white)

One of the most underrated of grapes, grown mainly in Alsace. In Italy it's called Pinot Grigio; in Germany and Austria it's Grauburgunder if it's dry and Rülander if it's sweet. Full-bodied white with lots of flavour. Some of the best come from Oregon.

Basic flavours: peach, citrus fruits

Pinot Noir (red)

A notoriously fickle grape that when fully ripe makes exquisite wines in Burgundy that age almost as long as red Bordeaux. Also successfully grown in Oregon, New Zealand, California and Ontario. Extensively used in the production of champagne, for which it is blended with Chardonnay. When used by itself it is called *Blanc de Noirs* (white wine from black grapes).

Basic flavours: raspberry, strawberry, cherry, violets

Riesling (white)

Perhaps the most versatile white wine; can range in style from steely dryness to honeyed sweetness. The bouquet is floral with a freshness from the acidity. It grows best in cool climates and reaches its apogee in Germany. The best wines come from Mosel and Rheingau in Germany; Alsace; Washington State; Australia's Clare Valley; and Ontario.

Basic flavours: dry—lime, grapefruit; sweet—honey, apricot, peach

Sangiovese (red)

The major grape in Chianti (along with Canaiolo), though now many Italian producers are beginning to make it as a varietal wine. It is 100 percent of Brunello di Montalcino and a constituent of Vino Nobile di Montepulciano. Highly acidic and tannic.

Basic flavours: cherry, truffle

Sauvignon Blanc (white)

This grape smells of grass, pea pods and elderberries. It is best known for the wines of the Loire—Sancerre and Pouilly-Fumé and as the signature varietal of New Zealand. It grows well in California and Chile too. In Bordeaux it is blended with Sémillon to produce such wines as Entre-Deux-Mers. Generally dry and crisp, it can make a sweet late harvest wine with good acidity.

Basic flavours: gooseberry, fig, asparagus

Sémillon (white)

Not often used as a varietal, this grape is generally blended with Sauvignon Blanc to make dry white Bordeaux. Similar in style to Sauvignon Blanc but more floral and not as herbaceous. Sémillon is the major grape in the sweet wines of Sauternes and Barsac.

Basic flavours: fig, green plum

Syrah (red)

Makes the powerful, rich dry wines of the Northern Rhône (Hermitage, Côte Rôtie) and is a constituent in the blend of Châteauneuf-du-Pape and the wines of the Southern Rhône. Ages well. Also grown successfully in California. In Australia it is called Shiraz, where it makes a varietal wine and is sometimes blended with Cabernet Sauvignon.

Basic flavours: blackberry, pepper, smoke

Tempranillo (red)

The major red grape of Spain, where it is also called Ull de Llebre. Has long-aging capabilities and produces wines that remind you of both red Burgundy and red Bordeaux.

Basic flavours: strawberry, spices

Viognier (white)

A rich, spicy varietal that has emerged from obscurity; originally a Northern Rhône grape famously made by the tiny appellation of Château-Grillet or used in small amounts to blend with Syrah. Now grown in California, Australia and even Ontario.

Basic flavours: honeysuckle, peach

Zinfandel (red)

Native to California, this grape is used to produce off-dry blush wines for immediate consumption as well as powerful dry reds for aging and port-like dessert wines.

Basic flavours: blackberry, raspberry, spices, pepper

REGIONAL LISTINGS

In this section you will find my perspective on the major wine regions of the world in terms of the "cellarability" of their wines. But first, a personal aside that will explain why I start where I do.

I received my initial wine education at Grants of St. James wine school in London in 1975. My teacher was the late Gordon Bucklitsch, a Falstaffian character who did not believe in corks—once a bottle of wine was opened the cork immediately became redundant. A former sailor, he taught me, amongst other things, that champagne is the best antidote for seasickness (during a force 9 severe gale on the English Channel). He was a great francophile and conveyed his love of French wines to all his students. Gordon became the model for my itinerant wine writer/detective hero Ezra Brant in a series of wine murder mysteries I wrote. In deference to his memory I begin this journey through the world of wine in France. I will then lead you through the rest of Europe. I cross over to the New World in the northern hemisphere and finally dip to the southern hemisphere. I have not covered all the wine regions of the world, as there are many other books that cover this subject. The reason is: lesser-known regions are not available in most markets outside their own country. One singular omission is English wine. Gordon would be pleased to know just how much the quality of these wines has improved in the past decade, especially in sparkling wines, so much so that some champagne houses in France are eyeing potential vineyard land in southern England.

When it comes to the specific regions, I have chosen the producers I recommend based on consistent performance of their wines in both great and "off" vintages. This is, of course, highly subjective, but isn't the pleasure we derive from wine a measure of personal taste?

I have also chosen wines for my Dream Cellar from each region. These are wines I would purchase to lay down in my imaginary cellar that best represent the terroir and talents of the local winemakers, irrespective of price.

I wrestled with whether to include recommendations for the best vintage years for each country but decided against it. A vintage chart ascribes a numeric value to the quality of the harvest, and it can be misleading when it comes to wines that have been properly cellared for a few years. I have tasted wines from years that were written off by the wine press when they were tasted in the barrel, only to find that they were absolutely delicious. And conversely, wines from heralded vintages have disappointed. A quick search of wine magazines and critics on the Internet will provide sufficient data on which to base a buying decision.

FRANCE

In the grand scheme of things, when you think about wine your mind first turns to France—unless you grew up in the Napa Valley and never left home. And when you think of the great wines of the world, you begin with Bordeaux and Burgundy. Before moving to Italy and the Rhine you might divert to the Rhône (north and south) and Champagne. If you are a wine writer or a wine professional you will include Alsace and the Loire, two regions that produce amazing wines that are, for some unknown reason, off the radar for many consumers. I am not touching on France's other fine regions, such as Cahors, Jura, Savoie and Provence, although I do put a toe in the vat in these places for wines for my Dream Cellar from other French regions.

With a few exceptions, no other country makes wines that have the potential to age for decades as the top French Bordeaux and Burgundies can do in great vintages. That is why I begin with Bordeaux and allot it as much space as I do. Does this betray a specific preference on my part? Perhaps it does. But in the world of wine investing you'll find that the real traffic is restricted mainly to the so-called blue-chip products: First Growth Bordeaux (Lafite, Latour, Margaux, Haut-Brion, Mouton-Rothschild), top Pomerol (Pétrus), Saint-Émilion (Cheval Blanc, Ausone) and Sauternes (Yquem). Then there are the fashionable châteaux of lesser prestige but equal quality, such as Lynch-Bages, Palmer and Léoville-Las-Cases. Burgundy domaines, being smaller, have less wine available, and Burgundy aficionados usually prefer to drink what they buy rather than invest for resale.

BORDEAUX

No other region in the world produces as much wine as Bordeaux. It also produces more than a quarter of all the wines grown in France. The region came into England's possession in the twelfth century, when Eleanor of Aquitaine married Henry II. It was a royal dowry that lasted for three hundred years—hence the British love of "claret," a corruption of the French *clairet*, meaning "pale" (which has nothing to do with the colour of contemporary red Bordeaux!).

While not the most beautiful of the world's winescapes—the scenery is rather flat and boring—Bordeaux has some ten thousand châteaux, some of which are architectural masterpieces, but most are more like farmhouses than fine country manors. Not all of them produce great wine, but the top classified growths produce some of the best wines you will ever have the good fortune to taste.

This top stratum is what makes red Bordeaux the most collectible wine in the world. In great years these top wines can live as long as the average human being. Much of Bordeaux's appeal has to do with the hierarchy of quality of its classified growths. In 1855, at the command of Napoleon III, the merchants of Bordeaux drew up a league table for the wines of Médoc and Graves, specifically for that year's Paris Exposition. The ranking was based on the historic price and reputation and the quality of the property's terroir. With minor adjustments over the years, the classification remains to this day.

The top five wines, known as First Growths, are

> **Château Lafite Rothschild (Pauillac)**
> **Château Latour (Pauillac)**
> **Château Margaux (Margaux)**

Château Haut-Brion (Pessac, Graves)
Château Mouton-Rothschild (Pauillac;
reclassified from Second Growth in 1973).

These are the A-list wines that, like Oscar nominees, have instant recognition around the world. Haut-Brion, incidentally, was the only Graves château to be accorded First Growth status; since its location is in a white wine–growing commune it is permitted to use its name for both red and white wines. Château Margaux, for instance, labels its white wine Pavillon Blanc du Château Margaux.

While it would be a delight to have a cellar full of First Growth Bordeaux, this is not a practical option unless you suddenly come into boatloads of money. So it is probably more in line with the majority of wine lovers' pockets to look for Second, Third, Fourth or Fifth Growths and, in some instances, the wines classified below these as Crus Bourgeois.

The Bordeaux area takes in four major regions: **Médoc** and **Graves**, on the left (west) bank of the Gironde, where the soil is gravelly, whose wines are made mainly with Cabernet Sauvignon blended with Merlot and Cabernet Franc (and maybe a little Malbec and Petit Verdot); and **Saint-Émilion** and **Pomerol** on the right (east) bank (where there is more limestone and alluvial sand and clay), whose wines are made mainly from Merlot and Cabernet Franc. Since the highly tannic Cabernet Sauvignon takes longer to soften up than Merlot, the wines of the right bank are usually more approachable sooner.

Médoc, which stretches north up the left bank of the Gironde from the city of Bordeaux, is perhaps the most famous wine real estate in the world. They say that its best wines are grown in sight of the Gironde River.

Four of the First Growths are to be found here, in its famous parishes of Pauillac (Châteaux Lafite, Latour, Mouton-Rothschild) and Margaux (Château Margaux).

Cut the *s* off the end of *Graves* and substitute an *l* and you will see how this appellation got its name. The soils along the banks of the Garonne River, south of Bordeaux city, are a mix of gravels, clay and sand. Home to the First Growth Château Haut-Brion and its neighbouring little sister Laville Haut-Brion, Graves produces white wines both sweet and dry, as well as robust reds based mainly on Cabernet Sauvignon.

The town of Saint-Émilion is a tourist site not to be missed, with its monolithic church carved into limestone cliffs. The region takes its name from a hermit who settled in a cave under what is now the hilltop town. This area of Bordeaux was the first to be planted by the Romans, in the second century A.D. The wines of Pomerol are not ranked as they are in Médoc, Graves and Saint-Émilion, but this relatively small appellation at 800 hectares provides some of Bordeaux's best wines, leading off with Pétrus and Le Pin, both much sought-after by collectors. Predominantly Merlot-based, these wines will last for fifteen years.

Usually red Bordeaux needs about seven years to soften up its tannins, while great wines need twice as long—sometimes twenty years or more.

Recommended Left-Bank Producers (leaving aside the five First Growths)

Château Léoville-Las Cases, Saint-Julien (Médoc)

Château Pichon Longueville Comtesse de Lalande, Pauillac (Médoc)

Château Cos d'Estournel, Saint-Estèphe (Médoc)

Château Montrose, Saint-Estèphe (Médoc)

Château Palmer, Cantenac-Margaux (Médoc)

Château Lynch-Bages, Pauillac (Médoc)

Château La Mission, Haut-Brion Pessac (Graves)

Château Léoville-Poyferré, Saint-Julien (Médoc)

Château Gruaud-Larose, Saint-Julien (Médoc)

Château Calon-Ségur, Saint-Estèphe (Médoc)

Recommended Right-Bank Producers (leaving aside Pétrus in Pomerol, which costs a king's ransom)

Château Ausone (Pomerol)

Château Cheval Blanc (Saint-Émilion)

Château Pavie (Saint-Émilion)

Château Troplong Mondot (Saint-Émilion)

Château Angélus (Saint-Émilion)

Château La Gaffelière (Saint-Émilion)

Château Figeac (Saint-Émilion)

La Croix de Gay (Pomerol)

Château Pavie Macquin (Saint-Émilion)

Château Berliquet (Saint-Émilion)

Laying Down a Claret Cellar

While preparing this section on Bordeaux I contacted Serena Sutcliffe, who is head of Sotheby's International Wine Department in London. Serena lives and breathes "claret" because it dominates the auction scene. Here are her thoughts on selecting red Bordeaux for your cellar from some more budget-friendly producers.

"Sadly, for most of us, the First Growths are now pretty out of sight, and so are some of the Super Seconds too. But this leaves an immense amount of Bordeaux châteaux from which to choose. Even some of the classified growths are still good value—one thinks of Giscours, du Tertre, Grand Puy Lacoste, Talbot, Langoa Barton etc., even Calon Ségur and Brane Cantenanc, all being made splendidly and not at greedy prices. And then those that missed the cut in the 1855 classification, such as Sociando Mallet, not to mention Angludet, Chasse Spleen, Monbrison, Phélan Ségur, de Pez, Siran etc. The list is endless. On the Right Bank, try Haut Chaigneau, Le Sergue, Bourgneuf, Beauregard and Larcis-Ducasse. In Pessac-Léognan, Bouscaut and Carbonnieux have greatly improved—and do not forget their dry whites too! There are scores of delicious wines.

"Then there are vintages—the 2004s are good value, and even in a very expensive vintage like 2005, the top growths are out of sight but beneath them there is a host of 'bonnes affaires.' Two thousand and one is very good, and less expensive than 2000, and 1995 and 1996 are still good value too. My advice is to think outside the box and to go to as many tastings as possible to find what you like."

Bordeaux's Sweet Wines: Sauternes and Barsac

In the 1855 classification, one wine was ranked as a Superior First Growth, elevating it above even the great First Growth reds: that was Château d'Yquem in Sauternes. In this region south of Bordeaux city, a climatic condition of warm, humid afternoons exists in autumn that generates a fungus called *Botrytis cinerea* (the French call it *pourriture noble*, or "noble rot"). This mushroom-like growth attaches itself to the skins of the ripe Sémillon, Sauvignon Blanc and Muscadelle grapes, punctures them and causes them to desiccate. The sugars and acids in the berries become very concentrated, and when the withered bunches are fermented they produce a lusciously sweet wine. If a vine on average will produce one bottle of dry wine, one subjected to botrytis will render a mere glassful of intensely sweet wine. Château d'Yquem is unquestionably the world's greatest sweet wine, with its flavours of honey, dried mango, marmalade and barley sugar. It is extraordinarily long lived; I have tasted vintages going back to 1921 and 1937. It is also the most expensive of dessert wines. But there are other producers in Sauternes and Barsac whose prices are more accessible.

Recommended Bordeaux Sweet Wine Producers

Château La Tour Blanche, Bommes (Sauternes)

Château Clos Haut-Peyraguey, Bommes (Sauternes)

Château de Rayne-Vigneau (Sauternes)

Château Suduiraut, Preignac (Sauternes)

Château Coutet (Barsac)

Château Climens (Barsac)

Château Guiraud (Sauternes)

Château Rieussec, Fargues (Sauternes)

Château de Fargues (Sauternes)

Château Gilette (Sauternes)

Bordeaux's White Wines

Eighty-five percent of wines produced in the Bordeaux region are red. Such is the prestige of red Bordeaux and its sweet dessert wines that we tend to overlook the fact that the region also produces dry white wines from Sémillon, Sauvignon Blanc and Muscadelle, mainly from the Graves region. Usually these wines are aged in wood, making them rounder and fuller in the mouth than the Sauvignon Blanc grown in the Loire Valley.

Recommended Bordeaux White Wine Producers (Graves)

Haut-Brion Blanc (Graves)

Le Pavillon Blanc, Château Margaux (Margaux)

Domaine de Chevalier (Graves)

Château Laville Haut-Brion (Graves)

Château La Tour Martillac (Graves)

Château La Louvière (Graves)

Château Olivier (Graves)

Château Carbonnieux (Graves)

Château Malatic-Lagravière (Graves)

Château Smith-Haut-Lafitte (Graves)

Tony's Dream Red Bordeaux Cellar

Château Lafite Rothschild (Médoc)

Château Margaux (Médoc)

Château Haut-Brion (Graves)

Château Latour (Médoc)

Château Mouton-Rothschild (Médoc)

Château Pétrus (Pomerol)

Château La Mondotte (Saint-Émilion)

Château Le Pin (Pomerol)

Château Valandraud (Saint-Émilion)

Château Cheval Blanc (Saint-Émilion)

Tony's Dream White Bordeaux Cellar

Château d'Yquem (Sauternes)

Château Haut-Brion Blanc (Graves)

Le Pavillon Blanc (Château Margaux)

Domaine de Chevalier (Graves)

Château Laville Haut-Brion (Graves)

Château Suduiraut (Sauternes)

Château Climens (Barsac)

Château Rieussec (Sauternes)

Château de Fargues (Sauternes)

Château Gilette (Sauternes)

BURGUNDY

When choosing Bordeaux reds and whites you can rely more on the broad strokes of a vintage chart than you can for Burgundy. Burgundy is a conundrum.

A *négociant* once told me, "Burgundy is a minefield. You can either be blown to heaven or blown to hell." A misstep is not necessarily fatal, only expensive. Consider the Clos de Vougeot, the quintessential Burgundian site with its historic Cistercian monastery and its fifty-one-hectare walled vineyard. Its vines were planted by the monks in the twelfth century. As one of the largest single vineyards in Burgundy producing Grands Crus wines, it is owned by eighty different corporations or individuals. Some have only a row or two of vines yet all have the right to label their wine as Clos Vougeot. The rectangular vineyard slopes from one high corner in the northwest down towards the south and east. The bottom part has poor drainage, while the area closest to the château is the best growing area because of the concentration of chalky clay soil. As Clos Vougeot is an expensive wine, you have to know which producer or *négociant* to go for, since the average production is one thousand bottles per owner.

The concept of terroir is at its most refined in Burgundy. While Bordeaux classifies its wines by the name of the château (the estate itself), in Burgundy it is the individual vineyard and its location on the slopes of the Côte d'Or that give the wine its distinction and reputation, so much so that villages have attached the name of the most prestigious sites within their boundaries to their names, as in Puligny-Montrachet, Gevrey-Chambertin and Vosne-Romanée.

Top Ten Collectible Red Burgundies

1. Domaine de la Romanée-Conti
2. Domaine de la Romanée-Conti La Tâche
3. Domaine de la Romanée-Conti Richebourg
4. Drouhin Chambertin Clos de Bèze
5. Domaine Georges Roumier Bonnes Mares Cuvée Vieilles Vignes
6. Domaine Henri Jayer Richebourg
7. Domaine Pierre Dugat Gevrey-Chambertin Vieilles Vignes
8. Domaine Leroy Chambertin
9. Domaine Ponsot Clos de la Roche Cuvée Vieilles Vignes
10. Domaine François Legros Nuits-Saint-Georges Les Bousselots

The Côte d'Or is made up of two distinct sub-regions, the Côte de Beaune (red and white wines) and the Côte de Nuits (mainly red wines). This is probably the most expensive agricultural real estate in the world.

Think of the classification of Burgundy as an archery target. Think of the bull's eye as the Grands Crus that come from small, favourably sited vineyards. The closest ring to the bull's eye is the Premiers Crus from good but not great soils, working out to the village or commune wines (which are usually located on flatter, less well-drained soils) and ultimately to the outer circle, the largest volume, made up of generic wines that can come from anywhere within the region. These will be labelled as Bourgogne Rouge or Blanc and usually bear the name of the grape—Pinot Noir or Chardonnay—on the label.

Burgundy is not one contiguous area. Chablis, the home of white wines, is 160 kilometres north of the region of Beaune, and Beaujolais, renowned for its light red wines, is south of Mâcon, a region celebrated for its white wines.

Understanding Burgundy

Robert Jull, proprietor of the Toronto importing agency Vinifera Wine, is a Burgundy specialist. Rob made wine in Burgundy in 1986 before getting into the business of importing it in 1991. He offers this advice on negotiating the minefield that is Burgundy.

Just where should you start?

"You have to know a little bit about producers— that's the primary thing to think about Burgundy. Buy some books and try to familiarize yourself with the best producers in the villages you like or in Burgundy in general. The trickiest part of Burgundy is that each village represents a different style. There is quite a broad range in the flavours coming out of Burgundy even though they're all Pinot Noir and Chardonnay. The character from the different villages is distinctly different. It's difficult to decipher that without tasting through them. There are villages making very delicate, lacy and feminine wines like Chambolle-Musigny in the Côte de Nuits and Volnay in the Côte de Beaune, and likewise there's very masculine, full-bodied styles of Pinot Noir coming out of Nuits Saint Georges, Côte de Nuits and Pommard in the Côte de Beaune. Distinctly different in character, and unless you have the opportunity to taste them and make a decision for yourself it's pretty tough to know what you're going to prefer."

And how significant is the vintage date on a bottle of Burgundy?

"Vintage is very significant but I still think it's of lesser importance than the producers themselves. These days, certainly with global warming and more importantly with modern winemaking techniques, the quality of wine being made at specific domaines is reasonably consistent. It you only had a cellar of great vintages of Burgundy at this time you wouldn't have much ready to drink. If you had a cellar full of, say, 2005s, 1999s, 1996s, 1993s, 1990s, really only the '90s and '93s are approaching drinkability. Great vintages of red Burgundy often need at least fifteen years to reach their peak of maturity. For whites, I'd say more the eight-to-ten-year range. If you have some of the lesser vintages that are well made by top growers, they provide a lot of pleasure for interim drinking. To have a well-stocked Burgundy cellar you really need to buy vintage in and vintage out of the top producers and enjoy every vintage for its merits when it's drinking best."

If you had a limited budget what would you go for?
"I would still go for top growers but lesser villages. So I'd be looking in reds for mostly the Côte de Beaunes, which is the easiest place [to] find some budget-oriented wines. You'd look for places in the Côte d'Or like Monthélie, Savigny-les-Beaune, Auxey-Duresse, Givry, Santenay, Marsannay, and farther south in the Mâconnais you find Mercurey—these types of villages that are a little bit off the beaten track, there's some great growers there and some exhilarating drinking to be done for a fraction of the price. With whites you could look at Auxey-Duresse as well, Mâcon—there are brilliant wines coming from Pouilly-Fuissé and Mâcon now—Rully in the Chalonnais, and there's some decent Savigny-les-Beaune Blanc. And there are a great number of producers in Chablis who are making tremendous wines, oak-aged or oak-fermented styles and in stainless steel styles. Chablis is outstanding value given the quality that's coming out of there, particularly at the Premier Cru level like Montée de Tonnerre and Blanchot, which really approach Grand Cru quality for Premier Cru prices. In this market where Premier Cru and Grand Cru Burgundy are $150 and up, Chablis in the $46 range represents fantastic value."

With global warming, are we going to see a string of better vintages from Burgundy?

"It's possible. There are some growers who say it's making winemaking more difficult. You don't have as long a growing season, which many argue is important in creating complexity. Pinot Noir—that needs a long, cool growing season. I think what we're seeing is greater consistency from year to year. We're not seeing these real washout super-cool summers where we're not getting any quality ripeness at all. It is creating challenges, particularly during harvest time if it's very hot, trying to keep your fermentation temperatures in check. All in all, I'm not convinced it's having a significant effect in terms of quality but it might create a greater quantity of quality wines over time.

"At the top level Burgundy is a rich man's pursuit. Finding the wines in the first place is difficult enough. More and more, whatever market you occupy in the world, if you want to source a particularly great producer, whether it be Ponsot or Roumier or Leroy, you really will be required to buy year in, year out to maintain an allocation. That can mean $5,000 per allocation per producer, year in, year out. So certainly it's a rich man's game to a certain degree. Top-notch Burgundy in the 2005 vintage is ranging in Europe from $150 a bottle for reasonable Premiers Crus. I've seen prices for the top Grands Crus approaching $2,000 a bottle now. Prices have gone through the roof and it's no longer Bordeaux that's occupying that blue-chip niche. Burgundy's moved in in a wholesale way and there's less of it. So there's stronger international demand for it and more pressure on prices."

What would be in your dream Burgundy cellar?

"It's important in any cellar to have balance. I could easily say I'd just want the greatest Burgundies from the greatest vintages going back to 1971; that would be fantastic but I think you lose perspective if you only drink great bottles of wine. I would build a cellar that would have balance. It could consist of the great growers and have lesser villages as well. What ideally I'd like to have is a selection of wines where I have something to drink continuously—good wines that went well with simple fare, also great wines that you could pull out occasionally with more complex dishes and tasting environments. I would look for a very broad variety of villages through Burgundy from all the top producers in their varying appellations. But I would not be afraid of weak vintages. For me I think I have had more pleasure from weaker vintages than I have from great vintages where the expectations are very high."

Recommended Côte d'Or Producers

Domaine de la Romanée-Conti

Domaine Leroy

Domaine Comte de Vogüé

Domaine d'Arlot

Domaine Armand Rousseau

Comte Lafon

Sylvain Cathiard

Bruno Clair

Denis Bachelet

Henri Jayer

Simon Bize

René Engel

Domaine Jean Grivot

Domaine Anne Gros

Daniel Rion

Domaine Jean Gros

Maison Louis Jadot

Domaine Leflaive

Domaine Ramonet

Etienne Sauzet

Méo-Camuzet

Michel Colin-Deléger

Albert Morot

Richard Fontaine-Gagnard

Hudelot-Noëllat

Drouhin

Jean-Marc Blain-Gagnard

Robert Chevillon

CHABLIS

Chablis, in the most northern part of Burgundy, has a similar hierarchy of quality to the Côte d'Or for its Chardonnay-based wines: Grand Cru, Premier Cru and Village. Given its geographic location, the weather is slightly cooler here than it is in the Côte d'Or or the Mâconnais. The climate, along with the limestone soil, imparts a vivid freshness to its white wines, giving them vibrant green apple and citrus flavours.

Recommended Chablis Producers

René & Vincent Dauvissat

Jean Dauvissat

Christian Moreau

William Fèvre

Christophe & Fils (Fyé)

Ravenau

Louis Michel

Rosemary George, M.W., who wrote the book *The Wines of Chablis and the Grand Auxerrois*, has this to say about recommended producers in Chablis: "Laurent Pinson and Jean-Paul and Benoit Droin (which has improved especially since Benoit started making the wine). . . . Sebastien Christophe is very good, but small. I also rate Daniel Defaix. I like Domaine des Malandes—and other good small producers include Domaine Oudin and Didier Picq. Jean Marc Brocard makes good wine, considering the quantities he produces. And of the big boys, Laroche is reliable and sometimes exciting. . . ."

BEAUJOLAIS

Beaujolais, the most southerly part of Burgundy, has the added distinction of having different levels of quality. The simply named Beaujolais comes from the southern part of the region, which is flat, with limestone and clay soil. The middle and northern sectors are hilly, with granite soil. This is Beaujolais-Villages country, where the wines are sturdier and have more extract. The top of the quality range comes from the named villages of Beaujolais in the north of the region. There are ten such named villages or *crus:* Brouilly, Chénas, Chiroubles, Côte de Brouilly, Fleurie, Juliénas, Morgon, Moulin-à-Vent, Régnié and Saint-Amour. In great years the best Beaujolais *crus* can age for decades. I recall in 1987 tasting a 1947 Moulin-à-Vent that had all the hallmarks of a well-aged Beaune. These village-named wines are prohibited from being made into Beaujolais Nouveau, only Beaujolais and Beaujolais-Villages.

Recommended Beaujolais Producers

Brunet

Duboeuf

Jadot

Trenel

Pascal Granger

Guy Bréton

Ferraud

Georges Descombes

Diochon

Joseph Drouhin

Tony's Dream Burgundy Cellar

Domaine Comte Ligier-Belair La Romanée

Domaine de la Romanée-Conti La Tâche

Armand Rousseau Le Chambertin

Domaine Bonneau du Martray Corton-Charlemagne

Denis Bachelet Charmes-Chambertin

Georgers Roumier Bonnes Mares

Louis Jadot Clos de Bèze

Clos du Tart

Anne Gros Richebourg

Comte Armand Pommard Clos des Epeneaux

CHAMPAGNE

Of all wines champagne is the most abused. Successful Formula One drivers spray spectators with large-format bottles and winning hockey teams shampoo each other with the stuff in locker rooms. Nor is this abuse confined to the sporting fraternity. Consumers keep bottles in the fridge against a time when they might get lucky and New Year revellers delight in creating as much noise as possible when opening bottles of bubbly. Then there's the "right occasion" syndrome: couples who keep a bottle from their wedding party to celebrate their first grandchild; by the time they open the bottle it will taste like skunky beer.

Champagne deserves a better fate. The winemakers of Champagne have laboured long and hard to get the bubbles into the bottle. So avoid those saucer-shaped glasses that have become the symbol for sparkling wine, because they're the worst receptacle for it—only slightly better than serving it out of a Wellington boot. Don't hang on to non-vintage champagne for years. You don't have to. The producers have already aged their wines for four years, which means you can drink it as soon as you buy it. Unless, of course, you're English and you enjoy the flavour the French call *le goût anglais*: the slightly maderized, nutty flavour of old champagne.

Now repeat after me: only wines coming from the designated Champagne region in northeastern France can be called champagne. All other wines with bubbles, even from France's other regions, are merely *vin mousseux* (sparkling wine).

Champagne is made from a blend of grapes: Chardonnay (white) and Pinot Noir and Pinot Meunier (black). If you see the term *Blanc de Blancs* on the label it means the wine was produced only from Chardonnay grapes, while *Blanc de Noirs* refers to the use of only black grapes. A rosé champagne can be made by macerating black grape skins with the wine for a matter of hours during fermentation to reach the requisite shade of pink. These days it is more likely made by blending red and white wines to the desired shade of pink and then putting that blend through a secondary fermentation in the bottle. Small amounts of still white and red wines are also made in the Champagne region; they are called Coteaux Champenois.

The bubbles are made by a secondary fermentation in the bottle. A solution of yeast and sugar is added to the still wine, which is then sealed with a crown cap. The fermentation that occurs creates carbonic gas that gets trapped in the wine because it has nowhere to go. The dead yeast cells have to be removed by a process called riddling. Originally done by hand over a series of weeks, in most champagne houses the cleaning process is now accomplished by a mechanical device that tilts the bottles in a large wire case. When the debris has collected under the crown cap, the bottles are immersed in brine to freeze their necks. When the cap is removed, the pressure of the gas (sixty to ninety pounds per square inch) forces out a plug of ice containing the dead yeast cells. At this point the house style of the producer's champagne determines the amount of sweetening wine that is added to top up the bottle. The label will tell you the style.

The World's Most Expensive Champagne

Clos Ambonnay is a walled vineyard enclosing little over an acre and a half of Pinot Noir vines in a village called Ambonnay on the Montagne de Reims. Krug, whose other single-vineyard Blanc de Blancs champagne, Clos de Mesnil, sells for more than $1,000 per bottle, produced a Blanc de Noirs champagne from the barrel-fermented Pinot Noir grapes. Clos Ambonnay is sold in New York for $3,000 to $3,500 a bottle. Its first vintage was 1995, and only 250 cases were made.

- **Brut Natural or Brut Zéro:** less than 3 grams of sugar per litre
- **Extra Brut:** less than 6 grams of sugar per litre
- **Brut:** less than 15 grams of sugar per litre
- **Extra Sec or Extra Dry:** 12 to 20 grams of sugar per litre
- **Sec:** 17 to 35 grams of sugar per litre
- **Demi-Sec:** 33 to 50 grams of sugar per litre
- **Doux:** more than 50 grams of sugar per litre

As I have mentioned, non-vintage champagne is ready for drinking when you purchase it. These products can be a blend of reserve wines from as many as seven different years. Vintage-dated champagne, which is made in good years, contains wines from a single year and has the possibility of being aged.

Recommended Champagne Producers

Krug

Bollinger

Louis Roederer

Gosset

Billecart-Salmon (rosé)

Salon

Dom Pérignon

Deutz

Jacquesson

Piper-Heidsieck

Pierre Gimmonet & Fils

Vilmart

Pol Roger

STORING CHAMPAGNE

Champagnes (and sparkling wines in general) are the only wines sealed with corks that do not have to be laid down in the literal sense. The pressurized CO_2 in the headspace is supersaturated (i.e., above 100 percent humidity), [and] thus keeps the cork moist and expanded, so you can keep bottles standing upright. This is not practical, of course, but at least it allows you to be relaxed about leaving the odd bottle upright. Champagne is particularly sensitive to temperature and light. Not just changes in temperature. I am between homes at the moment, but I had a natural cellar for twenty-one years, and in my next home, however good the natural cellar is . . . I will augment the ambient conditions with air-conditioning to ensure rigid control of temperature. I will store almost all of my red and white, dry and sweet, wines at a constant 14° Celsius (because that provides just the right rate of development as far as I'm concerned), but I will keep all my champagnes and any mature wines I buy (say twenty-plus years) in an inner sanctum at 9.5° Celsius. When disgorged, champagne is in an aerobic reductive state, and the longer it has been in that state (i.e., on its yeast lees) the more sensitive it is to oxygen. And what happens in disgorgement? That's right; it takes in a good deep breath of air. Reducing the storage temperature to 9.5° Celsius (the temperature in Pol Roger's cellars, compared to 10.5–11° Celsius in its competitors' cellars) slows the oxidation, encouraging the development of much finer post-disgorgement aromas (e.g., hints of toast, rather than blowsy toast). Lower temperatures also allow the CO_2 to combine, making the bubbles smaller before the gas bleeds away.

—Tom Stevenson, author of *Sotheby's Wine Encyclopedia* and *Christie's World Encyclopedia of Champagne and Sparkling Wine*

Tony's Dream Champagne Cellar

Krug Vintage

Krug Grande Cuvée

Bollinger Vieilles Vignes

Roederer Cristal Rosé

Taittinger Comte de Champagne

Billecart-Salmon Rosé

Dom Pérignon

Philipponat Clos des Goisses

Perrier-Jouët Belle Epoque Rosé

Piper-Heidsieck Brut Millésime

ALSACE

Tucked away on the French side of the Rhine, Alsace is Pied Piper land—a patchwork of 119 small half-timbered wine villages hard by each other. It is the only region in France that has historically labelled its wines by their grape variety rather than by the parish or commune where the vineyards are planted. About 90 percent of Alsace wines are white, grown from Riesling, Gewürztraminer, Pinot Gris (formerly known as Tokay Pinot Gris), Pinot Blanc, Muscat and Sylvaner grapes. The sole red wine is Pinot Noir, which is worth buying only in warm years, when the fruit can actually ripen. The most favoured slopes of the 15,298 hectares have been designated Grand Cru, although certain producers will not put the term on their labels. Hugel, for instance, the most prominent producer in Alsace—even though it produces great Riesling from the Grand Cru-designated Schoenenbourg vineyard—prefers to promote its name, believing the reputation of its brand is more significant than the vineyard name.

The glory of Alsace is its three major wines: Riesling, Gewürztraminer and Pinot Gris that can be made in a dry or sweet style (Vendange Tardive or Sélection de Grains Nobles). Sweet wines will always cellar well, and the style of Alsace dry wines has been growing noticeably sweeter with global warming. The most long-lasting and therefore the most cellar-worthy wines from Alsace, because of their fine acid structure, are Riesling. Without question, Alsace Gewürztraminer is the best expression of this aromatic variety; the wines are redolent of lychee and rose petals.

Though the wines of Alsace look like German wines in their long-necked green bottles, there is little similarity between the two wine styles. Alsace wines, being fermented to dryness, have significantly higher alcohol and lower residual sugar levels. They make excellent food wines. You'll also find an interesting sparkling wine called Crémant d'Alsace made by the *methode traditionelle* with Pinot Blanc, Pinot Gris, Pinot Noir, Riesling or Chardonnay grapes.

Recommended Alsace Producers

Hugel

Trimbach

Zind-Humbrecht

Léon Beyer

Domaine Weinbach

Josmeyer

Marcel Deiss

Schlumberger

René Muré

André Kientzler

Tony's Dream Alsace Cellar

Trimbach Frédéric Emile Riesling

Domaine Ostertag Grand Cru Riesling Muenchberg

Léon Beyer Riesling Les Escaliers

Domaine Zind Humbrecht Gewürztraminer Herrenberg

Gustave Lorenz Riesling Grand Cru Altenberg de
   Bergheim

Domaine Weinbach Riesling Grand Cru Cuvée Ste-
   Cathérine

Josmeyer Pinot Gris Grand Cru Hengst

Domaine Zind-Humbrecht Riesling Clos St-Urbain
   Grand Cru Rangen

Marcel Deiss Riesling Grand Cru Schoenenbourg

Hugel Gewürztraminer Sélection de Grains Nobles

LOIRE

The Loire Valley, with its chain of magnificent châteaux strung like pearls along the river bank, is basically a white-wine region. Some 300,000 hectares of vines produce a wide variety of white wines that are dry, semi-dry, sweet and sparkling, as well as rosé and red. After Champagne, incidentally, the Loire Valley is the second-largest producer of sparkling wine in France.

There are a bewildering number of appellations here, but basically all you need to know are the main sub-regions. Beginning in the west towards the Atlantic Ocean is **Muscadet**, the region and the grape (also known as Melon de Bourgogne just to confuse matters, although it is no longer grown in Burgundy) that produce a fresh, lively wine for drinking young that goes so well with the seafood of the area. The neighbouring **Anjou-Saumur** region has a predominance of Chenin

Blanc, which is made in a sweet style in Coteaux du Layon and an exquisite dry style in Savennières. In the southeastern corner of the appellation, in Saumur-Champigny, they grow Cabernet Franc and Cabernet Sauvignon. The best red wines of the Loire, however, come from **Touraine**. They are made from Cabernet Franc grapes grown around the towns of Bourgeuil and Chinon; the wines of Bourgeuil live longer than those of Chinon, but both can be delicious in good years.

Moving east, the next major appellation is **Vouvray**, and I must confess these are my favourite wines of the Loire. Made from Chenin Blanc that is harvested as late as November, they can be dry or semi-dry or, if affected by botrytis, they can be honey-sweet. The semi-dry and sweet wines are some of the longest-lived white wines available and are remarkably cellar worthy. For sheer longevity you can't beat the Chenin Blanc grape grown in Vouvray.

The best-known wines of the region come from **Sancerre** and **Pouilly-sur-Loire**, the home of Pouilly-Fumé (which should not be confused with Burgundy's Pouilly-Fuissé, made from Chardonnay grapes in the Mâconnais). The *Fumé* bit may come from the type of soil, called silex, which imparts a gun-flint smell to the wine, or it may be derived from the morning fog off the river that shrouds the vineyards in the morning. Here at the eastern limit of the Loire Valley, Sauvignon Blanc is king. There is an archipelago of smaller sub-regions—Menetou-Salon, Quincy and Reuilly—that produce the same tart gooseberry- and cut grass–flavoured wines.

Recommended Loire Producers

Didier Dagueneau (Pouilly-Fumé)

Jacky Blot (Domaine la Taille aux Loups, Montlouis)

Château Pierre-Bise, Claude Papin (Anjou, Savennières,
  Coteaux du Layon)

Yannick Amirault (Bourgueil)

Bernard Baudry (Chinon)

Jean-Maurice Raffault (Chinon)

Domaine Baumard (Savennières)

N. Joly (Savennières–Coulée de Serrant)

François Cotat (Sancerre)

Domaine Vacheron (Sancerre)

Tony's Dream Loire Cellar

Didier Dagueneau Pouilly-Fumé Pur Sang
  (and Pouilly-Fumé Silex)

Château de Villeneuve Saumur-Champigny
  Le Grand Clos

Château de Fesles Bonnezeau

Domaine la Taille aux Loups Montlouis Romulus

Domaine des Forges Quarts de Chaume

Château Pierre-Bise Coteaux du Layon Beaulieu
  Les Rouannières

Château du Hureau Saumur-Champigny Lisagathe

Domaine Vacheron Sancerre Rouge La Belle Dame

Domaines des Roches Neuves Saumur-Champigny
  Marginale

Domaines des Rochelles Anjou-Villages Brissac
  Les Millerits

RHÔNE

Some of France's finest wines come from the Rhône
Valley, and every self-respecting cellar should have some.
The Rhône is not one wine region but two. In the
Northern Rhône, with its continental climate, the only
red grape that is permitted is Syrah. But Syrah can be

blended with the white variety Viognier for Côte-Rôtie or Marsanne and Roussanne in the Saint-Joseph appellation (the Beaujolais of the Rhône), Crozes-Hermitage and Hermitage. The only appellation that must be 100 percent Syrah is Cornas. Only 5 percent of the Rhône's wine production is white, and in the northern part these wines are confined to Condrieu and Château-Grillet (made from Viognier grapes), while Marsanne and Roussanne are used for the whites of Crozes-Hermitage, Hermitage, Saint-Joseph and Saint-Péray (still and sparkling).

The Southern Rhône, with its Mediterranean climate, has a much less exclusive and democratic approach to grape varieties. Vintners here can blend up to thirteen different varieties in their wine if they so choose, red and white. And Domaine de Beaucastel does exactly that for its formidable Châteauneuf-du-Pape. The red varieties in terms of importance in the Southern Rhône are Grenache, Syrah, Mourvèdre, Cinsault, Carignan, Counoise and Picpoul. The white varieties are Grenache Blanc, Marsanne, Roussanne, Bourboulenc, Viognier and Picpoul Blanc.

Recommended Rhône Producers

Domaine Jean-Louis Chave (Hermitage)

E. Guigal Château d'Ampuis (Côte Rôtie, Hermitage)

Michel Chapoutier (Hermitage, Châteauneuf-du-Pape)

Domaine de Vieux Télégraphe (Châteauneuf-du-Pape)

A. Clape (Cornas)

Delas (Côte Rôtie)

Alain Voges (Cornas)

Château Rayas (Châteauneuf-du-Pape)

Domaine de Beaucastel (Châteauneuf-du-Pape)

Domaine Jamet (Côte Rôtie)

Tony's Dream Rhône Cellar

Chave Hermitage Cuvée Cathelin

Chapoutier L'Ermitage Ermite

Guigal Côte Rôtie La Landonne

Domaine Jamet Côte Rôtie

Georges Vernay Condrieu Coteaux de Vernon

Domaine de Beaucastel Châteauneuf-du-Pape

Domaine de Vieux Télégraphe Châteauneuf-du-Pape

A. Clape Cornas

M. Chapoutier Côte Rôtie La Mordorée

Jean-Michel Gérin Côte Rôtie La Landon

OTHER FRENCH REGIONS

I could have filled my cellar with French wines that were not even from the highly acclaimed and recognised regions of France. It would be wrong to overlook some of the great wines that are produced in the lesser-travelled regions, hence the following choice of a Dream Cellar.

Tony's Dream Cellar from Other French Regions

Jean Macle Château-Chalon (Jura)

André & Mireille Tissot Savagnin (Arbois)

Château du Cèdre Le Cèdre (Cahors)

Château Haut Monplaisir (Cahors)

Domaine Tempier Cabassaou (Bandol)

Gérard Bertrand Coteaux du Languedoc La Clape
    l'Hospitalet (Languedoc)

Château Bouscassé Vieilles Vignes (Madiran)

Château Simone Rouge (Palette)

Mas du Soleilla La Clape Clôt de l'Amandier
    (Languedoc)

Domaine Gardiés Côte du Roussillon-Villages La Torre
    (Roussillon)

ITALY

Wine is produced in all twenty of Italy's provinces, from Alto Adige in the northeast to Sicily in the south, and from Sardinia in the west to Puglia in the southeast. You might call it a wine-saturated country—depending on the vintage, it's the largest producer on the planet, with 20 percent of the world's wines coming from its 680,000 hectares of vineyards. Italy has more than 900,000 registered vineyards (and more that are not registered) and more than 770,000 wine estates. Some of their owners can trace wine-growing back through their noble family trees to the fourteenth century, such as the marcheses Antinori and Frescobaldi. But not only titled landowners have made wine for generations in Italy; every peasant farmer has a vineyard and every backyard supports a few rows of grapes for home winemaking. To the Italians, bless them, wine is both a food group and a heritage that stretches back to the Etruscans, long before the Romans ever planted a vine. (Personal aside: The very first wine article I ever wrote was under the "nom de vin" Perry Anders, an obscure reference to the tyrannical Greek general Periander, who introduced the vine to Rome.)

Italian wine regulations can be confusing but basically they fall into four categories. Vino da Tavola (table wine) is a class that ironically embraces both the simplest, most inexpensive gluggable wines and the costliest icon products such as Sassicaia and Tignanello. Because these Super Tuscan wines did not adhere to Chianti's appellation rules (they are made from unauthorized grape varieties), they could not be labelled as DOC (Denominazione di Origine Controllata) and were thus demoted to mere Vino da Tavola status. However, they were more expensive than the top Chianti Classico Riservas. So the bureaucrats, ever pragmatic, solved the problem by creating an appellation especially for them, Indicazione Geografica Tipica (IGT).

Technically, the higher level of quality is a category invented by more bureaucrats, this time in Brussels, for all the European Union wine-producing countries: QWPSR (Quality Wines Produced in Specified Regions). Italy has two levels of QWPSR: DOC and the more prestigious DOCG (Denominazione di Origine Controllata e Garantita). At the time of writing there were thirty-six designated DOCG regions, mainly in Tuscany and Piedmont, but for some unfathomable reason, Amarone from Veneto was not among them. The difference between DOC and DOCG is that the latter wines have to be blind tasted to ensure their regional typicity and quality. For DOC and DOCG wines there are more than 350 authorized grape varieties, but double this number are actually used for winemaking.

From a collector's point of view, the regions to concentrate on are **Piedmont** (think of this as Italy's Burgundy with its mono-varietal wines), **Tuscany** (more like Bordeaux with its blended reds and whites—and its preoccupation with Cabernet Sauvignon), **Veneto**, **Friuli** (for white wines) and **Sicily** (newly emerged as a source of fine wines at reasonable prices). There are, of course, some great wines to be found in other Italian regions, which I have dealt with in my "Dream Cellar from Other Italian Regions" list below.

Italian white wines are for the most part ready for drinking within a year of their vintage date, except, of course, for the sweet wines made from botrytized grapes, *vin santo* and the Marsalas of Sicily. The reds, especially those produced from Nebbiolo and Sangiovese grapes, can age for many years. Remember, the better the wine, the more likely it is to have a longer life. In Italy's case this means that wines labelled "Riserva" will have more concentration and potential aging ability than those without the designation.

PIEDMONT

The Nebbiolo grape produces the great long-lived Barolos and Barbarescos as well as less feted and as a result less costly wines from other parts of the region, such as Sforzato, Inferno, Sassella, Ghemme and Gattinara. The other notable red wines, lighter in style and faster maturing, are Barbera, Dolcetto, Freisa, Grignolino and Brachetto. The whites of the region should not be overlooked. The semi-sweet Moscato d'Asti is a delicious summer drink, and the Cortese grape from Gavi makes a lip-smacking dry white wine.

Recommended Piedmont Producers

Giacomo Conterno

Ceretto

Domenico Clerico

Gaja

Bruno Giacosa

Roberto Voerzio

Paolo Scavino

Elio Atare

Massolino

Silvio Grasso

Tony's Dream Piedmont Cellar

Bruno Rocca Barbaresco Rabatajà

Giacomo Conterno Barolo Cascina Francia

Bartolo Mascarello Barolo

Sandrone Barbera d'Alba

Marchese di Gresy Barbaresco "Martenenga"

Angelo Gaja Barbaresco "Costa Russi"

Antinolo Gattinara "Osso San Grato"

Fratelli Cavallotto Barolo "Bricco Boschis"

Giuseppe Mascarello Barolo Monprivato

Cavallotto Barolo Vignolo Riserva

TUSCANY

The first Italian wine you ever drank was probably Chianti. The Classico heart of the region stretches from Florence to Siena. Here the ubiquitous Sangiovese grape is blended with Canaiolo and sometimes Cabernet Sauvignon or Syrah or as a 100-percent varietal. In the southern part of the province it produces a 100-percent varietal Brunello di Montalcino and Vino Nobile di Montepulciano. In all of its expressions Sangiovese is a candidate for cellaring, especially as Morellino di Scansano. The grape produces wines with a dry, spicy cherry flavour and a fine spine of acidity. Maremma, on the Tuscan coast, is also home to several of Italy's renowned IGT wines such as Sassicaia and Ornellaia. They are based on Cabernet Sauvignon and would be hard to pick out of a line of red Bordeaux. Tuscany's white wine of note is Vernacchia de San Gimignano, which is best consumed young.

Recommended Tuscany Producers

Fattoria di Felsina (Chianti Classico)

Fontodi (Chianti Classico)

Poggio di Sotto (Montalcino)

Antinori (Chianti Classico, Maremma)

Frescobaldi (Chianti Rufina, Brunello di Montalcino)

Isole e Olena (Chianti)

Casse Basse Soldera (Montalcino)

Lisini (Montalcino)

Querciabella (Chianti Classico)

Fattoria Selvapiana (Chianti Rufina)

Tony's Dream Tuscany Cellar

Tenuta Il Poggione Brunello di Montalcino

Le Macchiole "Paleo"

Isole e Olena Cepparello

Tenuta dell'Ornellaia Toscana Masseto

Bibi Gaetz Toscana Testamatta

Antinori Toscana Solaia

Marchesi de' Frescobaldi Brunello di Montalcino
    Castelgiocondo Ripe al Convento Riserva

Fattoria Le Pupille Maremma Toscana Saffredi

Altesino Brunello di Montalcino Montosoli

Brancaia Toscana Il Blu

VENETO

From Lake Garda to Venice, the Veneto region is rich in wine culture. Its pre-eminent red is an anomaly. You can drink it young and fresh and chilled if you like as Valpolicella. But when the same wine is made by drying the Corvina, Rondinella and Molinara grapes for about four months before fermentation, it becomes Amarone, a higher-alcohol wine you can cellar for a decade or more, especially the sweeter version, Recioto della Valpolicella Amarone. Veneto is home to Prosecco, an inexpensive sparkling wine, and Soave, a crisp white that tastes of peaches. Soave in Recioto style is one of the world's great dessert wines.

Recommended Veneto Producers

Masi (Amarone)

Serego Aligheri (Amarone)

Roberto Anselmi (Soave)

Pieropan (Soave)

Montenidoli (Vernaccia di San Gimignano)

Giuseppi Quintarelli (Valpolicella, Amarone)

Romano Dal Forno (Amarone)

Allegrini (Amarone)

Tedeschi (Amarone)

Tony's Dream Veneto Cellar

Roccolo Grassi Amarone della Valpolicella "Vigneto
　　Roccolo Grassi"

Allegrini Verona La Poja (Corvina)

Masi Amarone della Valpolicella Costasera

Serègo Alighieri Vaio Armaron

La Salette Amarone della Valpolicella Classico
　　La Marega

Maculan Merlot Breganze Crosara

Quintarelli Vapolicella and Amarone

Suavia Soave Classico Le Rive

Vivani Amarone della Valpolicella Classico Casa
　　dei Bepi

Brunelli Amarone della Valpolicella Classico
　　Campo del Titari

SICILY

A long-time producer of sweet dessert wines such as
Marsala and Moscato, Sicily has emerged in the past fifteen years as a producer of quality red wines and
surprisingly—given the heat—rich, well-balanced white
wines. The warm weather makes for very ripe grapes

whose sugars ferment directly into higher alcohol than you find in Tuscany or Piedmont. As a result, the wines are full-bodied with a spicy plum flavour. Nero d'Avola, a local variety not dissimilar to Syrah, is producing some full-bodied dry reds, and top producers such as Planeta have come out with Chardonnays of quality.

Recommended Sicilian Producers

Planeta

Fazio

Sant'Anastasia

Donnafugata

Spadafora

Tasca d'Almerita

Morante

Fuedo Maccari

Cusumano

Tony's Dream Sicilian Cellar

Feudo Montoni Nero d'Avola Selezione Speciale "Vrucara"

Fuedo Maccari Nero d'Avola Saia

Planeta Syrah

Tenuta delle Terre Nere Prephylloxera La Vigna di Don Peppino

Donnafugata Passito di Pantelleria Ben Ryé

Firriato Nero d'Avola Syrah Santagostino Baglio Soria

Morante Nero d'Avola Don Antonio

Planeta Chardonnay

Tasca d'Almerita Rosso del Conte

Cusumano Nero d'Avola Sàgana

OTHER ITALIAN REGIONS

As I mentioned, Italy grows wine in all twenty of its provinces. There are some dazzling products from regions that don't have the same visibility as Tuscany, Piedmont, Veneto and Sicily. Although space precludes my profiling every part of the country, it would be churlish not to celebrate the best wines from these less-frequented regions.

Tony's Dream Cellar from Other Italian Regions

Valentini Trebbiano d'Abruzzo (Abruzzo)

Zaccagnini Montepulciano d'Abruzzo "San Clemente" (Abruzzo)

Elena Fucci Aglianico del Vulture (Basilicata)

Cantina Sociale di Santadi Valli di Porto Pino Latinia (Sardinia)

Cosimo Taurino "Patriglione" (Puglia)

Cantine Ciolli Cesanese di Olevano Romano "Cirsium" (Lazio)

Mastroberadino Taurasi Riserva "Radici" (Campagnia)

Antonelli Sagnatino di Montefalco (Umbria)

Odoardi Savuto Superiore "Vigna Mortilla" (Basilicata)

Produttori Cortaccia Merlot "Brenntal" (Trentino-Alto-Adige)

MARSALA

What sherry is to Spain, Marsala is to Italy. This fortified wine, which varies from 17 to 19 percent alcohol, can occasionally be dry but is more normally sweet to very sweet. The wine is named after the port city in Sicily where it was originally produced in the latter half of the eighteenth century, by English wine merchants who were looking for cheaper versions of sherry and port. The wine is made from the Grillo, Catarratto and Inzolia grapes and in its

David Gleave, M.W., proprietor of Liberty Wines in London, specializes in Italian wines. He makes the following vintage-dated suggestions for an Italian cellar.

2003: "Go for classic reds like Barolo, Barbaresco, Chianti Classico Riserva, Chianti Rufina Riserva or some of the top Super Tuscans."

2004: "Go for the best names. A Barolo from a mediocre *négociant* won't have the aging ability of one from Aldo Conterno or Bruno Giacosa."

2005: "In general, drink the wines young rather than older. Italy is still in an experimental phase, and only a handful of top producers are making wines that will age to the same extent as the classics from France."

2006: "I'd stuff my cellar full of Italian wines for short-term aging—Langhe Nebbiolo, good Valpolicella, Montepulciano d'Abruzzo, Primitivo from Puglia, Aglianico, Nero d'Avola, young Chianti and Chianti Riserva—this will provide great pleasure."

2007: "Go for good vintages—'06, '04, '01 and '99—for wines for long aging."

2008: "Go for the big wines from hot years—2000, 2003, 1997—for wines for early and intermediate drinking."

2009: "Don't underestimate Italy's whites: good Verdicchio, Lugana from producers like Ca' dei Frati, Soave from Pieropan and some of Friuli's and the Sud Tirol's whites can age wonderfully."

natural state, like sherry, it is dry. Marsala Vergine is the most sought after. Sweeter versions are made from grape must called *cotto*, which is concentrated by boiling down, or *sifone*, sweet wine with grape brandy. Four basic styles are designated under the DOC, Italy's wine law.

Marsala Fine: the lowest grade, of around 17 percent alcohol, which contains more concentrated must than sweetened wine. It can also bear the older designation of Italy Particular (IP) or Italia.

Marsala Superiore: has 1 percent more alcohol and at least two years of wood aging and ranges from dry to sweet, depending upon the producer. Initials on the label will indicate traditional descriptions—SOM (Superior Old Marsala), LP (London Particular), GD (Garibaldi Dolce).

Marsala Speciale: contains an extra 1 percent alcohol and flavouring additives such as coffee, cream, egg, banana or orange.

Marsala Vergine: dry to very dry, without any sweetening agents added. Must be aged for at least five years in wood and may spend time in a solera (see page 167). Vergine Stravecchio is aged for ten years.

Recommended Marsala Producers
Marco de Bartoli

Florio

Pellegrino

Tony's Dream Marsala Cellar
Marco de Bartoli Vecchio Semperi

Marco de Bartoli Bukkuram

GERMANY

Germany has the largest vineyard plantings of Riesling—accounting for nearly 62 percent of this variety globally—concentrated mainly in the Rheingau and Mosel regions. Giles MacDonogh, a British wine historian and a specialist in German wines, believes that Riesling, "of all white wines, is arguably the longest lasting. True, there are Chenin Blancs in the Loire and Sauternes that age for decades, but Riesling in all its styles from bone dry to honeyed sweet is more cellar worthy than Chardonnay, Sauvignon Blanc, Soave or Muscadet. Great Mosel Riesling can last forever." The reason for Riesling's cellar-worthiness is the high acidity of the grapes in this northerly region.

While acidity gives longevity to the wine, it is the sugar in the grapes at the time of harvest that preoccupies the growers, because their appellation system is based on how sweet they are. The sugar readings determine what will appear on the label. The driest German Riesling is labelled as QbA, the next level up is Kabinett, and then sweetness increases through Spätlese, Auslese, Beerenauslese, Trockenbeerenauslese and Eiswein. This is made a little more complicated when the term *trocken* (dry) is added; it means that the residual sugar has been fermented out and the wine is drier and higher in alcohol.

German Riesling at its driest will display a unique tension between crisp citrus acidity and sweet peach/apricot flavours, with an overlay of minerality and a beguiling floral note. The sweeter versions take on notes of honey and tropical fruits.

Surprisingly, Germany is also the third-largest grower, after France and the United States, of Pinot

Noir (a grape they call Spätburgunder, or late-ripening Burgunder, as opposed to the early-ripening Frühburgunder). With red Burgundy prices heading into the stratosphere, Spätburgunder from the Ahr, Rheingau and Baden regions becomes an attractive proposition, although its cellar life won't be as long as the best red Burgundy's.

German wines were the bargain-basement wines of Europe until fairly recently, and then Riesling came into vogue again. There is now a global market for German wines that means bargains are rare. A few estates have lots of wine and lots of vineyard land, so the prices have always been kept down. The top estates, such as J. J. Prüm, Ernst Loosen and Marcus Molitor, can be very expensive but their Estate Riesling—their lowest-priced wine in the Riesling category—is well worth buying.

In the past twenty years the German wine map has been redrawn. The best vineyards have been classified, which has led producers to divide their wines into three categories: the basic estate wine, then the classified growth and at the top the Great Growth (what the Rheingau calls Erstes Gewächs, a term it trademarked for its own region, forcing the Mosel to come up with its own term, Grosses Gewächs). These days you can pay more for these top-quality wines than for a Burgundy.

Red wine is creeping in all over Germany. From the Mosel plains, where the cheap wine used to come from, you can now find red-wine vineyards. The same is true of Rheinhessen, which will ultimately become a red-wine region.

In making the choices for my Dream Cellar my predilection for the old-style German wines, with their wonderful tension between sweetness and racy acidity and lightness on the palate, is transparent.

AHR

The region along the River Ahr, a tributary of the Rhine, is the most northerly of Germany's wine areas, yet it produces the country's best Spätburgunder (Pinot Noir).

Recommended Ahr Producers

Meyer-Näkel

Stodden

Kriechel

J. J. Adenauer

Linden Sonnenberg-Görres

Kreuzberg

Weingut Maibachfarm

Tony's Dream Ahr Cellar

Meyer-Näkel Dernau Pfarrwungert Spätburgunder

Jean Stodden Recher Herrenberg Spätburgunder

Weingut Kreuzberg Ahrweiler Silberberg Spätburgunder

Weingut Nelles Spätburgunder Goldkapsel

Weingut Burggarten Sonnenberg Spätburgunder Auslese

Weingut Deutzerhof—Cossmann-Hehle Kirchtürmchen
   Spätburgunder

BADEN

Baden, one of Germany's warmest growing regions, is in the southwestern corner of the country, directly across the Rhine from Alsace. The Pinot varieties (Weissburgunder, Grauburgunder and Spätburgunder) flourish here, and the alcohol levels tend to be the highest in Germany, especially in wines grown in the Kaiserstuhl.

Recommended Baden Producers

Fischer Inh-S. & J. Heger

Weingut Franz Keller

Salwey (Ziereisen)

Martin Wassmer

Harmut Schlumberger

Huber

Tony's Dream Baden Cellar

Franz Keller Spätburgunder

Salwey Spätburgunder

Gut Nägelsförst Chardonnay Trockenbeerenauslese

Weingut Bernard Huber Spätburgunder

Weingut Heger Schlossberg Weissburgunder Spätlese

Winzergenossenschaft Achkarren am Kaiserstuhl
   Schlossberg Gewürztraminer Eiswein

FRANCONIA

This region (a.k.a. Franken in Bavaria) is famous for its flask-shaped Bocksbeutel. The bottle design is said to have been inspired by a goat's scrotum; while decorative, it's difficult to store in a conventional cellar rack. The vineyards are clustered around the Main River, where the chalky soil is ideal for producing powerful dry Silvaner wines.

Recommended Franken Producers

Fürstlich Castell'sches Domänenamt

Rudolf Fürst

Hofmann

Staatliche Hofkeller

Schmitts Kinder

Juliusspital

Hans Wirsching

Horst Sauer

Ludwig Knoll

Tony's Dream Franken Cellar

Fürstlich Castell'sches Domänenamt Schlossberg Silvaner
Trocken Grosses Gewächs

Horst Sauer Centgrafenberg Riesling Eiswein

Rudolf Fürst Centgrafenberg Traminer "R" QbA

Juliusspital Würzberg Silvaner Grosses Gewächs

Weingut Bickel-Stumpf Johannisberg Scheurebe
Trockenbeerenauslese

Wirsching Iphöfer Julius-Echterberg Silvaner Grosses
Gewächs

Fürst Hunsrück Spätburgunder Trocken "R" Grosses
Gewächs

HESSISCHE BERGSTRASSE (HESSIAN MOUNTAIN ROAD)

This region is the second smallest of Germany's regions. Riesling is the major grape, although some Spätburgunder is planted as well.

Recommended Hessische Bergstrasse Producers

Bergsträsser Winzer eG

Hessische Staatsweingüter Kloster Eberbach

Simon-Bürkle

Weingut der Staat Benheim

Tony's Dream Hessische Bergstrasse Cellar

Bergsträsser Winzer eG Heppenheimer Edweg Riesling
Eiswein

Hessische Staatsweingüter Kloster Eberbach

Heppenheimer Centgericht Rieslaner
   Trockenbeerenauslese
Simon-Bürkle Aurbacher Höllberg Riesling Eiswein

MITTELRHEIN

As its name suggests, the Mittelrhein region is located along the middle stretch of the Rhine, between the Rheingau and Mosel regions, and is planted mostly to Riesling.

Recommended Mittelrhein Producers

Toni Jost

Weingut Peter Hohn

Weingut August & Thomas Perll

Heinrich Weiler

Jochen Ratzenberger

Florian Weingart

Matthias Müller

Weingut Didinger

Tony's Dream Mittelrhein Cellar

Toni Jost Bacharacher Hahn Riesling
   Trockenbeerenauslese
Florian Weingart Boppard Hamm Riesling
   Trockenbeerenauslese
Florian Weingart Boppard Hamm Feuerlay Riesling
   Auslese
Weingut Hermann Ockenfels Leutesdorf Rosenberg
   Riesling Auslese
Jochen Ratzenberger Bacharacher Wolfshöhle Riesling
   QbA Grosses Gewächs
Weingut August & Thomas Perll Boppard Hamm
   Mandelstein Riesling Beerenauslese Goldkapsel

MOSEL

Until 2007 this high-quality region was known as Mosel-Saar-Ruwer after the Moselle (Mosel) River and its two tributaries, the rivers Saar and Ruwer. Here Riesling is king; Mosel's precipitous vineyards on deep slate soil produce some of the finest Rieslings in the world. Mosel Rieslings are generally racier—with a lively acidity—and lighter in body than those of the Rheingau or Rheinhessen.

Recommended Mosel Producers

Reichsgraf von Kesselstatt Thanisch

Dr. Pauly-Bergweiler

Dr. Ernst Loosen

J. J. Prüm

S. A. Prüm

Reinhold Haart

St. Urbanshof

Van Volxem

Geltz-Ziliken

Clemens Busch

Weiser-Künstler

Weingut Markus Molitor

Tony's Dream Mosel Cellar

J. J. Prüm Wehlener Sonnenuhr Riesling Auslese Goldkapsel

Dr. Loosen Ürziger Würzgarten Riesling Auslese
    Goldkapsel

Weingut Markus Molitor Zeltingen Sonnenuhr Riesling
    Auslese

Weingut Heymann-Löwenstein Riesling
    Trockenbeerenauslese von Blauen Schiefer

Fritz Haag Brauneberger Juffer-Sonnenuhr Riesling
    Auslese Lange Goldkapsel

Clemens Busch Pündericher Marienburg Riesling

Trockenbeerenauslese

Van Volxem Scharzhofberger Pergentsknopp Riesling

Maximin Grünhauser Abtsberg Riesling Auslese

Dr. Pauly-Bergweiler Bernkastel Alte Badstube am

Doctorberg Riesling Trockenbeerenauslese

Egon Müller Scharzhofberger Riesling Auslese

NAHE

The River Nahe runs south from the Rhine at Bingen. The soils vary owing to prehistoric volcanic activity. It's mostly a white-wine region where Riesling does best and can rival Mosel and Rheingau in quality.

Recommended Nahe Producers

Prinz zu Salm-Dalberg'sches Weingut

Schäfer-Frölich

Korrell-Johannishof

Hans Crusius

Hehner-Kiltz

Hermann Dönnhof

Kruger-Rumpf

Paul Anheuser

Schlossgut Diel

Emrich-Schönleber

Tony's Dream Nahe Cellar

Weingut Joh. Bapt. Schäfer Dorsheimer Pittermänchen

Riesling Trockenbeerenauslese

Weingut Dr. Crusius Traisener Rotenfels Riesling

Trockenbeerenauslese

Weingut Emrich-Schönleber Monzingener Halenberg

Riesling QbA Grosses Gewächs

Schlossgut Diel Dorsheimer Goldloch Riesling Spätlese

Weingut Hermann Dönnhof Oberhäuser Brücke Riesling
Auslese

Weingut Emrich-Schönleber Monzingener Halenberg
Riesling Spätlese

Weingut Hermann Dönnhoff Niederhausen Hermannshöhle
Riesling Spätlese

Weingut Bürgermeister Willi Schweinhardt
Langenlonsheimer Königsschild Riesling
Trockenbeerenauslese

PALATINATE (PFALZ)

Formerly known as Rheinpfalz, the Pfalz region is overall the warmest and driest of Germany's wine regions. It makes rich Riesling in Alsace style and is the second-largest producing region in Germany. Pfalz's winemakers also produce some appealing red wines from Spätburgunder, Portugieser and Dornfelder grapes.

Recommended Pfalz Producers

Dr. Bürklin-Wolf

Müller-Cattoir

Kurt Darting

Bassermann-Jordan

J. L. Volk

Philip Kuhn

Knipser Friedrich Becker

Lingenfelder

Georg Mosbacher

Joseph Biffar

Tony's Dream Pfalz Cellar

Dr. Bürklin-Wolf Forster Kirchenstück Riesling Trocken

Reichsrat von Buhl Forster Ungeheuer Riesling Spätlese
Trocken

Reichsrat von Buhl Forster Jesuitengarten Riesling Spätlese

Weingut Koehler-Ruprecht Kallstadt Saumagen Riesling
Auslese

Weingut Georg Mosbacher Deidesheim Kieselberg
Riesling Spätlese Grosses Gewächs

Weingut Müller-Cattoir Gimmeldingen Schlössel
Rieslaner Beerenauslese

Bassermann-Jordan Deidesheimer Hohenmorgen Riesling
Auslese

Rebholz Birkweiler Konstanienbusch Riesling Spätlese
Trocken

Christmann Königsbacher IDIG Riesling Grosses Gewächs

RHEINGAU

The Rhine flows east–west for thirty kilometres through the small region of Rheingau before it turns north. The village names read like a first-class wine list.

Recommended Rheingau Producers

Schloss Johannesberg

Staatsweingüter Kloster Eberbach

Georg Breuer

Weingut Franz Künstler

Weingut Georg Müller

Kessler

Josef Leitz

Fürst von Löwenstein

Weingut Trenz

Langwerth von Simmern

Tony's Dream Rheingau Cellar

Georg Breuer Rüdesheimer Berg Schlossberg Riesling
Trocken

Saint Urbans-Hof Ockfener Bockstein Riesling Auslese

Staatsweingüter Kloster Eberbach Steinberger Riesling

Weingut Franz Künstler Hochheimer Kirschenstück
Riesling Spätlese

Robert Weil Kiedricher Grafenberg Riesling
Trockenbeerenauslese

Balthasar Ress Hattenheimer Nussbrunnen Riesling
Trockenbeerenauslese Goldkapsel

Langwerth von Simmern Hattenheimer Nussbrunnen
Riesling Beerenauslese

Josef Leitz Rüdesheimer Klosterberg Riesling Eiswein

Johannishof Rüdesheimer Berg Rottland Riesling Spätlese

Domdechant Werner'sches Hochheimer Domdechaney
Riesling Auslese Goldkapsel

RHEINHESSEN (RHENISH HESSE)

Rheinhessen is the largest wine region of Germany and
the home of Liebfraumilch, although this should not be
held against it—producers here are now making some
top-flight white and red wines.

Recommended Rheinhessen Producers

Gunderloch

Freiherr Heyl Zu-Herrnsheim

Keller

Wittmann

Kühling-Gillot

K. F. Groebe

Gutzler

Winter

Tony's Dream Rheinhessen Cellar

Balbach Niersteiner Oelberg Riesling Eiswein

Gunderloch Nackenheimer Rothenberg Riesling Auslese
  Goldkapsel

Gunderloch Nackenheimer Riesling Rothenberg
  Trockenbeerenauslese

Freiherr Heyl Zu-Herrnsheim Niersteiner Pettental
  Riesling Auslese

Weingut Keller Riesling Trocken G Max

Weingut Wittmann Westhofener Morstein Riesling
  Trocken

Wagner Stempel Siefersheimer Heerkretz Riesling
  Spätlese

Weingut Wittmann Westhofener Morstein Riesling
  Auslese

Kruger-Rumpf Binger Scharlachberg Riesling Spätlese

Franz Karl Schmidt Niersteiner Hipping Riesling Spätlese

SAALE-UNSTRUT

Germany's most northerly wine-growing region, Saale-Unstrut is named for the two rivers that flow through it; it was formerly one of the two regions in East Germany. This white-wine area is planted mainly to Müller-Thurgau, Weissburgunder and Silvaner grapes.

Recommended Saale-Unstrut Producers

Pawis

Gussek

Weingut Lützkendorf

Klaus Böhme

Kloster Pforta

Thüringer Weingut Bad Sulza

Tony's Dream Saale-Unstrut Cellar

Weingut Lützkendorf Karsdorfer Hohe Gräte
Weissburgunder Grosses Gewächs

Weingut Lützkendorf Karsdorfer Hohe Gräte Traminer
Auslese

Thüringer Weingut Bad Sulza Traminer Eiswein

Winzerhof Gussek Naumburg Steinmeister Müller-
Thurgau Trockenbeerenauslese

SAXONY (SACHSEN)

Saxony, the other former East German wine region, is along the River Elbe, in the southeastern corner of the country. It's the smallest wine-growing region in Germany and produces very dry wines. It is planted mainly to Riesling, Müller-Thurgau and Weissburgunder grapes.

Recommended Sachsen Producers

Klaus Zimmerling

Schloss Wacherbarth

Schloss Proschwitz

Sächsisches Staatsweingut

Weingut Vincenz Richter

Tony's Dream Sachsen Cellar

Weingut Schloss Proschwitz Weissburgunder QbA
Grosses Gewächs

Weingut Schloss Proschwitz Scheurebe Kabinett Trocken

Weingut Vincenz Richter

Meissener Kapitelberg Riesling Beerenauslese Sächsisches
Staatsweingut GmbH Schloss Wackerbarth

Radebeul Lößnitz Weissburgunder Spätlese Trocken

WÜRTTEMBERG

The Württemberg region is the largest producer of red wine in Germany, mainly from Trollinger, Schwarzriesling and Lemberger grapes.

Recommended Württemberg Producers

Weingut des Grafen Neipperg

Schnaitmann

Gerhard Aldinger

H. Bader

Kistenmacher-Hengerer

Kurz-Wagner

Schlossgut Hohenbeilstein

Weingärtner Brackenheim

Weingut Jürgen Ellwanger

Drautz-Able

Tony's Dream Württemberg Cellar

Weingut Jürgen Ellwanger Nicodemus Red Wine

Drautz-Able Jodokus Rotwein Trocken

Schnaitmann Riesling Trocken QbA

Weingut Birkert Adolzfurt Schneckenhof Riesling Eiswein

Weingut Graf Adelmann Kleinbottwar Süssmund
   Grauburgunder Trockenbeerenauslese

Weingut Albrecht Schwegler Granat Red Wine QbA

Karl Haidle Spätburgunder Trocken QbA

Weingut Ernst Dautel Lemberger Trocken QbA

Weingut Ernst Dautel Spätburgunder Trocken QbA

AUSTRIA

Grüner Veltliner, Austria's signature grape, is waiting in the wings for its moment on stage when the world tires of Chardonnay. This versatile variety, with flavours of peaches and white pepper, has been grown along the Danube since Roman times and today accounts for over a third of the country's vineyard surface. Vienna is the only world capital with vineyards within its city limits (Paris's tiny plot in Montmartre pales before Vienna's 651 hectares), and every year following the harvest the frothing new wine is served at *Heurigen*, local drinking establishments in Grinzing, a suburb of Vienna.

The Austrian wine industry was sorely tested by the diethylene glycol scandal of 1985 (some wines were found to be adulterated with a chemical used in antifreeze) but came through with a stringent new set of wine laws that have become a model for other regions. As a result, the quality of Austrian wines has improved immeasurably. The wines are classified by the sugar levels in the grapes at harvest, similar to the German system, although there are a few regional variations.

In total, Austria has nearly 52,000 hectares planted in the eastern sector of the country. Since 2001 the wine regions have been defined as four geographic areas under, curiously, the Latin designation Districtus Austriae Controllatus (DAC).

> Weinviertel DAC (Grüner Veltliner)
> Mittelburgenland DAC (Blaufränkisch)
> Traisental DAC (Grüner Veltliner and Riesling)
> Kremstal DAC (Grüner Veltliner and Riesling)

Lower Austria, particularly the regions of Kamptal, Kremstal and Wachau, is known for its well-balanced dry white wines. Sweet wines are made in Burgenland's Neusiedlersee and Neusiedlersee-Hügelland regions, around a shallow lake that provides botrytis conditions similar to those of Sauternes in Bordeaux. In the Styria region they grow many white wines, specializing in Sauvignon Blanc and Chardonnay, which they call Morillon. The four principal grapes for Austria's burgeoning red wine production are Zwiegelt, Blaufränkisch, Blauer Portugieser and St. Laurent, a Pinot Noir sibling.

KAMPTAL

The Kamptal region takes its name from the Kamp River, which flows into the Danube. With 4,000 hectares of wines, Kamptal is one of Austria's most important wine-growing areas. On its steep terraces Grüner Veltliner and Riesling flourish in fine-grained, friable soil, producing wines that age well. Pinot varieties and Blauer Zweigelt are also grown here.

Recommended Kamptal Producers

Alram

Kurt Angerer

Buchegger

Bründlmayer

Familie Brandl

Hiedler

Loimer

Schloss Gobelsburg

Sax

Rudi Rabl

KREMSTAL

The Kremstal region, which straddles the Danube, is named after the Krems River and the beautiful old town of Krems. The broad expanse of the Danube acts as a temperature regulator, reflecting light back onto the terraced slopes and warming the vineyards with accumulated heat in winter.

Recommended Kremstal Producers

Martin Nigl

Franz Proidl

Mantlerhof

Wolfgang Aigner

Franz Türk

Walter Buchegger

Salomon Undhof

Bio-Weingut Geyerhof

Weingut Petra Unger

WACHAU

In Wachau, the most prestigious region, poetic descriptors are given for the alcohol levels and residual sugar of their Rieslings and Grüner Veltliners: Steinfeder ("stone feather"), named for a local grass that grows in the vineyard, for QbA level; Federspiel (a falconry term) for Kabinett quality; and Smaragd (named after an emerald-coloured lizard that lives in the vineyards) for higher-alcohol wines made from the ripest grapes.

Recommended Wachau Producers

Alzinger

F. X. Pichler

Nikolaihof

Prager

Hirzberger

Knoll

Geyerhof

Heinrich Siegl

Rainer Wess

Frei Weingartner

Tony's Dream Lower Austria Cellar

Alzinger Loibenberg Riesling Smaragd (Wachau)

Bründlmayer Zöbinger Heiligenstein Riesling Alte Reben
(Kamptal)

Frei Weingärtner Achleiten Grüner Veltliner Smaragd
(Wachau)

Graf Hardegg V Viognier (Weinviertel)

Loimer Steinmassl Riesling (Kamptal)

Knoll Kellerberg Riesling Smaragd (Wachau)

Nikolaihof Vom Stein Riesling Smaragd (Wachau)

Nigl Riesling Privat (Kremstal)

F. X. Pichler Grüner Veltliner Smaragd "M" (Wachau)

Salomon-Undhof Riesling Kögl (Kremstal)

BURGENLAND

The sub-regions of Burgenland, Neusiedlersee and
Neusiedlersee-Hügelland border on the shallow Neusiedl
lake in the southeast of the country and offer a range
of grape varieties unparalleled in the rest of Austria.
Here you can find all three Pinots, Sauvignon Blanc and
Furmint as well as Grüner Veltliner and Blaufränkisch,
but Burgenland is best known for its sweet wines grown
close to the lake, which produces ideal conditions for
the generation of *Botrytis cinerea*.

Recommended Burgenland Producers

Feiler-Artinger (Neusiedlersee-Hügelland)

Kracher (Neusidlersee)

Kloster am Spitz (Neusidlersee)

Gabi Mariell (Neusiedlersee-Hügelland)

Prieler (Neusiedlersee-Hügelland)

Heidi Schrök (Neusiedlersee-Hügelland)

Wenzel (Neusiedlersee-Hügelland)

Umathum (Neusiedlersee)

Willi Opitz (Neusiedlersee)

Tony's Dream Burgenland Cellar

Anton Iby Dürrau Juwel Blaufränkisch QbA Trocken

Feiler-Artinger Ausbruch Pinot Cuvée

Kracher Trockenbeerenauslese Grande Nouvelle Vague
Cuvée No. 7

Nittnaus Grüner Veltliner Premium Eiswein

Willi Opitz Gewürztraminer Trockenbeerenauslese

Umathum Zweigelt Hallebühl

Umathum Joiser Kirschgarten Blaufränkisch QbA Trocken

Prieler Blaufränkisch Goldberg Ruster Ausbruch auf den
Flügeln der Morgenröte

Manfred Weiss Eiswein Neusiedlersee (Grüner Veltliner,
Welschriesling)

Judith Beck Pinot Noir

STYRIA

With its rolling Alpine foothills, Styria has often been scenically compared to Tuscany. This region, the smallest in Austria, makes lively white wines and even livelier rosés. Sauvignon Blanc and Morillon (Chardonnay) are worthy of the wine lover's attention—if you can find them.

Recommended Styria Producers

E. & M. Tement

Alois Gross

Erich Sattler

Walter & Evelyn Skoff

E. & W. Polz

Wolfgang Maitz

Erwin Sabathi

Tschermonegg

Tony's Dream Styria Cellar

Wolfgang Maitz Sauvignon Blanc Hochstermetzberg
   Vineyard

E. & W. Polz Hochgrassnitzberg Sauvignon Blanc

E. & W. Polz Weissburgunder Grassnitzberg Vineyard

Manfred Tement Sauvignon Blanc Reserve Zieregg

Alois Gross Morillon Steirische Klassik

Lackner-Tinnacher Weissburgunder Steinbach Vineyard

Erwin Sabathi Sauvignon Blanc Poharnig Vineyard

Walter & Evelyn Skoff Sauvignon Blanc "Edition"

Tschermonegg Blauer Zweigelt

SPAIN

Every time I open a wine magazine I read that Spain has a new wine region. Time was if you knew about Rioja, Navarra, Penedès, Ribera del Duero and Jerez you had pretty well covered the Spanish wine scene. Today there are some seventy-five QWPSR (Quality Wines Produced in Specified Regions) zones, including many exciting new regions such as Bierzo, Jumilla, Priorat, Montsant, Toro, Uteil-Requena and Yecla. For the purposes of this book I'm going to concentrate on the four major regions—Rioja, Priorat, Ribera del Duero and Penedès—with excursions into the less-renowned zones to pluck out the best wines for my Dream Cellar.

Of all wine-growing countries Spain, has the largest surface area of vines (1.17 million hectares) but in terms of production it lags behind both France and Italy. This has nothing to do with faulty vineyard work or question-able winemaking practices; it speaks to the low yields that growers get from the arid soils of many of the regions here. More than six hundred grape varieties are grown in Spain, and to confuse matters, the most popular have different names in different parts of the country. Rioja's Tempranillo, for example, is known as Tinto Fino or Tinto del Pais in Ribera del Duero, Cencibel in La Mancha and Valdepenas and Ull de Llebre in Catalonia.

The tradition in Spain is to give its wines long oak-aging. Coupled with the ripeness of the fruit, in most instances this allows for cellar-worthy wines that can age gracefully in your cellar for many years. They include white wines such as the spectacular Marques de Murrieta Castillo Ygay Gran Reserva Especial (this august winery did not release its 1942 Gran Reserva until 1983, giving it forty-one years of aging in the cellar!). In addition to table wines, Spain is renowned for its sherry and for its great-value sparkling wines made by the traditional method (secondary fermentation in the bottle) called *cava*.

Three regions of Spain have been accorded the higher appellation Denominación de Origen Calificada (DOCa) for the consistently high quality of their wines. These are Rioja, Priorat and, in 2008, Ribera del Duero. And while I would not dream of trying to influence the Spanish wine authorities, I am adding Penedès to the circle of DOCa's because they make darn fine wine there—and it's the home of cava, Spain's sparkling-wine industry.

RIOJA

Tucked behind the Cantabrian Mountains along the Ebro River in northern Spain, Rioja has three zones—Rioja Alavesa, Rioja Alta and Rioja Baja—each with its own distinct wine style. Eighty-five percent of Rioja's production is a blended red made from Tempranillo, Granacha, Graciano and Mazuelo grapes. The whites are made with Viura (also known as Macabeo) with some Malvasía and Garnacha Blanca. The unique flavour of Rioja wines (spicy sandalwood) comes from the traditional use of American oak, although many wineries now age their wines in both American and French barrels. Reserva and Gran Reserva reds from Rioja are the ones to choose for your cellar.

Recommended Rioja Producers

Alvaro Palacio (Rioja Baja)

Bodegas Lan (Rioja Baja)

Bodegas Muga (Rioja Alta)

Marques de Murrieta (Rioja Alta)

Marcos Eguren (Rioja Alavesa)

Lopez de Heredia Vina Tondonia (Rioja Alta)

Benjamin Romeo (Rioja Alta)

Viñedos de Páganos (Rioja Alavesa)

Bodegas Sierra Cantabria (Rioja Alavesa)

Tony's Dream Rioja Cellar
Bodegas Lan Rioja Edición Limitada

Bodegas Muga Rioja Torre Muga

Bodegas Sierra Cantabria Rioja Amancio

Bodegas Muga Rioja Aro

Viñedos de Páganos Rioja La Nieta

Bodegas Marques de Murrieta Rioja Castillo Ygay Gran
    Reserva Especial

Bodegas Sierra Cantabria Rioja Colección Privada

Benjamin Romeo Rioja Contador

Bodegas y Viñedos Pujanza Rioja Cisma

Artadi Rioja Pagos Viejos

PRIORAT
Wild, rugged and barren, the tiny Catalonian region of
Priorat (about a quarter the size of Rioja with 1,680
hectares of vines) is not a tourist destination unless
you're a lover of powerful, meaty red wines. Twelfth-
century monks from the Scala Dei ("Ladder of God")
monastery planted the first vineyards on terraces much
as they appear today. These ancient vines on mountain-
goat slopes produce some of Spain's best offerings.
Made principally from Garnacha (known in France as
Grenache) and Cariñena (Carignan) grapes alongside
international varieties such as Cabernet Sauvignon,
Merlot and Syrah, the wines are rich in minerality

because of the thin black and red slate soil. The quality of the soil adds complexity to the wine's flavour as the roots of the vines absorb trace elements from it. The white wines, made from Chenin Blanc, Macabeo, Garnacha Blanca and Pedro Ximenez (PX, the grape of sweet sherry), are fruity and herbal.

Recommended Priorat Producers

Alvaro Palacios

Costers del Siurana (Clos de l'Obac)

Clos Mogador

Bodegas Mas Alta

Celler Melis

Mas Perinet

Mas d'En Gil

Domini de la Cartoixa

Celler Mas Doix

Celler de L'Encastell

Tony's Dream Priorat Cellar

Alvaro Palacios L'Ermita

Clos Mogador Priorat

Laurel Priorat

Cellar Mas Doix Vinyes Velles

Priorat Costers de Vinyes Velles

Vall Llach Priorat

Ardevol Priorat Terra d'Hom

Cellers Capafons-Osso Priorat Mas de Masos

Cellers de la Cartoix Priorat Montgarnatx

Clos Berenguer Priorat Selecció

Melis Priorat

Torres Salmos

RIBERA DEL DUERO

With its cold winters and hot summers, Ribera del Duero has an ideal climate for the early-ripening Tempranillo grape. Some producers blend it with Garnacha, Cabernet Sauvignon, Merlot or Malbec. The region's two most famous wines are Vega Sicilia (a favourite of Winston Churchill) and Pasquera, although their pre-eminence is being challenged these days by a host of young winemakers. Situated on an elevated plateau, the region is one of five along the Duero River, which becomes the Douro as it enters neighbouring Portugal on its way to the Atlantic.

Spanish Wine Labels

Wines are named for the amount of aging they receive prior to leaving the winery.

Sin Crianza: a young wine usually aged without oak in stainless steel tanks.

Crianza: red wines aged for two years, at least six months of which is in oak barrels. For white wines and rosés, at least one year of aging with a minimum of six months in oak.

Reserva: red wines aged for three years with at least one year in oak. For whites and rosés, two years minimum aging with at least six months in oak.

Gran Reserva: reds from the best vintages, requiring a minimum of five years aging, at least eighteen months of which has to be in oak. For whites and rosés, at least four years aging and at least six months in oak.

Ribera del Duero's most prestigious vineyards are to be found towards the west, near Valladolid. The white wine made here is from the Albillo grape. This wine is rarely seen in the export market, since the locals like it so much; it has delicate flavours of grapefruit and pineapple.

Recommended Ribera del Duero Producers

Dominio de Atauta

Bodegas Aalto Ribera del Duero Aalto

Viñedos Alonso del Yerro Vega Sicilia

Alejandro Fernández

Dominio de Pingus

Hermanos Sastre

Bodegas Cuevas Jimenez Ferratus

Bodegas Emilio Moro

Condado de Haza

Tony's Dream Ribera del Duero (Tempranillo) Cellar

Dominio de Atauta Llanos del Almendro

Dominio de Atauta Valdegatiles

Dominio de Pingus Pingus

Bodegas Emilio Moro Malleolus de Sanchomartin

Bodegas Felix Callejo Gran Reserva

Pago de los Capellanes Ribera del Duero Parcela
   El Nogal

J. C. Conde Delgado y Otros Neo Bodegas Los Astrales
   Christina Bodegas Hermanos Sastre Pesus

PENEDÈS

Although it is not yet designated a DOCa like Rioja, Priorat and Ribera del Duero, Penedès produces a wide range of fine wines and is also home to Spain's sparkling-wine industry. The story of Penedès table wines is basically the story of the Torres family, whose name is synonymous with the region; they have grown grapes here for more than three hundred years. Their winery is located at Vilafranca del Penedès, the regional capital, not far away from Barcelona and San Sadurni de Noya, the home of cava—Spain's sparkling wine—production. Phoenicians planted Chardonnay here in the sixth century B.C. Today white varieties predominate, thanks to cava production, which uses Xarel·lo, Macabeo and Parellada grapes; Chardonnay, Muscat of Alexandria, Riesling, Chenin Blanc and Gewürztraminer are also grown. In addition to the ubiquitous Tempranillo and Garnacha, Cabernet Sauvignon and Pinot Noir are grown here, and the reds of the region deserve a place in your cellar.

Recommended Penedès Producers

Torres

Jean Léon

Albet i Noya

Agusti Torello

Alemany i Corrio

Vallformosa

Can Ràfols Dels Caus

Parés Balta

Alemany i Corrio

Jané Ventura

Tony's Dream Penedès Cellar

Torres Mas La Plana Cabernet Sauvignon

Torres Reserva Real (Cabernet Sauvignon, Merlot,
   Cabernet Franc)

Jané Ventura Mas Viella Cabernet Sauvignon

Jean Léon Chardonnay

Juvé y Camps Casa Vella D'Espiells Cabernet Sauvignon

Parés Balta Calcari Xarel·lo

Vallformosa Gemma de Vallformosa Merlot

Alemany i Corrio Pas Curtei (Merlot, Cabernet
   Sauvignon, Cariñena)

Albet i Noya Finca La Milana (Cabernet Sauvignon,
   Tempranillo, Syrah, Merlot)

Can Ràfols Dels Caus Caus Lubis (Merlot)

CAVA

In the 1960s the French champagne houses launched a lawsuit against Spanish sparkling-wine producers in a London court over the use of the term *champagne* on their labels. The Spanish responded by coining the term *cava* to denote a fizzy wine made by the champagne method (secondary fermentation in the bottle). Initially they used a blend of indigneous varieties—Macabeo, Parellada and Xarel·lo—then began using Chardonnay and Pinot Noir. Cava is generally inexpensive, although at its best it can rival champagne. Like champagne it can have a range of residual sugar, which is indicated by the following terms:

- **Extra Brut:** 0–6 grams residual sugar per litre (the driest)
- **Brut:** 0–15 grams residual sugar per litre
- **Extra Seco:** 12–20 grams residual sugar per litre
- **Seco:** 17–35 grams residual sugar per litre
- **Semi-Seco:** 33–50 grams residual sugar per litre
- **Dulce:** more than 50 grams residual sugar per litre (the sweetest).

Recommended Cava Producers

Freixenet

Juvé y Camps

Huguet

Codorníu

Lemby

Segura Viudas

Mont-Marçal

Castillo Perelada

Gramona

Rovellats

OTHER SPANISH REGIONS

As mentioned above, Spain has an ever-growing number of designated wine regions from which I could have chosen a Dream Cellar. Here is my pick of what I'd like to have in my cellar from regions not given a full treatment.

Tony's Dream Cellar from Other Spanish Regions

Bodegas Numanthia Termanthia (Tempranillo; Toro)

Perez Barquero La Cañada PX (Pedro Ximenez; Montilla-Moriles)

Capcanes Cabrida (Grenache; Monstant)

Estefania Tilenus Pieros (Tempranillo; Bierzo)

Dominio de Tares P3 (Mencia; Bierzo)

Ponce Manchuela Clos Lojen Bobal (Bobal; Castilla, La Mancha)

Bodega Mustiguillo Bobal (Bobal; Valencia)

Agricola Falset-Marca Etim Old Vines Grenache (Montsant)

Ricardo Benito Vinos de Madrid Divo (Tempranillo; La Mancha)

Bodegas Ribera de Pelazas Bruñal (Juan Garcia; Arribes)

SHERRY

Of all beverage alcohol, sherry is perhaps the most underappreciated in our time, and consequently the best value for collecting. It is produced mainly from the Palomino grape around the towns of Jerez, Sanlúcar de Barrameda and El Puerto de Santa María in southern Spain. Sherry gets its name from an English corruption of the name Jerez. While the term *sherry* is loosely used in New World wine regions to describe a fortified white wine, its true form belongs to the region of southwest Spain centred on the town of Jerez de la Frontera.

Sherry is fortified not to stop fermentation but after fermentation is complete, which means that in its natural state it is a dry wine. The various styles and sweetness levels of sherry are achieved by blending and by aging.

The production of sherry is an act of God as well as of man. When the fermentation of Palomino grapes starts, the vintner does not know whether the wine he makes will be a fino or an oloroso. Finos develop a blanket of yeast cells, called *flor*, on the surface of the wine. It looks rather like heavy cottage cheese and protects the young wine from air, dramatically reducing oxidation. Olorosos develop only partial flor or none at all, and thus mature differently.

As a fortified wine, sherry is allowed to oxidize in the barrel. Once the flor has grown on the surface of the wine it is then introduced into a *solera* (from the Latin *solum*, "floor"). This is a set of barrels, usually stacked four or five high, to which the wine is added and fractionally topped up as blended wine is removed from the lowest barrel.

Finos are fortified to about 15 percent alcohol (so as not to inhibit the growth of flor) and olorosos to 18 percent (to kill the yeast). The cellar master then classifies the wine as either fino or oloroso with a chalk mark on the butt. Both are then sweetened with fresh wine or concentrate from Pedro Ximenez (PX) grapes. From this point the two styles develop very differently. Manzanilla is a special kind of fino grown around the Atlantic coastal town of Sanlucar de Barrameda. The salt air is said to impart a saline quality to the wine.

The young wines are introduced into their solera systems, where they are blended and aged. One-quarter to one-third of the sherry is drawn off from the oldest butts, at the lowest level, for bottling. Then these butts are topped up from those above, which contain wines a year younger, and so on up the stack. The younger wine quickly takes on the character of the older wine. This process is repeated until the youngest butts are refreshed with the new vintage.

When finos age for several years, they deepen in colour and turn into a style called amontillado. The quirky nature of flor growth can cause an oloroso to take on the style of a fino, in which case it is called a palo cortado.

Since sherry is a blended product, you will rarely find one that is vintage dated.

Sherry Styles

- **Manzanilla**: the lightest, driest and most delicate of sherries (from Sanlucar de Barrameda); hard to find.
- **Fino**: as dry as manzanilla but usually fuller bodied; deteriorates quickly; very dry—an excellent aperitif. Best purchased in half-bottles.
- **Amontillado**: an aged dry fino; deeper in colour, with a nutty flavour.
- **Medium**: an amontillado sweetened with PX.
- **Palo Cortado**: an oloroso displaying the finesse and character of an amontillado; rare and tends to be more expensive.

- **Oloroso:** full-bodied and raisiny, dry to medium sweet.
- **Cream:** Rich and sweet, usually very deep in colour.
- **Brown:** The sweetest sherry of all.

Recommended Jerez Producers

Emilio Lustau

Gonzales Byass

Emilio Hidalgo

José Estévez

Bodegas Dios Baco

Bodegas Osborne

Pedro Romero

Hidalgo—La Gitana

Williams & Humbert

Sánchez Romate

Tony's Dream Sherry Cellar

Emilio Lustau Palo Cortado

Herederos de Argüeso San Léon Manzanilla

Sánchez Romate Pedro Ximenez Jerez Cardenal
    Cisneros

Bodegas Rey Fernando de Castilla Pedro Ximenez

Bodegas Dios Baco Oloroso

Gonzales Byass Noé Pedro Ximenez Muy Viejo

Gonzales Byass Amontillado Jerez Del Duque Muy Viejo

Domecq Sibarita Oloroso

Emilio Hidalgo Oloroso Jerez Gobernador Seco

Emilio Lustau Fino Jerez Jarana Solera Reserva

PORTUGAL

The country that gave us two of the world's great drinks—port and Madeira—is now providing some excellent red table wines that can have a long cellar life. Port, incidentally, was the first wine in the world to introduce an appellation system. If you visit the Douro Valley, a World Heritage Site, you can see granite pillars dating back to 1757 that the Marquis of Pompal ordered erected as markers to demarcate the limits of the vineyards. The Portuguese wine industry used to be known for its fizzy medium-dry rosés such as Mateus and Lancers, but today its red wines from the Douro Valley, Alentejo and Dão can rival the best in the world.

Portugal has more than 400,000 hectares of vines in regions as diverse in climate as Vinho Verde in the north (producing those light, tart green wines ideal for summer sipping) to the blistering hot plains of the Alentejo, the temperate mountainous Dão plateau and the arid schist hills of the Douro Valley. The deeply coloured, tannic wines of the Bairrada region near the Atlantic are the longest-lived Portuguese wines. Made from the indigenous Baga grape and frequently blended with international varieties, this wine is one of the most cellarable wines; it can live for forty years.

In the Lisbon metropolitan area is the Setúbal Peninsula, renowned for its sweet wine made from Moscatel. A rare red version of this grape, Moscatel Roxo, produces a wine that is released to market only after twenty years of aging.

Here I am concentrating on the major Portuguese regions—the Douro Valley, Dão, Alentejo and Bairrada—

and have not touched Vinho Verde, where the wine is made for drinking, not for cellaring.

DOURO VALLEY

The Douro Valley, with its massive man-made terraces cornrow-braided with vines, is one of the most dramatic winescapes in the world. No other region has so many indigenous grape varieties; in fact, port can be made from a combination of any of seventy different grapes. This was rationalized in the early 1980s, when José Rosas, director of Ramos Pinto, and his nephew, João Nicolau de Almeida, selected a shortlist of twelve as the best varieties for port. They further refined this number to the five basic grapes that are used today: Touriga Nacional, Aragonês, Touriga Franca, Tinta Barroca and Tinto Cão. These grapes are also used to make Douro red table wines, and such is the worldwide demand for red wine from the Douro that it now equals the production of port.

Recommended Douro Producers

Sogrape (Barca Velha, Ferreirinha, Quinta de Leda)

Quinta do Vale Raposa

Niepoort

Quinta do Vale Dona Maria

Quinta do Vale Meão

Quinta do Crasto

Quinta do Cotto

Quinta do Infantado

Ramos Pinto

Quinta de la Rosa (Poeira)

Quinta do Passadouro

I asked Charles Metcalfe, co-author with Kathryn McWhirter of *The Wine and Food Lover's Guide to Portugal,* his ideas on how to start a Portuguese cellar.

"If you like port, that's an obvious choice. I have a lot of vintage port in my cellar that seems to stay in my cellar and not get drunk. My wife is not a great lover of port so possibly this is one of the reasons. A variety of port that spends a shorter time in my cellar is aged tawny ten-year-old and, even better, twenty-year-old. At thirty years old you're getting into a more mature, elegant, light, sometimes slightly woody wine. Twenty-year-old, I think, is the choice for most normal cellars, because the rule in Portugal is that it has to taste like a twenty-year-old tawny. You can actually incorporate younger wine to freshen it up if it seems to be getting older, so most twenty-year-old blends have wines that are older than twenty years but also might well have wines that are between five and ten years. It's a lovely wine style, brilliant when chilled in summer, and for me the best port style to drink with Stilton cheese at Christmas, which is the way in the U.K. because it goes much better [than vintage].

"Aside from port I think what Portugal does very well is reds. They do have some good white wines and wines that are delicious to drink if you visit Portugal, but Portuguese reds are really some very distinguished wines. There are the wines of the Douro, of course. The Douro has the advantage in that they have the expertise in making and marketing port and so they had a running start at making table wines. It's not that red wines weren't always made here, but no one really cared about them before the mid-1980s, when they started planting varietally for table wines, which is a much more efficient way of doing it—although some of the great Douro reds are from old, mixed-variety vineyards. The Douro reds are terrific. They're quite high in alcohol. They keep extremely well. You can keep a Douro red in the cellar for ten years and it will come out smiling."

Tony's Dream Douro Cellar

Alves de Sousa Abandonado (port varieties)

Barca Velha (Tinta Roriz, Touriga Franca, Touriga Nacional)

Chryseia (Touriga Nacional, Touriga Franca, Tinta Roriz)

Duas Quintas (Touriga Nacional, Tinta Barroca)

Neipoort Redoma Branco Reserva (Rabigato, Codego, Donzelhino, Viosinho, Arinto)

Niepoort Batuta (field blend of port varieties)

Quinta de la Rosa Poeira (Touriga Nacional, Touriga Franca, Tinta Roriz, Tinta Barroca)

Quinta do Crasto Reserva Old Vines (port varieties)

Quinta do Cotto Grande Eschola (Touriga Nacional, Tinta Roriz)

Quinta do Vale Meão (Touriga Nacional, Tinta Franca, other indigenous varieties)

DÃO

This region of granite soils fifty kilometres south of the Douro River is surrounded on three sides by mountain ranges that protect it from the harsh Atlantic weather on the coast. While it's not Shangri-La with its winter rains, it does enjoy a more Mediterranean climate during the growing season. Vineyards are planted among eucalyptus and pine forests at altitudes up to 900 metres, which mitigates the summer heat, allowing the grapes to maintain their natural acidity. Touriga Nacional and Tinta Roriz (a.k.a. Tempranillo) grapes, varieties that produce the ports of the Douro Valley, do well here for the region's spicy, peppery table wines.

Recommended Dão Producers

Quinta de Säes

Quinta da Pellada

Quinta dos Roques

Quinta dos Carvalhais

Casa de Cello

Quinta de Cabriz

Casa de Santar

Sociedade Agricola Seixais

Tony's Dream Dão Cellar

Quinta dos Roques Touriga Nacional

Quinta de Cabriz Touriga Nacional

Fontes da Cunha Munda Red

Quinta de Cabriz Virgilio Loureiro

Casa de Santar Reserva (Touriga Nacional, Alfrocheiro, Tinta Roriz)

Sociedade Agricola Seixais Dom Fradique (Touriga Nacional)

Sogrape Callabriga (Touriga Nacional)

ALENTEJO

The Alentejo is a vast, prairie-like region that stretches from the Tagus River in the north of Portugal to the Algarve in the south. Much of the country's cork comes from this region as well as wheat (it's the breadbasket of Portugal), olive oil and, of course, wine. Choose the red wines from this region made from Aragonez (the local name for Tempranillo), Trincadeira Preta (or Castelão, just to confuse you) and Periquita—which is even more confusing since it's the name of a wine introduced by J. M. de Fonseca more than 150 years ago that is made with Castelão and Aragonez grapes.

Recommended Alentejo Producers

Herdade do Mouchão

Quinta do Carmo

Fundação Eugénio de Almeida

Herdade da Malhadinha Nova

Herdade da Mingorra

Quinta do Mouro

Herdade do Esporão

Fita Preta

Paolo Laureano Vinus

Casa Santa Vitória

Tony's Dream Alentejo Cellar

Cortes de Cima Incógnito (Syrah)

Herdade de Cartuxa Pera Manca (Trincadeira, Aragones, Cabernet Sauvignon)

Herdade do Mouchão (Alicante Bouschet, Trincadeira)

Herdade do Esporão Reserva (Tempranillo, Cabernet Sauvignon, Trincadeira)

Quinta do Mouro Gold Label (Aragones, Trincadeira, Alicante Bouschet)

Júlio Bastos Dona Maria Reserva (Alicante Bouschet, Syrah, Cabernet, Aragones)

Adega Cooperativa de Borba Touriga Nacional

Margarida Cabaço Montes dos Cabaços (Syrah, Cabernet Sauvignon, Touriga Nacional, Aragones)

Quinta do Carmo Reserva (Aragones)

BAIRRADA

West of the Dão region, Bairrada has an indigenous grape called Baga that is unique to the region and by law must constitute at least 50 percent of its red wines. This thick-skinned variety, grown on clay (the Portuguese for

clay is *barro*, from which the region's name is derived),
produces a highly tannic acidic wine that can age well—
even though a large portion of the crop goes into the production of Mateus Rosé.

Recommended Bairrada Producers

Luis Pato

Filipa Pato

Manuel dos Santos

Caves do Freixo

Caves Aliança

Campolargo

Aveleda

Quinta do Encontro

Caves São João

Quinta do-Carvalinho

Tony's Dream Bairrada Cellar

Luis Pato Quinta do Ribeirinho Pé Franco (Baga)

Luis Pato Vinha Barrosa (Baga)

Quinta das Baceladas Single Estate (Baga, Merlot,
    Cabernet Sauvignon)

Campolargo Termeão (Touriga Nacional, Castelão,
    Cabernet Sauvignon)

Quinta do Encontro Encontro 1 (Baga)

Caves São João Frei João Reserva (Baga)

Quinta de Baixo Garrafeira (Baga)

Quinta das Bágeiras Reserva (Baga, Touriga Nacional)

OTHER REGIONS OF PORTUGAL

From the less-trodden paths of Portugal's wine regions I have selected the following wines that will cellar well.

Recommended Producers from Other Portuguese Regions

Quinta da Bacalhôa (Terras de Sado)

José Maria da Fonseca (Setúbal Peninsula)

Quinta de Chocapalha (Estremadura)

Quinta do Monte d'Oiro (Estremadura)

Casa Cadabal (Ribatejo)

Quinto da Covela (Minho)

Casa da Alorna (Ribatejo)

DFJ Vinhos (Estremadura)

Quinta dos Cozinheiros (Beiras)

Quinta da Ribeirinha (Ribatejo)

Quinta do Barranco Longo (Algarve)

Hero do Castanheiro (Terras do Sado)

Tony's Dream Cellar from Other Portuguese Regions

José Maria da Fonseca Setúbal Moscatel Roxo 20 Years (Setúbal)

Luperlegacy—Vinhos Quinta da Carolina (Tinta Roriz, Touriga Francesa; Trás-Os-Montes)

Quinta de Pancas Cabernet Sauvignon Special Selection (Estremadura)

Quinta de Chocapalha Vinho Tinto (Touriga Nacional, Tinta Roriz, Alicante Bouschet; Estramadura)

Quinta d'Aguieira Touriga Nacional (Alto Trás-os-Montes)

Quinta da Cortezia Touriga Nacional (Estremadura)

Casa Agrícola da Quinta do Falcão Paco dos Falcoes (Periquita, Cabernet Sauvignon; Ribatejo)

PORT STYLE	AVERAGE AGE	DESCRIPTION
Ruby	3 years	Basic port; young, sweet, full-bodied.
Late-bottled vintage (LBV)	4–6 years	Aged longer in wood. May carry a vintage date but will not improve in the bottle; drink immediately.
Vintage character	4–6 years	Same quality as LBV but a blend of different years.
Tawny	3–5 years	Ruby blended with white port; usually drier than ruby.
Aged tawny	5–10 years	Superior ruby long-aged in wood until it loses colour. Labels saying ten, twenty, thirty or forty years are a blend of old and young wines.
Colheita	vintage dated	Tawny port of a single harvest, aged at least seven years in wood before bottling; bears a vintage date.
Single quinta	vintage dated	Made from a single farm, usually in vintage style; bears a year.
Vintage	vintage dated	Superior ruby bottled after two years and allowed to mature for a decade or more. Each house declares whether it considers its port good enough to be a vintage two years after it is produced.
White port	3–5 years	Can be dry or medium-dry; serve as an aperitif, chilled or on the rocks.

PORT

The home of port is the Douro Valley in the northern part of Portugal, though, like sherry, the name has been adopted by New World wine producers for their fortified red wine. But port can be white and dry too.

The wine can be made from forty-eight different grape varieties, but the major ones are Touriga Nacional, Touriga Francesa, Tinta Cão, Tinta Roriz and Tinta Barroca (Tinta Amarela, Mourisco and Sousão are also used by some producers). White port is made from white varieties, particularly Malvasia Fina and Malvasia Grosso.

The finest port is still made in the traditional way, by crushing the grapes by foot. The wine matures in large barrels called pipes that contain 534.2 litres. When the wine has reached the right alcoholic strength, the fermentation is stopped by adding brandy—100 litres for every 450 litres of wine. In the spring following the vintage the young port is assessed for quality to determine its future. The best will be bottled after two years to become vintage port. The rest will go to ruby or late-bottled vintage (LBV).

Only vintage port needs to be aged once you have bought it; the other categories can be consumed immediately. Vintage port and some unfiltered LBVs will throw a deposit that must be separated from the wine by decanting. One of the great taste sensations is port and Stilton cheese, a sweet-and-salty combination that is absolutely delicious.

Recommended Port Producers

Taylor Fladgate

Fonseca

Dow's

Warre's

Quinta do Noval

Graham's

Niepoort

Sandeman

Quinta do Crasto

Quinta do Infantado

Tony's Dream Port Cellar

Taylor Fladgate Vintage

Fonseca Vintage

Graham's Vintage

Ramos Pinot 20-Year-Old Tawny

Quinta do Noval Nacional Vintage

Niepoort Vintage

Quinta do Infantado Vintage

Quinta do Crasto LBV

Gould Campbell Vintage

Barros 20-Year-Old Tawny

MADEIRA

The mountainous Portuguese island of Madeira, located in the Atlantic Ocean five hundred kilometres west of Casablanca, produces a remarkable fortified wine in almost as many styles as sherry. The best are named after the noble grape varieties from which they are made. The wine is first fermented in oak casks and then fortified with grape brandy at different times according to the grape variety. The sweeter the style, the earlier the fortification, to leave residual sugar in the wine. In January following the harvest, the new wines are "cooked" by the heat from hot water pipes for six months to one year. The best madeiras are allowed to oxidize naturally in the heat of the sun. They are placed in barrels at the top of the lodges and left there for five to eight years or more. Madeira is one of the longest-lasting wines—bottles from the mid-eighteenth century are still drinkable. Unlike table wines, the bottles should be stored standing upright. Once opened, the wine will remain fresh for a long time if securely stoppered.

Madeira Styles

- **Sercial:** pale in colour; the driest style of Madeira. Grown in the highest vineyards, this wine resembles a dry sherry. Drink chilled.
- **Verdelho:** deeper in colour; medium dry. "Rainwater" is the name given to a very pale and light style, produced accidentally in the eighteenth century when casks were left on the beach at Funchal awaiting shipment and absorbed rainwater during a storm. Good with soups or as an aperitif.
- **Bual:** amber colour; sweet. Try with cake, sweet biscuits or blue cheese.
- **Malmsey:** deep gold to brown; very sweet. Try as a dessert wine or digestif.

Madeira Classifications

- **Fine Old/Choice/Selected:** five years old. The grape variety named on the label refers to the style (sweetness) of the wine. Made from the lesser variety, Tinto Negra Mole, with some 15 percent of the named variety blended in to improve the aroma.
- **Reserve:** the youngest wine in the blend will be ten tears old. At least 85 percent noble varieties, whose names will appear on the label.
- **Special Reserve:** similar to Reserve. The youngest wine will be ten years old; at least 85 percent noble grape varieties.

- **Colheita:** as with port, the year of the harvest. From a single vintage rather than being a blend and bears the date on the bottle; not aged for as long as true Madeira.
- **Vintage:** 100 percent of a single named noble variety from a stated year, aged in a cask for a minimum of twenty years; usually heated naturally under the eaves of the lodge's warehouses.

Recommended Madeira Producers

Blandy's

Henriques & Henriques

D'Oliveira

Barbeito

H. M. Borges

Cossart Gordon

Tony's Dream Madeira Cellar

D'Oliveira Verdelho

D'Oliveira Sercial

Barbeito Malvasia

Julio Barros Moscatel

Favilla Viera Malvasia

Quinta do Serrado Boal

Broadbent Terrantez

Henriques & Henriques Boal 10-Year-Old

Acciaioly Terrantez

Cossart Gordon Sercial

GREECE

If winemaking is a measure of civilization, then human-kind has been civilized for 6,500 years. The earliest evidence of crushed grapes was found in Greece and dates back some 4,500 years B.C.—which is perhaps only fitting given that the evidence was found at a Neolithic site in eastern Macedonia; after all, the Greeks gave us Dionysus, the god of wine. The ancient Greeks, with their love of sweet wine, spread the vine throughout Europe, and many of the varieties we know today owe their ancestry to Greek farmers. Witness Italy's Greco di Tufo, for example.

Wine is grown throughout Greece and its Aegean and Ionian Islands. Today most casual consumers can name one Greek wine—retsina, the beverage almost everybody loves to hate until they drink it in a Mediterranean taverna with grilled sardines and stuffed vine leaves. But since the 1970s there has been a revolution in the quality of wines produced here, using local grapes as well as international varieties. Without a classical education the multiplicity of indigenous Greek grapes can be confusing, but they are worth the effort to get your tongue around, both figuratively and literally. The major white varieties are Assyrtiko (similar to Riesling in character); low-acid Athiri (used to make retsina); fruity Lagorthi; aromatic Malagousia; floral, fresh Moschofilero (my favourite); smoky Robola; and Rhoditis and the widely planted Savatiano (both used in retsina). The poetic-sounding red varieties are even more challenging to pronounce: noble Agiorghitiko ("St. George's"), Nebbiolo-like Xinomavro ("black acid"), deeply coloured Mandelaria (used mainly for blending) and Mavrodaphne ("black laurel"), which makes great dessert wines. If you're looking for long-cellaring Greek reds, head for Xinomavro-based wines, which are not dissimilar to Piedmont's Nebbiolo in its sinewy, dried cherry flavours.

Recommended Greek Producers

Ktima Gerovassiliou

Ktima Kosta Lazaridi

Tselepos

Gaia Wines

Kir Yianni

Ktima Mercouri

Paraparousis

Oenoforos

Sigalas

Domaine Carras

Tony's Dream Greek Cellar

Gentilini Robola Cellar Selection

Ghi ke Uranos (Xinomavro)

Kir Yianni Ramnista (Xinomavro)

Alpha Estate Red (Xinomavro, Syrah, Mourvèdre)

Sigalas Santorini (Assirtiko, Athiri)

Gerovassiliou Malagousia

Parparousis Muscat de Rio Patras

Sigalas Vin Santo (Assirtiko, Aidani)

Voyatzi Estate Red (Xinomavro, Cabernet Sauvignon,
    Merlot, indigenous Moschomavro and Vapsa)

Kir Yianni Paranga (Xinomavro, Merlot, Syrah)

HUNGARY

Had Hungary not been locked behind the Iron Curtain its wine culture would be as esteemed today as that of France or Italy. The Romans first planted vines in the Danube Basin of Pannonia, and by the fifth century A.D. extensive vineyards throughout Hungary supported a flourishing wine industry. Records show that as early as the sixteenth century a sweet white wine was made from botrytized grapes in the foothills of the Carpathian Mountains in northeastern Hungary, long before the vintners of Bordeaux started producing Sauternes. This wine—Tokaji Aszú—was the first wine in the world to have its own controlled appellation, several decades before the delimitation of port in the Douro Valley and 120 years before Bordeaux merchants classified their wines for the 1855 Paris Exposition. When he tasted Tokaji for the first time, Louis XIV of France pronounced it to be the "wine of kings and the king of wines," a phrase eagerly taken up by contemporary marketers of this nectar.

Tokaji is unique in its production. The grapes, affected by botrytis (called *aszú* in Hungarian), are put into large vats; the juice pressed out by the weight of the berries is fermented over three or four years to make Tokaji Esszencia, which is very rare and very expensive. The residual grape pulp from the production of Tokaji Esszencia is mashed up into a paste and portioned into 25-kilogram baskets called *puttonyos*. The number of these baskets emptied into the traditional 140-litre cask for fermentation will determine the sweetness level and richness of the finished wine; this number will appear on the label as "4 puttonyos" or "5 puttonyos" or even six.

The most common grape used for Tokaji is Furmint, which also makes a delicious dry white wine. But perhaps the best-known Hungarian wine is red: that old student standby Szekszárdi Bikavér (*bikavér* translates as "bull's blood"), a blend of Blaufränkisch, Cabernet Sauvignon, Merlot and Kadarka grapes.

Recommended Hungarian Producers

Szepsy

Királyudvar

Domaine de Disznókó

Oremus

Malatinszky Kúria

Gere Atila

Weninger

Dobogó

Vylyan

Tony's Dream Hungarian Cellar

Szepsy Tokaji Aszú 6 Puttonyos

Château Dereszla Tokaji Aszú Esszencia

Royal Tokaji Company Tokaji Esszencia

Royal Tokaji Company Tokaji Aszú 5 Puttonyos Red
　　Label

Arvay Tokaji Esszencia

Gere Atila Solus Merlot

Bock Pince Syrah

Weninger Kékfrankos Selection

Malatinszky Kúria Villány Cabernet Franc

ISRAEL

The extraordinary thing about the Israeli wine industry is that it supports more than two hundred wineries in a country with a population of 7.3 million, many of whom do not consume alcohol for religious reasons. With 4,000 hectares under vine—all the classic European varietals—Israel is one of the smallest wine-producing countries, and most of its wineries are also small.

At a latitude of 32 degrees north, farther south than Morocco, Israeli growers look for the coolest sites to plant grapes. The first thing winemakers talk about when you ask them about their vineyards is elevation. It's the height of the vineyard, they say, that gives the wine quality and is the key to flavour. The Jerusalem Hills can rise up to 800 metres, Galil (Upper Galilee) and the Golan Heights to 1,200 metres. Barkan, a winery with the largest vineyard holdings in Israel, markets a series of three Cabernet Sauvignons under the Altitude label that are grown at different elevations: above 412 metres, above 624 metres and above 720 metres.

There are six growing regions: Galil; the Judean Hills around Jerusalem; Shimshon, between the Judean Hills and the coastal plain; the Negev Desert; the Sharon coastal plain south of Haifa; and the Golan Heights, along the Syrian border.

The other remarkable thing about the Israeli wine industry is the youth of its winemakers. They all seem to be in their mid-twenties. And nearly all of them have studied their craft abroad, in France, Italy, Australia or California. They are making up the rules as they go along, rather like the Aussies and the Californians did in the 1960s. There is a confidence in the industry that

their wines, especially their Cabernets, Syrahs and Chardonnays, will be recognized soon enough on the world
stage. The thing that bugs these winemakers the most
is that Israeli wines get placed on the "Kosher" shelves
of wine shops abroad rather than under "Mediterranean"
or "Israel." But not all Israeli wine is kosher.

Recommended Israeli Producers

Margalit

Domaine du Castel

Golan Heights

Yatir

Vitkin

Clos de Gat

Flam

Galil Mountain

Pelter

Salove

Tony's Dream Israeli Cellar

Domaine du Castel Grand Vin (Bordeaux blend)

Margalit Cabernet Sauvignon Special Reserve

Karmei Yosef Bravdo Cabernet Sauvignon

Seahorse Elul 2004 (Cabernet Sauvignon, Syrah,
    Petite Sirah)

Ella Valley Merlot

Flam Classico 2006 (Cabernet Sauvignon, Merlot)

Flam Cabernet Sauvignon Reserve

Recanati Special Reserve Galilee (Cabernet Sauvignon,
    Merlot)

Chateau Golan Geshem 2005 (*geshem* means "rain" in
    Hebrew; Grenache, Syrah)

Golan Heights Yarden Cabernet Sauvignon El Rom
    Vineyard

LEBANON

The Lebanese will tell you that their local white grape, Obaideh, is the predecessor of Chardonnay. If this is the case, then the gift they bequeathed to Burgundy was returned in full measure in the 1930s with the range of French red vinifera varietals that was planted in the Bekaa Valley: Cinsault, Carignan, Cabernet Sauvignon, Merlot, Mourvèdre, Grenache and Syrah. Today Lebanon has 15,000 hectares under vine, and despite the vicissitudes of wars and insurrections, winemakers such as Serge Hochar at Château Musar have been able to bring in an annual harvest and the industry has exported more than two million bottles. It was Château Musar that brought the spotlight onto Lebanese wines in the 1970s with its cellar-worthy blend of Carignan, Cabernet Sauvignon and Cinsault (sometimes with a little Grenache) that could well be mistaken for a fine exotic claret. Lebanese wine writer Michael Karam has described Serge Hochar, without a hint of hyperbole, as "the man who has done more since Bacchus to put Lebanon on the world wine map."

If you like to have wines in your cellar that will age fifteen years at least, you need not only Château Musar red but the winery's white wine too. Made from the aforementioned Obaideh and another local variety, Merwah (believed to be Sémillon), this wine with its rich barley-sugar and apricot flavours has a strong spine of acidity.

The majority of Lebanon's wine is grown in the Bekaa Valley at elevations between 1,000 and 1,300 metres to ensure cool nights to build up acidity in the grapes. Château Ksara, the country's largest and oldest winery (some 70 percent of the production), was until 1972 under the supervision of the Jesuit monastery of Tanail. The following year it was purchased by a consortium of Lebanese businessmen.

Recommended Lebanese Producers

Château Musar

Château Ksara

Château Kefraya

Cave Kouroum

Massaya

Clos St. Thomas

Domaine Wardy

Domaines des Tourelles

Vin Nakad

Elias Tanios Touma & Sons

Tony's Dream Lebanese Cellar

Château Musar Red (Carignan, Cabernet Sauvignon, Cinsault)

Château Musar White (Obaideh, Merwah)

Massaya Reserve (Cabernet Sauvignon, Mourvèdre)

Château Kefraya Comte de M (Cabernet Sauvignon, Syrah)

Domaines des Tourelles Marquis de Beys (Cabernet Sauvignon, Syrah)

Clos St. Thomas Château St. Thomas (Cabernet Sauvignon, Merlot, Syrah)

Château Ksara Red (Cabernet Sauvignon, Arinarnoa)

UNITED STATES

French Huguenot settlers in the 1560s made the first wine on American soil, from a grape indigenous to the Carolinas called Scuppernong. Over the following centuries many attempts were made to grow the noble grapes of Europe along the eastern seaboard, but it was the West that would prove to be the real engine of the wine industry, particularly California.

The modern wine industry in the United States owes much to the drive of one particular Californian, Robert Mondavi. In the 1960s he established the precedent of naming wines by their grape variety rather than their geographical location, as is still the custom in Europe. Mondavi coined the term Fumé Blanc, playing off the French Pouilly-Fumé, to describe a Sauvignon Blanc that is aged in oak—just one of his lasting inspirations for the California wine industry.

Wine is now made in every state of the Union—even in Hawaii. I found a winery on Maui called Tedeschi that makes not only pineapple wine but also a blended red from Cabernet Sauvignon and Syrah. And what's more, they get two grape crops per vintage.

As the fourth-largest wine producer in the world, the United States is home to two of the world's largest winery operations: Constellation Brands, headquartered in New York's Finger Lakes region, and E. & J. Gallo in Modesto, California. I don't intend to cover every state here, only those whose products can be found in wine merchants' stores in most cities. This includes California, Oregon, Washington and New York State.

CALIFORNIA

More than 90 percent of wines produced in the United States is grown in California. And when you think of California wine, the mind immediately turns to Napa. But this valley, even with its international reputation, produces a mere 4 percent of the state's total. Sonoma may get less attention than Napa but I'm a great fan of its wines, especially its Chardonnays and Pinot Noirs. California's 1,200 wineries bottle more than the entire production of Australia, and its winemakers, unfettered by European traditions and techniques, have created a wine style that is fruit driven and table ready.

The industry owes a debt to eighteenth-century Spanish missionaries who planted vines for wine to celebrate Mass. They planted the first vineyard in San Diego, and as they moved north into Sonoma to open more missions they brought cuttings from that original vineyard with them. The gold rush of 1849 created a demand for the local wines but the industry went into decline with the arrival of Prohibition. It took thirty years for the California wine industry to recover. What drew world attention to California wines (and spawned two movies) was Steven Spurrier's "Judgment of Paris" tasting in 1976, when eight French professionals, in a blind tasting, placed 1973 Chateau Montelena Chardonnay above the top white Burgundies and 1973 Stag's Leap Wine Cellars Cabernet Sauvignon above the best red Bordeaux.

California has 173,000 hectares of vines planted over a 700-mile (1,100 km) area from Mendocino County in the north to Riverside County in the south. Varying climatic conditions from Pacific Ocean breezes create a wide diversity of macroclimates. These have been defined through heat analysis as five climate regions that correspond to European wine regions. California has areas as cool as Champagne and Germany's Rhine regions, and as hot as North Africa. This means vintners can grow all of Europe's grapes. Over a hundred varieties are available to winemakers but the major ones are Cabernet Sauvignon, Chardonnay, Merlot, Pinot Noir, Sauvignon Blanc, Syrah and Zinfandel. Zinfandel is California's signature grape, accounting for more than 10 percent of the state's vineyard surface. A versatile black grape, it can produce wines in a variety of styles, even as an off-dry white.

To California goes credit for having dreamed up the term *Meritage* to describe a Bordeaux-style blend of Cabernet Sauvignon, Merlot and Cabernet Franc. The word itself is a blend of *merit* and *heritage*, so it rhymes with *heritage*, not *Taj* (Mahal).

California has four main regions:

- **North Coast:** stretching up from San Francisco Bay; includes Napa and Sonoma, Mendocino and Lake County
- **Central Coast:** Santa Clara Valley, Santa Cruz Mountains, San Lucas, Paso Robles, Santa Maria Valley and Santa Ynez Valley
- **South Coast:** the coastal regions south of Los Angeles down to the border with Mexico, including Temecula Valley, Antelope Valley/Leona Valley, San Pasqual Valley and Ramona Valley
- **Central Valley:** a 300-mile (480 km) valley where 70 percent of California's grapes are grown; includes Sierra Foothills and Lodi.

Dan Berger publishes a private weekly wine newsletter, *Dan Berger's Vintage Experience*. His recommendations for laying down a California cellar: buy Russian River Valley and Santa Lucia Highlands Pinot Noirs for six to ten years of cellaring but don't ask for more than a decade from any California Pinot. Dan is particularly partial to Santa Barbara Pinots. "They can be superb, but you must try them at five years from the vintage to see if they are aging."

"While this [is] a somewhat technical point, be wary of any red wine with a pH over 3.75 if you want to cellar it for more than twelve months [pH is the measure of acidity in a solution, and it's acid that gives a wine its structure and staying power. Pure water has a pH of 7; lemon juice has a pH of 2.3; dry wines will have a pH between 3 and 4].

"Buy some extra California Sauvignon Blancs with low pH levels and those that are not aged in [the] barrel for aging. Remember, the lower the pH, the higher the perception of acidity in the wine. Most people are amazed what a decade will do to these wines," says Dan.

"And," he adds, "do not forget Sémillon or dry Riesling for aging, starting with Trefethen. But do not buy Viognier. The grape isn't meant for aging, and it transmogrifies into a mongrel if you try to age it."

And what about California's signature grape?

"The best California Zinfandels are being made these days for immediate consumption, and those high alcohol levels (15 to 16 percent) do not decline with cellar aging. The few claret-style Zins that will become better with age will also lose some fruit and become less like Zin over time. *Caveat emptor.*"

California Cabernets are cellar worthy, but what about other red varietals?

"I know of no California Sangioveses that age very well," says Dan. "Syrah from cooler climates [Russian River, Carneros, Central Coast] can be fascinating with age, but beware of those with *Brettanomyces*. They get worse, not better, with time. Petite Sirah may be one of the best 'sleeper' cellar buys. A decade usually is rewarded. Old-vine Grenache and Carignan are also treats when aged, but again, watch that pH!"

And for those California Chardonnay lovers?

"The only Chardonnays worth cellaring are those with no malolactic fermentation. So try for Stony Hill, Chateau Montelena, Mayacamas, Grgich Hills, Far Niente, Iron Horse, Silverado Vineburg and a few others. Full malolactic Chardonnays can be okay with some cellaring, but you generally have to like white wines that are acid-deficient to appreciate them."

Recommended Napa Producers

Caymus

Robert Mondavi

Dominus

Flora Springs

Joseph Phelps

Spottswoode

Stag's Leap Wine Cellars

Quintessa

Franciscan Cellars

Pine Ridge

Tony's Dream Napa Cellar

(I have not included Screaming Eagle, Colgin Family,
Harlan Estate and other cult Napa wines because
they're impossible to get!)

Joseph Phelps Insignia

Gary Farrell Zinfandel

Stag's Leap Wine Cellars Cask 23 Estate Cabernet
Sauvignon

Paul Hobbs Stagecoach Vineyard Cabernet Sauvignon

Schrader Cabernet Sauvignon

Araujo Sauvignon Blanc Eisele Vineyard

Caymus Cabernet Sauvignon Napa Valley Special
Selection

Bryant Family Cabernet Sauvignon Napa Valley

Merus Cabernet Sauvignon Napa Valley

Bond Cabernet Sauvignon

Recommended Sonoma Producers

Dutton Goldfield

Gary Farrell

Gundlach Bundschu

Iron Horse

Kistler

Sonoma Coast Vineyards

Marimar Torres

Williams Selyem

Marcassin

Peter Michael

Tony's Dream Sonoma Cellar

Williams Selyem Pinot Noir

Rochioli Pinot Noir (any block)

Marimar Torres Earthquake Pinot Noir

Marcassin Chardonnay Sonoma Coast Three Sisters
Vineyard

Kistler Vineyard Chardonnay (Dutton Ranch or McRae
Vineyard)

Kosta Browne Pinot Noir (any single vineyard)

Gary Farrell Chardonnay Russian River Valley Russian
River Selection

Landmark Chardonnay Sonoma County Damaris Reserve

Dumol Pinot Noir Ryan Green Valley

Dehlinger Russian River Pinot Noir

Recommended Producers from Other Californian Regions

Au Bon Climat (Santa Maria Valley)

Bonny Doon (Santa Barbara)

Calera (San Benito County)

Eberle (Paso Robles)

Morgan (Monterey)

Navarro (Mendocino)

Ridge Vineyards (Santa Cruz Mountains)

Qupé (Santa Barbara)

Tony's Dream "Rest of California" Cellar

Linne Caldo Problem Child Zinfandel (Santa Rosa)

Ridge Vineyards Monte Bello (Cabernet Sauvignon;
Santa Cruz Mountains)

Qupé Syrah Bien Nacido Hillside Estate (Santa Maria
Valley)

Bonny Doon Le Cigare Volant (Santa Cruz)

Tondre's Grapefield Pinot Noir (Santa Lucia Highlands)

Kendall-Jackson Highland Estates Syrah Alisos (Santa
Barbara County)

Navarro Muscat Blanc (Anderson Valley)

Calera Pinot Noir Mount Harlen Jensen Pinot Noir

Mount Eden Vineyards Chardonnay (Santa Cruz
Mountains)

Au Bon Climat Pinot Noir (Santa Barbara County, San
Benito County)

OREGON

If you're a Pinot fan then you'll love Oregon. The Pinot Noir, Pinot Gris and Pinot Blanc grown here are some of the best New World wines you'll find. The industry really took off in the 1970s, when disaffected California winemakers headed north looking for cooler growing regions. Even the prestigious Burgundy house of Joseph Drouhin recognized the potential for making top-flight Pinot Noir here, so they bought land, planted a vineyard and built their own winery in Dundee. Of all the U.S. wine regions it is arguably the greenest in both landscape and environmental consciousness. The state boasts more than 350 wineries, the majority of them boutique enterprises (Oregon's largest producer ships 125,000 cases a year, and most are under 35,000 cases), and most of them are to be found in the Willamette Valley.

The other two regions are southern Oregon (Rogue and Umpqua Valleys) and the Columbia Gorge, which bites into Washington State across the Columbia River. The newest viticultural area is the Snake River to the extreme east, bordering on Idaho, where it is cold enough in winter to produce icewine. Ste. Chapelle makes an award-winning Riesling icewine. But the wine for your cellar from Oregon is Pinot Noir.

Recommended Oregon Producers

Argyle

Drouhin

Beau Frères

Chehalem

Ponzi

Roco

Archery Summit

Shea

Domaine Serene

Ken Wright

Tony's Dream Oregon Cellar

Brick House Pinot Noir Les Dijonnais

Ken Wright Abbott Claim Pinot Noir

Cristom Estate Pinot Gris

Deponte Pinot Noir Baldwin Family Reserve

Laura Volkman Pinot Noir Rachel Estate

Domaine Drouhin Pinot Noir Laurène

Roco Pinot Noir Chehalem Mountains Private Stash

Shea Pinot Noir Shea Vineyard Estate

Archery Summit Pinot Noir Dundee Hills Arcus Estate

WASHINGTON

After California, Washington is the largest producer of wine in the United States. With 17,500 hectares under vine, all but 1 percent of the grapes are grown east of the Cascade Mountains, an area that gets only six to eight inches of rain a year (like the southern Okanagan Valley in British Columbia, to its immediate north). Three hundred of Washington's five hundred wineries are located in the vast Columbia Valley appellation, a semi-desert that includes, bizarrely, a piece of Oregon across the Columbia River. The major red grape varieties grown here are Cabernet Sauvignon, Cabernet Franc, Syrah and Merlot, and in white, Chardonnay, Riesling, Sauvignon Blanc and Gewürztraminer. Many of the best wines are blends. The appellation names in Washington have a poetic ring—Walla Walla Valley, Horse Heaven Hills, Rattlesnake Hills, Wahluke Slope, Yakima Valley AVA, Red Mountain (famous for its Syrah).

Recommended Washington Producers

Leonetti

Woodward Canyon

Quilceda Creek

Betz Family

DeLille Cellars

Andrew Will

Brookwalter

Pepper Bridge

Chateau Ste. Michelle

Cayuse

Tony's Dream Washington Cellar

Andrew Will Sorella Horse Heaven Hills (Cabernet Sauvignon, Cabernet Franc, Merlot, Petit Verdot)

Leonetti Merlot

Leonetti Red Wine Reserve

Bergevin Lane Syrah

Seven Hills Ciel de Cheval Vineyard Red Mountain
   (Cabernet Sauvignon, Merlot, Cabernet Franc, Petit
   Verdot)

Mark Ryan Wild Eyed Red Mountain Syrah

Chateau Ste. Michelle Ethos Syrah

Cayuse Syrah Walla Walla Valley Bionic Frog

K Vintners Syrah the Beautiful

Woodward Canyon Cabernet Sauvignon Old Vines

NEW YORK STATE

There are 212 wineries in New York State in four appellations: Lake Erie, Finger Lakes, Hudson River and Long Island. Dutch settlers first planted vines in the Hudson Valley in the seventeenth century. The Brotherhood Winery in the Hudson Valley was established in 1839 and is still operating. However, the hero of the modern industry is the late Dr. Konstantin Frank, an immigrant from Ukraine who, in the early 1950s, convinced his peers to plant the noble European vinifera varieties in the Finger Lakes region—such as Riesling, Chardonnay, Pinot Noir, Gewürztraminer and Cabernet Sauvignon—rather than the foxy North American Labrusca varieties such as Concord and Niagara, which are delicious as grape juice, jams or jellies but are not great for wine.

Riesling is New York's strong suit as well as late-harvest whites, along with Chardonnay and Merlot on Long Island and Cabernet Franc in the Hudson Valley.

Recommended New York Producers

Dr. Konstantin Frank (Finger Lakes)

Wöllfer (Long Island)

Bedell (Long Island)

Lamoreaux Landing (Finger Lakes)

Lenz (Long Island)

Anthony Road (Finger Lakes)

Standing Stone (Finger Lakes)

Hermann Wiemer (Finger Lakes)

Paumanok (Long Island)

Macari (Long Island)

Millbrook Vineyards (Hudson Valley)

Tony's Dream New York Cellar

Anthony Road Martini-Reinhart Selection Riesling

Bedell Merlot

Ravines Meritage

Hermann Wiemer Riesling

Lamoreaux Landing Riesling Icewine

Paumanok Assemblage (Cabernet Sauvignon, Merlot)

Bedell Taste White (Chardonnay, Gewürztraminer,
   Viognier, Riesling)

Fox Run Riesling Reserve

Standing Stone Riesling

Macari Merlot

CANADA

Winemaking in Canada dates from European settlement at the beginning of the nineteenth century. It's a history shared with all Commonwealth countries. As in Australia, South Africa and New Zealand, the Canadian palate was influenced by the British predilection for port and sherry, and wines from the 1800s to the Second World War mimicked those products. They were sweet and powerful, with alcohol volumes of 20 percent or more.

The mid-twentieth century saw a veritable revolution in taste for wine. When Canadian servicemen and women returned from the battlefields after the Second World War, they remembered the wines they had tasted in Europe. And with the waves of European immigration to Canada after the late 1940s, the desire for such wines meshed with knowledge of how to produce them.

In the span of a generation the Canadian wine industry has changed beyond recognition. Today the wineries of Ontario and British Columbia are winning gold medals in international competitions, not only for icewine but also for Chardonnay, Riesling, Cabernet blends and Pinot Noir. What has caused this sea change in Canadian wines? Basically, four factors coalesced in 1988: the Free Trade Agreement with the United States, which prohibited the imposition of tariffs on imported wines; the introduction of the appellation system Vintners Quality Alliance (VQA) in Ontario (two years later in British Columbia); the banning of Labrusca varieties from table wines; and the planting of vinifera varietals instead of hybrids.

ONTARIO

Ontario is a horizontal region, with an even (cool) climate across its four designated VQA regions: Niagara Peninsula, Lake Erie North Shore, Pelee Island and Prince Edward County. Conditions are ideal for producing good Riesling, Chardonnay and Pinot Noir. Although its vineyards are situated on the same latitude as the Languedoc and Chianti Classico, Ontario's long, harsh winters, which can last into late March, make it a challenge for growers to ripen red varieties in some years. Historically, because of its large European immigrant population, Ontario has modelled its wine styles on France, Italy and Germany. Justifiably renowned for its icewine, Canada's most populated province grows more varieties than it should, including Cabernet Sauvignon and Syrah. The most successful red varieties are Pinot Noir, Cabernet Franc and Gamay. Icewine and Riesling are the most successful cellar candidates over the long haul, although Ontario Cabernet Sauvignon and Chardonnay should not be overlooked.

Recommended Ontario Producers

Le Clos Jordanne (Niagara Peninsula)

Hidden Bench (Niagara Peninsula)

Tawse (Niagara Peninsula)

Flat Rock Cellars (Niagara Peninsula)

Stratus (Niagara Peninsula)

Château des Charmes (Niagara Peninsula)

Inniskillin (Niagara Peninsula)

Huff Estate (Prince Edward County)

Cave Spring (Niagara Peninsula)

Closson Chase (Prince Edward County)

Tony's Dream Ontario Cellar

Le Clos Jordanne Claystone Vineyard Pinot Noir

Hidden Bench La Brunate (Bordeaux blend)

Cave Spring CSV Riesling

Closson Chase The Iconoclast Chardonnay

Tawse Robyn's Block Chardonnay

Stratus White (Chardonnay, Gewürztraminer, Sauvignon
   Blanc, Sémillon, Riesling)

Flat Rock Cellars Nadja's Riesling

Jackson Triggs Delaine Vineyard Gewürztraminer

Thirty Bench Triangle Vineyard Riesling

Charles Baker Stratus Riesling

BRITISH COLUMBIA

In British Columbia the natural tendency is to look south of the border rather than east to the rest of Canada. Vintners here tend to model their wines on California and Washington State, although there is still a lingering German influence, with grapes such as Bacchus, Ehrenfelser, Kerner, Ortega and Schönburger first planted by German immigrants.

Given its geography, British Columbia resembles Chile writ small. It's a vertical wine region stretching from Salmon Arm in the north to the Washington state border. The range in temperature and rainfall, as well as soils, is enormous. The town of Oliver, the self-styled "Wine Capital of Canada," boasts 318 days with temperatures over 18° Celsius; Cowichan Bay on Vancouver Island has a mere 52 days over that mark. Thus the Island and the northern Okanagan feature early-ripening hybrids, while Oliver and the Osoyoos region (Canada's only pocket desert) can ripen Bordeaux varieties such as Cabernet Sauvignon and Merlot and the Rhône variety Syrah. Those bold reds, both varietals and blends, are the ones to lay down.

Recommended Okanagan Producers

Jackson-Triggs

Mission Hill

Burrowing Owl

Osoyoos Larose

Quails' Gate

Road 13

CedarCreek Estate

Sandhill

Blue Mountain

Wild Goose Vineyards

Tony's Dream British Columbia Cellar

Black Hills Nota Bene

Blue Mountain Pinot Noir Stripe Label

Jackson-Triggs Grand Reserve Shiraz

CedarCreek Platinum Reserve Meritage

Pentage Winery Reserve Syrah

Sumac Ridge White Meritage

Mission Hill Reserve Riesling Icewine

Quails' Gate Stewart Family Reserve Pinot Noir

La Frenz Viognier

Nk'Mip Qwam Qwmt Pinot Noir

NOVA SCOTIA has a nascent wine industry that is starting to produce some excellent white wines. Leading by example is Benjamin Bridge Vineyards, which is making the best sparkling wine I have tasted in Canada (they leave it on the lees for five years, which extracts flavours of great complexity). They also make a delicious white blend of Muscat and Perle of Csaba called Nova. Also worthy of cellaring is Gaspereau Vineyards Riesling.

ARGENTINA

Like Chile, Argentina owes a debt to Spain for its wine industry. During the Spanish colonization of South America in the latter half of the sixteenth century, the Cross travelled with the Sword as Juan Cedrón's forces took possession of Argentina in 1557. The priests needed wine for Mass and the grape variety they brought with them was Criolla Chica, an inoffensive vinifera with a pink skin. The Chileans called it Pais (today they make pisco from it), and as the conquering expeditionary forces travelled into North America, planting vineyards as they went, the grape became known as Mission.

Today Argentina is the fifth-largest wine producer in the world, after France, Spain, Italy and the United States. But because the lion's share of its production is consumed within its borders, we haven't seen much Argentinian wine in northern hemisphere markets until recently.

The country's signature grape is the thin-skinned Malbec, a minor member of the six varieties used in the Bordeaux blend and a major contributor to the "black" wines of Cahors, a descriptor that refers to their dense, inky colour. Malbec—thought to have been named after a Hungarian peasant who first planted the variety in France—requires more sunshine and heat to ripen than its more celebrated sisters Cabernet Sauvignon and Merlot. It provides lots of colour and muscle-flexing tannins, making it a paradigm variety for Argentina and an ideal candidate for your cellar.

The major growing regions are the Mendoza, San Juan and Rio Negro Valleys, Catamarca, Salta, La Rioja and Neuquén. Mendoza, with 148,200 hectares, accounts for nearly 70 percent of all Argentina's vineyards. After Malbec, the most heavily planted red grapes are Bonarda, Cabernet Sauvignon, Syrah, Merlot and Tempranillo, with a little Pinot Noir in the cooler Rio Negro region. While the emphasis is on red varieties, Argentina produces some tasty whites, led by the Torrontes grape (very similar in style to Alsace's dry Muscat but not really something you want to age), Chardonnay and Chenin Blanc.

Recommended Argentinian Producers

Catena Zapata (Mendoza)

Noemia de Patagonia (Rio Negro)

Pulenta Estate (Mendoza)

Cheval des Andes (Mendoza)

Bodega O. Fournier (Mendoza)

Norton (Mendoza)

Val de Flores (Mendoza)

Alta Vista (Mendoza)

Trapiche (Mendoza)

Bodega Lurton (Mendoza)

Tony's Dream Argentinian Cellar

Noemia Malbec

Catena Zapata Malbec Argentino

Achaval Ferrer Malbec Altamira

Alta Vista Alto (Malbec, Cabernet Sauvignon)

Norton Gernot Langes (Malbec, Cabernet Sauvignon, Cabernet Franc)

Viña Cobos Malbec

Luca Malbec Altos de Mendoza Nico

Bodega O. Fournier Malbec Uco Valley Alta Crux

Bodegas Mendel Unus Mendoza (Malbec, Cabernet Sauvignon)

Trivento Malbec Mendoza Eolo

CHILE

Chile is a long, skinny country delimited by the Pacific Ocean to the west and the Andes to the east. As long as Canada is wide, with arid deserts in the north and the Antarctic to the south, Chile has a wide range of climates as well as soils. The average width of the country is 100 kilometres, which creates an interesting phenomenon: the climate is more varied east to west than it is north to south because of the wind patterns off the ocean and the mountain ranges.

With some 120,000 hectares under vine Chile is roughly the same size as Bordeaux, but with only two hundred commercial wineries. The vineyards are concentrated in an 800-kilometre band in the centre of the country cut across with twelve valleys, some with their own sub-appellations.

Chile is a paradise for grape growers—you could plant a walking stick and it would sprout grapes. Okay, it should be a young vine. The point is that Chile is the only country in the world that is free of phylloxera, protected as it is by its geographical boundaries. As a result Chilean vines can trace their ancestry back to the original rootstock imported from Bordeaux in the mid-nineteenth century by wealthy local business people.

One anomaly is the presence of Carmenère in Chile. This rare Bordeaux variety, wiped out during the phylloxera plague, flourished in Chilean soil, although the vintners thought it was Merlot and treated it as such in terms of harvesting and fermentation. For generations it was thought to be a Chilean clone of Merlot because it behaved very differently from its Bordeaux sister: the leaf formation, the colour of its shoots, the fact that it ripened a month later than Merlot and tasted more like Cabernet Franc. In 1994 a French ampelographer did a DNA study of the vine and found that much of what was thought to be Merlot, and labelled as such, was in fact the rare variety Carmenère. Making a virtue of necessity, Chilean vintners embraced the variety as their signature grape, either in its own right or blended with Cabernet Sauvignon or Syrah.

Chile continues to offer some of the best quality-for-price wines you will find on the market, in both red and white. Seventy-five percent of the vines in the ground are red—in order of importance, Cabernet Sauvignon, Merlot, Carmenère, Syrah, Pinot Noir and Petit Verdot. The white varieties are Sauvignon Blanc, Chardonnay and Viognier with some Gewürztraminer, Riesling and Muscat.

Recommended Chilean Producers

Almaviva (Maipo Valley)

Casa Lapostolle (Rapel Valley)

Casa Marin (San Antonio Valley)

Concha y Toro (Maipo Valley)

De Martino (Maipo Valley)

Altair (Cachapoal Valley)

Cono Sur (Colchagua Valley)

Montes (Colchagua Valley)

Miguel Torres (Curicó Valley)

Casa Silva (Colchagua Valley)

Amayna (Leyda Valley)

Errazuriz (Aconcagua Valley)

Tony's Dream Chilean Cellar

Concha y Toro Carmin de Peumo (Carmenère)

Casa Lapostolle Clos Apalta (Merlot, Carmenère)

Almaviva (Cabernet Sauvignon, other Bordeaux
varieties)

Matetic EQ Syrah

Cono Sur Ocio Pinot Noir

Miguel Torres Manso de Velasco (Cabernet Sauvignon)

Vina Anakena ONA Pinot Noir

Concha y Toro Don Melchor Cabernet Sauvignon

Perez Cruz Liguai (Syrah, Cabernet Sauvignon,
Carmenère)

Casa Silva Altura (Carmenère, Cabernet Sauvignon,
Petit Verdot)

AUSTRALIA

The wines of Australia are a liquid expression of the national character. They are friendly, boisterous, slap-you-on-the-back, no-nonsense beverages that are easy to drink and table ready. They have been described as "fruit bombs" (concentrated, over-extracted wines) but at their best they rival the wines from any region in the world. Australia has no native grapes of its own but it took the Rhône's Syrah grape, planted it in the Barossa Valley, renamed it Shiraz and metamorphosed it into a wine style that has captured the palate of the planet. Shiraz reaches its highest expression in wines such as Penfolds Grange, Henschke's Hill of Grace, Elderton's Command, Clarendon Hills' Astralis and Torbreck's Run Rig.

On the less elevated level of everyday drinking wines, the accessibility of Australian reds and whites has made this country the fourth-largest exporter in the world. They also export their talented winemakers, who are much in demand in the northern hemisphere to introduce New World techniques to Old World cellar practices. With close to 175,000 hectares under vine and 2,146 wineries concentrated in the coastal regions of the southeast and southwest, Australia is a major force in the wine world. With New Zealand, it was the first to embrace the screw cap and to introduce the pet (plastic) bottle. The use of rotary fermenters and water-saving drip irrigation are just two of the technological advances that have made Australia a leading wine-producing country. Elgo Estate in northeastern Victoria uses a wind turbine to power its winery and leaves no carbon footprint.

In addition to Shiraz, Australia has extensive Cabernet Sauvignon vineyards, as well as Merlot, Pinot Noir, Grenache and Mourvèdre. Chardonnay is the leading white variety, followed by Sémillon, Sauvignon Blanc and Riesling. South Australia is the major region where more than half of Australia's wineries are located, in appellations such as Adelaide Hills, Barossa Valley, Coonawarra and McLaren Vale. The other major regions are Victoria (Yarra Valley, Rutherglen), New South Wales (Hunter Valley, Mudgee, Riverina) and Western Australia (Margaret River). Cool-climate Tasmania also produces some delectable Pinot Noir and Chardonnay.

SOUTH AUSTRALIA

Over half the country's wine comes from South Australia, from the bold, muscular Shiraz of the Barossa Valley to the fresh lively Rieslings of the Clare Valley, from the baking plains of the Riverland region (similar to California's Central Valley) to the cool, luxuriant Adelaide Hills, where top-flight sparkling wines are produced. The range of wine styles produced in this state is impressive, particularly the Cabernet Sauvignon grown in the red soil of Coonawarra and the Chardonnays of the coastal areas. Shiraz and Shiraz-Cabernet blends make ideal wines to lay down. Penfolds reds, in particular, have a great cellar pedigree.

Recommended South Australia Producers

Penfolds

Henschke

Balnaves

Wynns

Petaluma

De Bortoli

Jim Barry

Peter Lehmann

Shaw & Smith

Charles Melton

Tony's Dream South Australia Cellar

Penfolds St. Henri Shiraz

Penfolds Block 42 Special Bin Cabernet Sauvignon

Jeffrey Grossett Polish Hill Riesling

Penfolds Yattarna Chardonnay

Wendouree Cabernet Malbec

Wolf Blass Gold Label Shiraz Viognier

Leasingham Single Vineyard Release Schobers Cabernet
   Sauvignon

Tim Smith Barossa Mataro Grenache Shiraz

Yalumba The Virgilius Viognier

Wynns Coonawarra John Riddoch Cabernet Sauvignon

VICTORIA

Poised above Tasmania, the state of Victoria is a study in contrasts. It's Australia's smallest state yet it has more wineries than South Australia (568 compared to 419). The cool coastal regions of the Yarra Valley, Geelong and Mornington Crescent produce elegant Pinot Noir and Chardonnay, while the hot, arid Mildura, Murray, Darling and Swan Hill regions in the northwest make gutsy, long-lived Shiraz and Cabernet Sauvignon. This northwestern zone is Australia's grape basket, providing the industry with a quarter of its annual crush. Victoria is renowned for its intense dessert wines (what the Aussies call "stickies") made from the Muscat grape.

Recommended Victoria Producers

Coldstream Hills

Clyde Park Vineyard

Shadowfax

Diamond Valley Vineyards

Tahbilk

Turner's Crossing

All Saints Estate

Stanton & Killeen

Dominique Portet

Maygars Hill Winery

Tony's Dream Victoria Cellar

Tomboy Hill The Tomboy Pinot Noir

Yabby Lake Vineyard Roc Shiraz

Coldstream Hills Pinot Noir

Turner's Crossing Vineyard Cabernet Sauvignon

Bannockburn Geelong Pinot Noir

By Farr Sangreal Pinot Noir

Tahbilk Eric Stevens Purbrick Shiraz

Mount Langi Ghiran Langi Shiraz

Clyde Park Vineyard Megan's Block Shiraz Viognier

Kooyong Single Vineyard Selection Faultline Pinot Noir

NEW SOUTH WALES

One hundred and twenty kilometres north of Sydney is the Hunter Valley, the first of Australia's wine regions to be planted by European settlers in the early 1800s. Here you can find Australia's most cellarable white wine, Hunter Valley Sémillon. An ugly duckling when young, after five years it begins to blossom into a complex wine with honey, citrus, apple and beeswax flavours. The Mudgee region, west of the Hunter Valley, is hotter and more elevated, producing Shiraz and Cabernet Sauvignon with great structure and longevity. The major area here is Riverina, which produces a lot of commercial wines; look for Botrytis Sémillon, especially from De Bortoli.

Recommended New South Wales Producers
De Bortoli

Brokenwood

Tyrrell's

Capercaille

McWilliam's Mount Pleasant

Lake's Folly

Tulloch

Tower Estate

McWilliam's (Riverina)

Clonakilla

Tony's Dream New South Wales Cellar
De Bortoli Noble One (Botrytis Sémillon)

Brokenwood Graveyard Vineyard Hunter Valley Shiraz

Tyrrell's Single Vineyard Stevens Hunter Sémillon

Chalkers Crossing Cabernet Sauvignon

Chatto Wines Hunter Valley Shiraz

Clonakilla Shiraz Viognier

Printhie Wines Cabernet Merlot

Tower Estate Hunter Valley Sémillon

Tulloch Pokolbin Dry Red Private Bin Shiraz

Trentham Estate Heathcote Shiraz

WESTERN AUSTRALIA
As far as the Okanagan Valley of British Columbia is from Ontario's Niagara Peninsula, Sydney is from Perth,

the city that is the epicentre of this exciting region. I must confess that I have a definite partiality for the elegance and balance of the wines of Western Australia. The major region here is Margaret River, a windswept area jutting out into the Indian Ocean that accounts for less than 1 percent of Australia's total wine production—but what wines! The Chardonnay, Cabernet Sauvignon and Sauvignon-Sémillon blends are a must for any cellar.

Recommended Western Australia Producers

Cullen Wines

Leeuwin

Brookland Valley

Cape Mentelle

Ashbrook

Devil's Lair

Vasse Felix

Moss Wood

Pierro

Woodside Valley Estate

Tony's Dream Western Australia Cellar

Cullen Margaret River Chardonnay

Leeuwin Art Series Chardonnay

Leeuwin Art Series Cabernet Sauvignon

Cape Mentelle Wallcliffe Sauvignon Blanc Sémillon

Moss Wood Cabernet Sauvignon

Sandalford Prendville Reserve Cabernet Sauvignon

Pierro Reserve Cabernet Sauvignon Merlot

Cullen Diane Maeline (Bordeaux blend)

Houghton Jack Mann (Cabernet Sauvignon, Malbec)

Voyager Estate Sauvignon Blanc Sémillon

NEW ZEALAND

The defining moment for New Zealand wines happened in 1986, when the British wine press got its first taste of a product from the Marlborough region that would become an instant international icon wine: Cloudy Bay Sauvignon Blanc 1985. A new style had been created, and just as Ontario captured the world's attention with icewine, overshadowing its German antecedent, so New Zealand co-opted the Sauvignon Blanc grape from the Loire Valley and made it its own. While Marlborough is Sauvignon Blanc's spiritual home (they grow top-flight Pinot Gris here as well), you can also find delicious Sauvignons from Martinborough, Waipara and Nelson.

But this remarkable country, stretching 1,600 kilometres through ten wine regions from Northland to Central Otago, on both of its islands, is not a one-trick pony. Having established itself as the benchmark for Sauvignon Blanc, it is well on the way to rivalling Oregon as the best place to shop for Pinot Noir if your budget doesn't extend to fine Burgundy. There are very few places on the planet where Pinot Noir feels at home; Central Otago, Canterbury and Martinborough have proven to be conducive to the production of this most pernickety of grapes.

If it's Bordeaux varieties that appeal to you, then head for Hawke's Bay on the North Island, which boasts 80 percent of New Zealand's plantings of Cabernet Sauvignon, Merlot and Syrah, varieties that can ripen well in its warm maritime climate. This region, with its gravelly soil, also produces some of New Zealand's richest and most complex Chardonnays. The coolest region is Nelson, where Seifried Winery produces a range of delicious Rieslings in both dry and sweet styles, including Sweet Agnes Riesling Ice Wine.

If you have the opportunity to visit New Zealand you must not miss my favourite wine region: Waiheke Island, a thirty-five-minute ferry ride east of Auckland in the Hauraki Gulf. Thirty-six square miles of rolling beauty, supporting eleven wineries, this island is home to the most famous New Zealand red wine (and its most expensive), Stonyridge Vineyard Larose, an organic Bordeaux-style blend.

Recommended New Zealand Producers

Stonyridge Vineyard (Auckland)

Cloudy Bay (Marlborough)

Neudorf (Nelson)

Craggy Range (Hawke's Bay)

Astrolabe (Marlborough)

Felton Road (Central Otago)

Ata Rangi (Wairarapa)

Villa Maria (Auckland and Hawke's Bay)

Saint Clair (Marlborough)

Dry River (Wairarapa)

Tony's Dream New Zealand Cellar

Stonyridge Vineyard Larose (Auckland)

Kumeu River Chardonnay Kumeu Maté's Vineyard
    (Auckland)

Cloudy Bay Sauvignon Blanc (Marlborough)

Nautilus Four Barriques Pinot Noir (Marlborough)

Selaks "The Favourite" Merlot Cabernet (Hawke's Bay)

Church Road Cuvé Series Cabernet Sauvignon
    (Hawke's Bay)

Crossroads Winery Elms Vineyard Hawkes Bay
    Reserve Syrah

Mount Difficulty Long Gully Pinot Noir (Central Otago)

Craggy Range Le Sol Syrah (Hawke's Bay)

Neudorf Home Vineyard Pinot Noir

SOUTH AFRICA

While South Africa is included in the geography of New World wines, stylistically its wines are more French but with the boldness of New World fruit. Like Chile and Argentina, it offers the wine lover good value in terms of the price–quality ratio. For the collector, the reds can be long-lived. South Africa's signature grape, Pinotage, a cross between Pinot Noir and Cinsault, is something of an acquired taste with its gamy, smoky, tarry notes, but the Cabernets and Syrahs have a more international appeal.

Quiescent during the apartheid era, South Africa has begun to make a name for its wines in the past decade. Long known for its Chenin Blanc (also known here as Steen) and Muscat-based sweet wines, South Africa is now making first-rate Sauvignon Blanc, Chardonnay, Cabernet Sauvignon and Syrah. Some of the most intriguing Pinot Noir and Chardonnay are grown around Hermanus in Walker Bay, the town that bills itself "the world's best land-based whale-watching spot."

South African wine production, from 110,000 hectares of vines tended by some 4,000 growers, is concentrated in the Western Cape province. The major regions are Constantia, in the southern suburbs of Cape Town, Elgin, Franschhoek, Paarl, Robertson, Stellenbosch, Swartland, Walker Bay and Worcester.

CONSTANTIA

A cool-climate area south of Cape Town, Constantia is the country's oldest wine region and home to the picture-book estate Groot Constantia, a historic wine farm founded by the Dutch colonial governor Simon van der Stel in 1684. Famous since the eighteenth century for its sweet Muscat wine, the region produces some top-flight Cabernet Merlot blends, Chardonnay and Riesling.

Recommended Constantia Producers

Buitenverwachting

Groot Constantia

Klein Constantia

Constantia Uitsig

Steenberg

Tony's Dream Constantia Cellar

Buitenverwachting Christine (Cabernet Sauvignon, Merlot, Cabernet Franc, Malbec)

Klein Constantia Sauvignon Blanc

Klein Constantia Marlbrook (Cabernet Sauvignon, Merlot, Cabernet Franc)

Groot Constantia Pinotage

Constantia Uitsig Constantia Red (Merlot, Cabernet Sauvignon, Cabernet Franc)

Steenberg Sauvignon Blanc Reserve

ELGIN

There are more apple orchards than vineyards in Elgin, South Africa's coolest region, which is a forty-five-minute drive from Cape Town along the coast. This scenic valley of forests and mountain peaks is known for its Sauvignon Blanc, Pinot Noir and Shiraz. Elgin is the home of an interesting experiment called Thandi; its aim is "to empower previously disadvantaged farming communities." Vineyard land is set aside for indigent farmers, who are mentored by experienced winemakers in production techniques. Thandi wines are now being exported around the world.

Recommended Elgin Producers

Paul Culver

Iona

Newton Johnson

Ataraxia

Tony's Dream Elgin Cellar

Oak Valley Mountain Reserve Sauvignon Blanc

Ataraxia Chardonnay

Paul Culver Weisser Riesling Noble Late Harvest

Newton Johnson Pinot Noir

Iona Sauvignon Blanc

FRANSCHHOEK

The French influence is everywhere in this valley (*franschhoek* in Afrikaans means "French corner"), an area first settled by French Huguenots in 1688. Many of the wineries still bear French names. The vineyards are planted to Sauvignon Blanc, Chardonnay, Sémillon and Chenin Blanc for whites, and Cabernet Sauvignon, Shiraz, Pinot Noir and Merlot for reds.

Recommended Franschhoek Producers

Rupert & Rothschild

Boekenhoutskloof

La Motte

L'Ornarins

Tony's Dream Franschhoek Cellar

Boekenhoutskloof Syrah

Rupert & Rothschild Baron Edmond (Cabernet, Merlot)

Boschendal Reserve Collection Shiraz

Plaisir de Merle Cabernet Franc

Bellingham Maverick Syrah

PAARL

North of Stellenbosch, Paarl is South Africa's wine capital and home to its largest wine cooperative, KWV. The range of soils and microclimates here supports a range of grape varieties and wine styles. The most successful are Shiraz, Cabernet Sauvignon, Mourvèdre and Viognier.

Recommended Paarl Producers

Fairview Estate

Backsberg

Anura

Coleraine

David Frost Estate

KWV

Landskroon

Nederburg

Glen Carlou

Tony's Dream Paarl Cellar

Fairview Solitude Shiraz

Fairview The Beacon Shiraz

Nelson Estate Cabernet Sauvignon–Merlot

Seidelberg Wine Estate Roland's Revenge Merlot

Vilafonté Series C (Cabernet Sauvignon, Cabernet
  Franc, Merlot)

Glen Carlou Chardonnay

David Frost Par Excellence (Cabernet Sauvignon,
  Cabernet Franc, Merlot)

Veenwouden Private Cellar Classic (Bordeaux blend)

Welgemeend Estate Reserve (Bordeaux blend)

ROBERTSON

Roses, horses and wine, especially Chardonnay—that's the Robertson Valley, 160 kilometres east of Cape Town. The spectacular sweep of the Langeberg mountain range to the north traps the sea breezes and cools the grapes. A major producer of sparkling wines, Robertson also has some nifty Pinotage and Cabernet Sauvignon.

Recommended Robertson Producers

Van Loveren

De Wetshof

Graham Beck

Zandvliet

Tony's Dream Robertson Cellar

De Wetshof–Bateleur Chardonnay

De Wetshof–Edeloes (Riesling dessert wine)

Graham Beck The Ridge Syrah

Graham Beck Barrel Select The William (Cabernet
  Sauvignon, Pinotage)

Zandvliet Kalkveld Shiraz French Oak Matured

STELLENBOSCH

Many of South Africa's best wineries can be found in the Stellenbosch region, which boasts the best wine route in the country. The red wines demand your attention, but don't overlook the Chardonnays and Sauvignon Blancs. The town from which the region takes its name is the second-oldest in South Africa and full of gleaming white Dutch farmhouses.

Recommended Stellenbosch Producers

Kanonkop

Vergelegen

Thelema

Meerlust

Rust en Vrede

Beyerskloof

Hartenberg

Tony's Dream Stellenbosch Cellar

Vergelegen V (Cabernet Sauvignon)

Kanonkop Paul Sauer (Cabernet Sauvignon, Cabernet Franc, Merlot)

Neil Ellis Vineyard Selection Cabernet Sauvignon

Kaapzicht Estate Steyler Range Vision (Cabernet Sauvignon, Merlot, Pinotage)

Meerlust Rubicon (Cabernet Sauvignon, Merlot, Cabernet Franc)

Warwick Estate Trilogy (Cabernet Sauvignon, Cabernet Franc, Merlot)

Rust en Vrede Shiraz

Hartenberg Shiraz

Saxenburg Shiraz Select

Neelingshof Estate Laurentius (Cabernet, Merlot, Shiraz)

SWARTLAND

Swartland, a hot, arid region north of Cape Town, is planted mainly to bush vines (untrellised) that are South Africa's traditional varieties, Pinotage and Chenin Blanc (Steen). But recent plantings of Shiraz, Viognier, Malbec and Grenache are beginning to bear fruit—literally and figuratively. This region is also known for its sweet wines, particularly port.

Recommended Swartland Producers

Sadie Family

Allesverloren

Tony's Dream Swartland Cellar

Sadie Family Columella (Shiraz, Mourvèdre)

Allesverloren Port

Swartland Winery Idelia (Cabernet, Shiraz, Merlot,
    Pinotage)

WALKER BAY

The coastal winds of the Walker Bay region, on the Garden Route south of Cape Town, provide ideal conditions for the slow ripening of Pinot Noir and Chardonnay. A more delicate style of Pinotage is grown here and Sauvignon Blanc does well too.

Recommended Walker Bay Producers

Raka

Hamilton Russell

Bouchard Finlayson

Southern Right

Sumaridge

Tony's Dream Walker Bay Cellar

Hamilton Russell Pinot Noir Hemel-en-Aarde Valley

Hamilton Russell Chardonnay

Bouchard Finlayson Galpin Peak Pinot Noir

Sumaridge Chardonnay

Southern Right Pinotage

De Trafford Chenin Blanc

Raka Figurehead Cape Blend (Pinotage, Cabernets,
Merlot, Malbec, Petit Verdot)

WORCESTER

Home to the largest brandy distillery in the world
(KWV), Worcester is a hot region 120 kilometres northeast of Cape Town. This region boasts the most vineyard
acreage in South Africa and its fruit is generally des-
tined for brandy production. Most of the grape production is sold to co-operatives.

Recommended Worcester Producers

Hex River Crossing Private Cellar

Groot Eiland

Conradie Family Vineyards

Tony's Dream Worcester Cellar

Hex River Crossing Private Cellar The Auction Crossing
Syrah Viognier

Hex River Crossing Private Cellar Viognier

THE DESSERT WINE CELLAR

I don't know anyone who has a wine cellar devoted exclusively to sweet wines, but a balanced cellar will contain a selection of dessert wines. Sweet wines cellar very well because residual sugar protects the fruit. I have tasted Sauternes that are as brown as shoe polish but still delicious and well-balanced after fifty years. The same can be true of fortified wines such as port and sherry.

Sweet wines can be classified into two basic groups: those that are naturally sweet after fermentation (less than 14 percent alcohol) and those that have grape spirits added to stop the sugar from fermenting (16 to 20 percent alcohol).

Various techniques are employed to make sweet wine:

- stopping fermentation to leave residual sugar in the wine. This can happen naturally if the yeast exhausts itself consuming the sugar (Muscats) and converting it to alcohol, or it can be done mechanically with sulphur to kill the yeast.
- adding concentrated grape juice to finished wine
- allowing the grapes to dry (Recioto della Valpolicella) or to be attacked by *Botrytis cinerea* (Sauternes) to concentrate their sugars
- allowing the grapes to freeze and pressing them in their frozen state to drive off water (icewine)
- fortifying a wine before it has finished fermenting to dryness (port).

The classic naturally fermented dessert wines (and the grapes they are made from) are as follows. They would all cellar well.

France

- **Bordeaux:** Sauternes, Barsac, Cérons, Loupiac, Ste-Croix-du-Mont (Sémillon, Sauvignon Blanc)
- **Loire:** Anjou, Vouvray, Coteaux du Layon, Quarts de Chaume, Bonnezeaux (Chenin Blanc)
- **Alsace:** Sélection de Grains Nobles, Vendange Tardive (Late Harvest) (Riesling, Gewürztraminer, Pinot Gris)
- **Southwest France:** Jurançon (Petit Marseng), Monbazillac (Sémillon, Sauvignon Blanc, Muscadelle)
- **Jura:** Vin de Paille (Savagnin)
- **Rhône:** Muscat Beaumes-de-Venise
- **Roussillon:** Rivesaltes, Frontignan (Muscat), Banyuls (red: Grenache Noir)

Italy

- **Veneto:** Recioto di Soave (Garganega), Recioto della Valpolicella (Corvina, Rondinella, Molinara)
- **Piedmont:** Asti Spumante (sparkling Muscat)

Serving Dessert Wines

The trick to matching sweet wines with food is to ensure that the wine is sweeter than the dish; otherwise, the wine will taste sharp. That's why fruit-based desserts with good acidity go well with sweet wines. The sweetest dessert wines I have found are made with the Muscat grapes grown in warm climates such as Greece and Cyprus. Since you will pour only about two ounces per person, it's advisable to buy dessert wines in half-bottles unless you're in the habit of entertaining a dozen people at one sitting.

- **Tuscany/Umbria:** Vin Santo (Malvasia, Grechetto, Trebbiano)
- **Friuli-Venezia-Guilia:** Verduzzo, Picolit
- **Sardinia:** Malvasia
- **Aeolian Isles:** Muscat

Other European Countries
- **Germany/Austria:** Auslese, Beerenauslese, Trockenbeerenauslese and Eiswein of any designated grape varieties
- **Hungary:** Tokaji Aszú (Furmint, Hárslevelü, Muskotalyi)
- **Greece:** Samos (Muscat), Mavrodaphne (red)
- **Cyprus:** Commandaria (sun-dried grapes: Mavro, Xynisteri)

New World
- **United States:** Late Harvest or Botrytis-Affected (Johannisberg Riesling, Gewürztraminer, Sauvignon Blanc, Chardonnay, Muscat)
- **Canada:** icewine, Late Harvest, Select Late Harvest, Special Select Late Harvest (Vidal, Riesling, Gewürztraminer, Cabernet Franc)
- **Australia (South Australia):** Late Harvest and Noble Rot (Sémillon, Riesling), Liqueur Muscat
- **South Africa:** Late Harvest, Special Late Harvest, Noble Rot (Chenin Blanc, Riesling)
- **South America:** Late Harvest (Sauvignon, Gewürztraminer, Muscat)

FORTIFIED WINES
Of all wines, those that have been fortified have potentially the longest cellar life; their alcohol content protects

them. A fortified wine is one to which grape brandy or a neutral spirit has been added, such as sherry, port or vermouth. They have an alcoholic content ranging from 15 percent by volume to 25 percent. Once a wine has been fortified it will no longer develop, but it will last longer in a bottle once it is opened because of the higher alcohol content. Wines were originally fortified for practical reasons: they travelled better on long sea voyages to foreign markets, and the addition of brandy helped to mask deficiencies in the quality of the product at a time when winemaking was haphazard rather than an art and science.

Not all fortified wines are sweet; they can range from very dry (fino sherry and Sercial Madeira) to very sweet (cream sherry and Marsala Superiore). They are usually served chilled to lower their perception of sweetness and to bring out their freshness (acidity), except for port, which is served just below room temperature (although white port should be chilled).

Tony's Dream International Dessert Wine Cellar

Château d'Yquem (Sauternes)

Maculan Breganze Torcolato (Veneto)

Roberto Anselmi Veneto Passito I Capitelli

Gunderloch Nackenheim Rothenberg Riesling
    Trockenbeerenauslese (Rheinhessen)

Château des Charmes Riesling Icewine (Ontario)

Arvay Tokaji Esszencia (Hungary)

De Bortoli Noble One (Sémillon; Australia)

Weinbach Riesling Schlossberg Vendanges Tardives Trie
    Spéciale (Alsace)

Avignonesi Vin Santo (Grechetto, Trebbiano Toscano,
Malvasia; Tuscany)

Gonzalez Byass Pedro Ximenez Noe Muy Viejo (Jerez)

THE MOST COMMON WINE MISTAKES

- **Confusing Pouilly-Fuissé with Pouilly-Fumé.** The first is a Burgundy made from Chardonnay grapes. The second is a Loire wine made from Sauvignon Blanc.

- **Spelling and pronouncing Riesling incorrectly.** Rhyme it with "freezing": *reezling*, not *rise-ling*.

- **Thinking that red wine is more fattening than white.** The number of calories in wine relates directly to the alcohol content or the alcohol and residual sugar. A Beaujolais, at 11 percent alcohol by volume, is less fattening than a Chardonnay at 13 percent.

- **Opening champagne by levering the cork out with the thumbs.** Any sparkling wine should be opened by holding the cork firmly and twisting the bottle away from it. The cork does not move. That way, you avoid the *pop* and the ensuing fountain.

- **Calling all sparkling wines *champagne*.** Only sparkling wine from the delimited region of Champagne in northeastern France, made by the traditional method, is legally entitled to the name.

- **Branding all rosés as sweet or medium-dry.** The best are dry. Try Tavel or Lirac rosé from the Rhône.

- **Assuming that the vintage date tells you when the wine was bottled.** The year on the label denotes the year the grapes were harvested and fermented.

- **Supposing that Burgundy is a style of wine.** Burgundy is not a style but a region that produces red, white, rosé and even some sparkling wines. Wines from other countries that call themselves Burgundies are invariably blends that have never seen a Chardonnay or Pinot Noir grape.

- **Considering Alsace to be a German wine region.** Alsace wines come in tall green bottles that look like Mosel wines, but they are distinctively and defiantly French. The region borders on Germany west of the Rhine.

- **Holding a wine glass by the bowl.** The heat of the fingers will warm up white wines and cover up the beautiful colour of reds. Hold your glass by the stem or the base.

- **Filling the glass to the brim.** This may be a sign of generous hospitality, but it does not allow the wine lover to swirl and sniff the wine. Fill to a maximum of two-thirds of the glass.

- **Placing glasses for sparkling wine in the freezer or in the ice bucket.** An iced glass or a wet one will turn a sparkling wine flat in no time. Chilling the wine is sufficient to bring it down to the proper serving temperature.

- **Supposing that dry wines are completely dry.**
There is no such thing as a totally dry wine—there is always a measure of unfermented grape sugar, although it may be as low as 3 grams per litre. Most so-called dry wines have up to 5 grams per litre, but high acidity enhances the perception of dryness. Dryness denotes the absence of sugar, not the tactile sensation from the tannin in red wine that can leave the mouth feeling dry.

- **Leaving unopened champagne or wine for weeks in the fridge.** Sparkling wine will lose its bubbles and still wines will oxidize if left too long in the fridge. The agitation of the compressor can shake them into old age very quickly.

- **Trying to find a wine without sulphites.** Even organic wines that are made without recourse to sulphur products will contain some sulphites, because anything that ferments will create sulphites. So those warnings on American wine labels should read "Guaranteed To Contain Sulphites."

WINE PROFILES

You may select your wines based on how they feel in your mouth or how they match the food you are ordering or preparing. You'll want to know the "weight" of the wine and the amount of sugar it contains. The following chart divides white and red wines from around the world into categories: very dry, dry, fruity (off-dry) and sweet; and light-bodied, medium-bodied, full-bodied, heavy duty and sweet.

WHITE WINES	VERY DRY; LIGHT-BODIED	DRY; MEDIUM-BODIED
FRANCE	Aligoté Crepy Jura Muscadet Petit Chablis Quincy Riesling Saumur Savoie Silvaner Touraine	Beaujolais Blanc Chablis Entre-Deux-Mers Graves Mâcon Blanc Pouilly-Fumé Sancerre Sauvignon Blanc
GERMANY/ AUSTRIA	Grüner Veltliner Riesling Trocken Silvaner	Müller-Thurgau Riesling (QbA) Silvaner (Pfalz) Silvaner (Rheinhessen) Weissburgunder Welschriesling
ITALY	Castelli Romani Colli Albani Collio Est! Est!! Est!!! Frascati Grüner Veltliner Marino Riesling Italico Riesling Renano Tocai Friulano	Chardonnay Cortese di Gavi Lacrima Christi Orvieto Pinot Bianco Pinot Grigio Soave Tocai di Lison Torre di Giano Traminer Trebbiano Verdicchio Vernaccia di San Gimignano

RY; LL-BODIED	FRUITY (OFF-DRY); LIGHT-, MEDIUM- & FULL-BODIED	SWEET; LIGHT-, MEDIUM- & FULL-BODIED
ardonnay (south) ondrieu ôte de Beaune ewürztraminer not Gris ouilly-Fuissé (estate) ône white	Anjou (L) Château Chalon (F) Edelzwicker (L) Gaillac (L) Gewürztraminer (Late Harvest) (F) Jurançon (L) Muscat (M) Pinot Blanc (M) Riesling (Late Harvest) (F) Sauternes (dry) (F) Savennières (M) Pinot Gris (F) vin jaune (F) Vouvray (F)	Banyuls (F) Barsac (F) Beaumes-de-Venise (F) Cérons (L) Coteaux du Layon (L) Loupiac (M) Rivesaltes (F) Sauternes (F) Ste-Croix-du-Mont (M) vin de paille (F) Vouvray (M)
aden whites rauburgunder uscat ylvaner aminer Veissburgunder	Gewürztraminer Liebfraumilch Pinot Blanc (Austria) Rülander Scheurebe Spätlese Auslese	Beerenauslese (M) Eiswein (M) Trockenbeerenauslese (F)
hardonnay (estate) orvo ano di Avelino reco di Tufo ocorotondo egaleali orbato ebbiano d'Abruzzo	Frascati Superiore	Albana di Romagna (M) Aleatico (M) Malvasia di Lipari (F) Moscato (L) Orvieto Abboccato (L) Passito (F) Picolit (M) Recioto di Soave (F) Verduzzo (M) Vin Santo (F)

WHITE WINES	VERY DRY; LIGHT-BODIED	DRY; MEDIUM-BODIED
SPAIN/ PORTUGAL	Azietao Valdepenas Vinho Verde	Bairrada Chardonnay Dão white Penedès white Rioja white Rueda white Sauvignon
OTHER EUROPEAN	Auxerrois (Luxembourg) Fendant (Switzerland) Furmint (Hungary) Riesling (Bulgaria) Riesling (Hungary) Riesling (Switzerland) Trakya (Turkey)	Chardonnay (Hungary/Bulgaria) Demestica (Greece) Muscat Dry Retsina Sauvignon (Slovenia) Sylvaner
CANADA	Aligoté Auxerrois Gamay Blanc Riesling Seyval Blanc	Chardonnay Gewürztraminer Muscat Pinot Blanc Pinot Gris Sauvignon Blanc Vidal

UNITED
STATES
	Riesling (New York)
	Riesling (Washington)
	Seyval (New York)
		Chardonnay
		  (New York,
		  some California)
		Fumé Blanc
		Pinot Gris
		Sauvignon Blanc

RY; ULL-BODIED	FRUITY (OFF-DRY); LIGHT-, MEDIUM- & FULL-BODIED	SWEET; LIGHT-, MEDIUM- & FULL-BODIED
hardonnay (Penedès) olares white ão white arrafeira oja white erdejo		Granjo (M) Malvasia (M) Muscatel (M) Sétubal (F)
	Pinot Gris (Hungary) Riesling (Hungary) Tokaji (dry) (Hungary)	Samos Muscat (F) Tokaji (F)
me Chardonnay inot Gris (British Columbia) me Sauvignon Blanc	Chenin Blanc Ehrenfelser Late Harvest Gewürztraminer Riesling (British Columbia) Scheurebe Vidal	icewine (F) Late Harvest Riesling (M) Late Harvest Vidal (M)
hardonnay (estate) umé Blanc (estate) infandel (white)	Symphony Gewürztraminer Riesling Vignoles/Ravat (New York)	Late Harvest Riesling (M) Late Harvest Sauvignon Blanc (M)

WHITE WINES	VERY DRY; LIGHT-BODIED	DRY; MEDIUM-BODIED
AUSTRALIA/ NEW ZEALAND	some Rieslings some Sauvignons	some Chardonnay Riesling (New Zealand) Sauvignon Blanc Sémillon/Chardonnay
SOUTH AMERICA	Torrontes	Chardonnay Riesling Sauvignon Blanc
SOUTH AFRICA		Colombar Chenin Blanc Sauvignon Blanc

DRY; FULL-BODIED	FRUITY (OFF-DRY); LIGHT-, MEDIUM- & FULL-BODIED	SWEET; LIGHT-, MEDIUM- & FULL-BODIED
Chardonnay (estate) Marsanne Muscat Sauvignon Blanc (estate)	some Chardonnay Chenin Blanc Riesling Sémillon/Chardonnay	Late Harvest Sauvignon (F) Late Harvest Sémillon (F) Muscadel (F) Muscat (F)
some Chardonnay some Sauvignon Blanc some Sémillon	Riesling	Late Harvest Gewürztraminer Late Harvest Muscat Late Harvest Sauvignon (F)
Fumé Blanc some Chardonnay	Chenin Blanc	Edelkeur (F) Late Harvest Chenin Blanc (F) Late Harvest Sauvignon Blanc (F) Muscat (F)

RED WINES	LIGHT-BODIED	MEDIUM-BODIED
FRANCE	Alsace Pinot Noir Anjou Gamay Beaujolais Bouzy Rouge Cassis Chinon Clairette Côtes d'Auvergne Fronsac Haut Poitou Jura Savoie	Beaujolais-Villages Bordeaux (non-vintage) Bourgueil Burgundy villages Corbières Côtes de Bergerac Côtes du Ventoux Gaillac Loire Cabernet Franc
GERMANY/ AUSTRIA	most reds	Auslese reds Dornfelder
ITALY	Bardolino Freisa Grignolino Lago di Caldaro Lambrusco Marzemino Santa Maddelena Valpolicella	Barbera Bonarda Cabernet Carema Chianti Dolcetto Ghemme Pinot Nero Sangiovese Valpolicella Ripasso Valtellina

FULL-BODIED	HEAVY-DUTY	SWEET REDS
Bandol	Côte Rôtie	Banyuls
Bergerac	Hermitage	Rasteau
Bordeaux (château-bottled)		
Burgundy (domaine-bottled)		
Cahors		
Châteauneuf-du-Pape		
Fitou		
Lirac		
Perchamant		
Provence		
Rhône		
Barbaresco	Amarone	Giro
Barolo	Brunello di Montalcino	Recioto della Valpolicella
Cannonau	Castel del Monte	
Carmignano		
Chianti Classico Riserva		
Gattinara		
Montepulcianio d'Abbruzzo		
Nebbiolo d'Alba		
Refosco		
Rubesco		
Sassicaia		
Sfursat		
Spanna		
Taurasi		
Tignanello		
Vino Nobile di Montepulciano		

RED WINES	LIGHT-BODIED	MEDIUM-BODIED
SPAIN/ PORTUGAL	Galician reds Somontano Vinho Verde (red)	
OTHER EUROPEAN	Luxembourg reds Swiss reds	Demestica Kratosija Merlot Nemea Pinot Noir
CANADA	Gamay Pinot Noir	Baco Noir Cabernet Franc Cabernet Sauvignon Marechal Foch Merlot Syrah/Shiraz
UNITED STATES	Gamay	Barbera East Coast reds Pinot Noir (Oregon)

FULL-BODIED	HEAVY-DUTY	SWEET REDS
Alentejo Bairrada Colares Dão Douro Navarra Penedès Priorato Ribera del Duero Rioja	Garrafeira	
Bulgarian reds Château Musar (Lebanon) Greek reds Hungarian reds Israeli reds	Bull's Blood (Egri Bikavér) Kasteler Postup	Mavrodaphne (Greece)
Baco Noir Reserve Cabernet/Shiraz (British Columbia)		Cabernet Franc icewine
Cabernet Sauvignon Merlot Petite Sirah Syrah Zinfandel	some Cabernets some Petite Sirah some Zinfandel	

RED WINES	LIGHT-BODIED	MEDIUM-BODIED
AUSTRALIA/ NEW ZEALAND		Pinot Noir Merlot
SOUTH AMERICA		Argentinian reds Pinot Noir Uruguayan reds
SOUTH AFRICA		Pinot Noir

FULL-BODIED	HEAVY-DUTY	SWEET REDS
Cabernet Sauvignon Shiraz	some Cabernet/Shiraz some Shiraz	Sparkling Shiraz
Cabernet Sauvignon (Chile) Carmenère (Chile) Malbec (Argentina) Shiraz (Chile)		
Cabernet Sauvignon Pinotage Syrah		

WINE FIND

If the name of a wine is unfamiliar to you, this section will help you determine its style, the region where it is grown, its ability to age and whether it is considered a quality wine or not. It also indicates the grape(s) from which the wine is produced.

KEY TO SYMBOLS

bold	wines that need aging
*	quality wines that are cellar-worthy
†	light-bodied wines suitable for early drinking
italics	predominant grape variety in blend
+	additional grape varieties in blend beyond those mentioned

WINE NAME	STYLE	REGION	GRAPE VARIETY
Abymes	dry white†	Savoie	Jacquère
Aglianico del Vulture	dry red	Basilicata	Aglianico
Ahn	dry white	Luxembourg	Traminer
Ahrweiler	dry red†	Ahr	Pinot Noir
Aigle	dry white†	Swiss	Chasselas
Ajaccio	dry rosé/**red**	Corsica	Sciaccarello
Albana di Romagna	dry/sweet white/sparkling	Emilia-Romagna	Albana di Romagna
Aleatico	sweet white/red	Central/S. Italy	Muscat clone
Alicante	red	Spain	Monastrell
Aligoté	dry white	Burgundy	Aligoté
Aloxe Corton*	dry red	Burgundy	Pinot Noir
	dry white		Chardonnay
Amarante	dry white†	Portugal	Alvarhino, Loureiro
Amarone*	dry red	Veneto	Corvina, Rondinella, Molinara
Amigne	dry white†	Swiss	Amigne
Anghelu Ruju*	sweet red	Sardinia	Cannonau (Grenache)
Anjou	off-dry white	Loire	Chenin Blanc
	rosé/dry red		Cabernet Franc, Cabernet Sauvignon, Gamay
Apremont	dry white†	Savoie	Jacquère, Chardonnay, Aligoté
Arbois	dry white†	Jura	Savignin, Chardonnay, Pinot Blanc
	dry red/rosé		Poulsard, Trousseau, Pinot Noir

WINE NAME	STYLE	REGION	GRAPE VARIETY
Arneis*	dry white	Piedmont	Arneis
Assmannshausen*	dry red†	Rheingau	Pinot Noir
Asti Spumante	sparkling off-dry/sweet	Piedmont	Muscat
Auxey Duresses*	dry red	Burgundy	Pinot Noir
	dry white	Burgundy	Chardonnay
Baco Noir	dry red	New York/Ontario	Baco Noir
Bairrada	dry red	N. Portugal	Baga +
Bandol	dry red/rosé	Provence	*Mourvèdre, Grenache, Cinsault* +
Banyuls	sweet red	Roussillon	*Grenache Noir, Maccabéo, Tourbat, Muscats*
Barbaresco*	dry red	Piedmont	Nebbiolo
Barbera	dry red	Piedmont	Barbera
Barca Velha*	dry red	Portugal	Tinta Roriz, Tourega Francesa, Tinta Barocca
Bardolino	dry red†	Veneto	*Corvina, Molinara, Rondinella*
Barolo*	dry red	Piedmont	Nebbiolo
Barsac*	sweet white	Bordeaux	*Sémillon, Sauvignon, Muscadelle*
Bâtard-Montrachet*	dry white	Burgundy	Chardonnay
Béarn	dry red†	SW France	*Tannat, Cabernets, Fer, Manseng* +
Beaujolais	dry red	Burgundy	Gamay
Beaumes-de-Venise	sweet white	S. Rhône	Muscat
Beaune*	dry white	Burgundy	Chardonnay
	dry red		Pinot Noir
Bellet	dry red	Provence	Braquet, Cinsault, Folle Noir +
Bergerac	**dry red**	Dordogne	Cabernet Sauvignon, Cabernet Franc, Merlot
	dry/sweet white		Sémillon, Sauvignon, Muscadelle
Bernkastel	dry/sweet	Mosel	Riesling
Bianco di Custoza	dry white	Veneto	Garganega, Trebbiano, Tocai Friulano, Cortese
Bienvenue-Bâtard-Montrachet*	dry white	Burgundy	Chardonnay
Blagny*	dry white	Burgundy	Chardonnay
	dry red		Pinot Noir
Blanquette de Limoux	sparkling	Languedoc	*Mauzac, Chardonnay, Chenin Blanc*
Blaye, Côte de (Blayais)	dry white	Bordeaux	Sauvignon, Sémillon, Muscadelle
	dry red		Cabernet Sauvignon, Cabernet Franc, Merlot, Malbec
Bonnes Mares*	dry red	Burgundy	Pinot Noir
Bonnezeaux*	sweet white	Loire	Chenin Blanc
Bordeaux*	dry/sweet white	Bordeaux	Sémillon, Sauvignon, Muscadelle
	dry red*		Merlot, Cabernet Sauvignon, Cabernet Franc, Malbec
Bourg, Côte de (Bourgeais)	dry/sweet white	Bordeaux	Sémillon, Sauvignon, Muscadelle
	dry red		Cabernet Sauvignon, Cabernet Franc, Merlot
Bourgogne	dry white	Burgundy	Chardonnay
	dry red		Pinot Noir
Bourgogne Passe-Tout-Grains	dry red	Burgundy	*Gamay, Pinot Noir*

WINE NAME	STYLE	REGION	GRAPE VARIETY
Bourgueil	dry red†	Loire	*Cabernet Franc*, Cabernet Sauvignon
Bouzy Rouge	dry red†	Champagne	Pinot Noir
Brouilly*	dry red	Beaujolais	Gamay
Brunello di Montalcino*	dry red	Tuscany	*Sangiovese*
Bucellas*	dry white	Portugal	Arinto
Bugey	dry white	Savoie	Chardonnay, Altesse, Aligoté +
	dry red		Gamay, Pinot Noir, Mondeuse +
Bull's Blood			
(see Egri Bikavér)			
Buzet, Côtes de	dry/sweet white	SW France	Sémillon, Sauvignon, Muscadelle
	dry red/rosé		*Merlot*, Cabernet Sauvignon,
			Cabernet Franc, Malbec
Cadillac*	sweet white	Bordeaux	Sémillon, Sauvignon, Muscadelle
Cahors	dry red	SW France	Malbec, Jurançon, *Merlot*, Tannat
Canon Fronsac	dry red	Bordeaux	Cabernet Sauvignon, Cabernet Franc,
			Merlot, Malbec
Carema*	dry red	Piedmont	Nebbiolo
Carmignano*	dry red	Chianti	*Sangiovese, Canaiolo*, Cabernet Sauvignon
Cassis	dry white	Provence	Ugni Blanc, Sauvignon, Grenache Blanc +
	dry red/rosé		Grenache, Carignan, Mourvèdre +
Castel del Monte	dry white	Apulia	Pampanuto, Trebbiano, Bombino
	dry rosé/**dry red***		Montepulciano, Nero di Troia, Bombino Nero
Castelli Romani	dry white	Latium	Malvasia, Trebbiano
Cerons	sweet white	Bordeaux	*Sémillon*, Sauvignon, Muscadelle
Chablis (Grands,			
Premiers Crus*)	dry white	Burgundy	Chardonnay
Chagny*	dry white	Burgundy	Chardonnay
Chambertin*	dry red	Burgundy	Pinot Noir
Chambolle-Musigny*	dry red	Burgundy	Pinot Noir
champagne*	sparkling dry	Champagne	Chardonnay
	off-dry/rosé		Pinot Noir, Pinot Meunier
Chapelle-Chambertin*	dry red	Burgundy	Pinot Noir
Charmes-Chambertin*	dry red	Burgundy	Pinot Noir
Chassagne-Montrachet*	dry white	Burgundy	Chardonnay
	dry red	Burgundy	Pinot Noir
Château-Chalon*	dry white	Jura	Savagnin
Château-Grillet*	dry white	N. Rhône	Viognier
Châteauneuf-du-Pape*	dry red	S. Rhône	*Grenache, Syrah*, Mourvèdre, Picpoul +
	dry white	S. Rhône	*Roussanne*, Clairette, Bourboulenc +
Chénas*	dry red	Beaujolais	Gamay
Chevalier-Montrachet*	dry white	Burgundy	Chardonnay
Cheverny	dry white	Loire	Chenin Blanc, Arbois, Chardonnay +
	dry red/rosé†		Gamay, Cabernet Sauvignon, Pinot Noir +
Chianti (Riserva*)	dry red	Tuscany	*Sangiovese, Canaiolo*
Chinon	dry red†	Loire	*Cabernet Franc*, Cabernet Sauvignon
Chiroubles*	dry red	Beaujolais	Gamay

WINE NAME	STYLE	REGION	GRAPE VARIETY
Chorey-lès-Beaune*	dry red	Burgundy	Pinot Noir
Ciro	dry red	Calabria	Gaglioppo
Clairette de Die	sparkling/dry white	N. Rhône	*Clairette*, Muscat
Clos de la Roche*	dry red	Burgundy	Pinot Noir
Clos de Tart*	dry red	Burgundy	Pinot Noir
Clos des Lambrays*	dry red	Burgundy	Pinot Noir
Clos Saint-Denis*	dry red	Burgundy	Pinot Noir
Colares	dry red	Portugal	Ramisco
Colli Albani	dry white	Latium	Malvasia, Trebbiano
Colli Berici	dry red	Veneto	Cabernet, Merlot, Tocai Rosso
Collioure	dry red	Roussillon	*Grenache*, Syrah, Cinsault, Carignan +
Commandaria	sweet white	Cyprus	Muscat
Condrieu*	dry white	N. Rhône	Viognier
Constantia*	sweet white	S. Africa	Muscadelle
Corbières	dry red	Languedoc	*Carignan*, Cinsault, Syrah +
Cornas*	dry red	N. Rhône	Syrah
Cortese	dry white	Piedmont	Cortese
Corton*	dry red	Burgundy	Pinot Noir
Corton-Charlemagne*	dry white	Burgundy	Chardonnay
Corvo	dry white	Sicily	Inzolia +
Costières du Gard	dry red	Languedoc	*Carignan*, Grenache, Cinsault +
Côte de Beaune (-Villages)	dry white	Burgundy	Chardonnay
	dry red		Pinot Noir
Côte de Brouilly*	dry red	Beaujolais	Gamay
Côte de Castillon	dry red	Bordeaux	*Merlot*, Cabernets, Malbec
Côte de Nuits (-Villages)	dry red	Burgundy	Pinot Noir
	dry white		Chardonnay
Côte Roannaise	dry red/rosé†	Auvergne	Gamay
Côte-Rôtie*	dry red	N. Rhône	*Syrah*, Viognier
Coteaux Champenois	dry white†/red	Champagne	Chardonnay/Pinot Noir, Pinot Meunier
Côteaux d'Aix	dry red/rosé	Provence	Cabernet Sauvignon, Carignan, Cinsault +
Coteaux d'Ancenis	off-dry white	Loire	Pineau de la Loire, Chenin Blanc, Malvoisie
	dry red		Gamay, Cabernet Franc
Coteaux du Layon*	sweet white	Loire	Chenin Blanc
Coteaux du Tricastin	dry red	S. Rhône	Grenache, Syrah, Cinsault, Mourvèdre
Côtes de Duras	dry white	SW France	*Sauvignon*, Sémillon, Muscadelle +
	dry red		Cabernet Franc, Cabernet Sauvignon, Merlot, Malbec
Côtes du Frontonnais	dry red	SW France	*Negrette*, Cabernet, Malbec +
Côtes du Luberon	**dry red**/rosé	S. Rhône	Carignan, Grenache, Syrah, Mourvèdre, Cinsault +
Côtes du Rhône (-Villages)	dry rosé/**red**	S. Rhône	*Grenache*, Syrah, Mourvèdre, Picpoul, Cinsault, Carignan
Côtes du Roussillon (-Villages)	dry red	Roussillon	*Carignan*, Cinsault, Grenache, Syrah +

WINE NAME	STYLE	REGION	GRAPE VARIETY
Côtes du Ventoux	**dry red**	S. Rhône	*Grenache*, Syrah, Mourvèdre, Picpoul, Cinsault, Carignan
	dry white		Clairette, Bourboulenc +
Coulée de Serrant*	sweet white	Loire	Chenin Blanc
Crémant d'Alsace	white/rosé sparkling	Alsace	Riesling, Pinot Blanc, Pinot Gris, Pinot Noir
Crémant de Bourgogne	red/white sparkling	Burgundy	Pinot Noir/Blanc, Pinot Gris, Chardonnay
Crémant de Loire	white/rosé sparkling	Loire	Chenin Blanc, Cabernet Franc, Pinot Noir, Chardonnay
Crépy	dry white†	Savoie	Chasselas
Criots-Bâtard-Montrachet*	dry white	Burgundy	Chardonnay
Crozes-Hermitage	dry red*	N. Rhône	Syrah
	dry white		*Marsanne, Roussanne*
Dão (garrafeira*)	dry red	Portugal	Touriga, Tinta Pinheira, Tinta Carvalha, Alvarelhao, Bastardo
	dry white		Arinto, Dona Branca, Barcelo, Cerceal
Debröi Hárslevelü	dry white	Hungary	Hárslevelü
Dolcetto	dry red†	Piedmont	Dolcetto
Dôle	dry red†	Swiss	Gamay, Pinot Noir
Dornfelder	dry red	Germany	Dornfelder
Échezeaux (Grands)*	dry red	Burgundy	Pinot Noir
Edelzwicker	dry white	Alsace	Pinot Blanc, Silvaner, Gewürztraminer, Riesling +
Egri Bikavér	dry red	Hungary	Kékfrankos, Kadarka, Cabernet, Merlot
Entre-Deux-Mers	dry white	Bordeaux	Sémillon, Sauvignon, Muscadelle
Erbaluce	dry white	Piedmont	Erbaluce
Est! Est!! Est!!!	dry white†	Latium	Trebbiano
Étoile*	dry white	Jura	Chardonnay, Poulsard, Savagnin
Falerno	dry red	Latium	Barbera, Aglianico
Faugères	dry red	Languedoc	Carignan, Grenache, Syrah, Mourvèdre +
Fendant	dry white†	Switzerland	Chasselas
Fiano di Avellino*	dry white†	Campania	Fiano di Avellino
Fitou	dry red	Languedoc	Carignan, Grenache +
Fixin*	dry red	Burgundy	Pinot Noir
Fleurie*	dry red	Beaujolais	Gamay
Franciacorto Rosso*	dry red	Lombardy	*Cabernet Franc*, Barbera, Nebbiolo, Merlot
Frascati	dry white†	Latium	*Malvasia*, Trebbiano
Freisa	dry red†	Piedmont	Freisa
Fronsac	dry red	Bordeaux	Merlot, Cabernet Franc, Cabernet Sauvignon, Malbec
Frontignan, Muscat de	sweet white	Languedoc	Muscat
Gaillac	dry-sweet white/sparkling	SW France	Len de L'El, Mauzac, Muscadelle, Sauvignon +
	rosé/red		Duras, Fer, Gamay, Syrah +
Galestro	dry white†	Tuscany	Trebbiano, Malvasia
Gambellara	dry white	Veneto	Garganega, Trebbiano
Gamza	dry red	Bulgaria	Kadarka
Gattinara*	dry red	Piedmont	Nebbiolo

WINE NAME	STYLE	REGION	GRAPE VARIETY
Gavi*	dry white	Piedmont	Cortese
Gevrey-Chambertin*	dry red	Burgundy	Pinot Noir
Ghemme*	dry red	Piedmont	Nebbiolo
Gigondas*	dry red	S. Rhône	Grenache, Syrah, Mourvèdre, Cinsault
Givry*	dry red	Burgundy	Pinot Noir
	dry white		Chardonnay
Granjo	sweet white	Portugal	Malvasia Fina, Malvasia Rei +
Graves (G. de Vayres)	dry red	Bordeaux	Cabernet Sauvignon, Merlot,
			Cabernet Franc, Malbec, Petit Verdot
	dry white		Sémillon, Sauvignon, Muscadelle
Greco di Tufo*	dry white	Campania	Greco di Tufo
Grignolino	dry red†	Piedmont	Grignolino
Griotte-Chambertin*	dry red	Burgundy	Pinot Noir
Grumello	dry red	Lombardy	Nebbiolo
Grüner Veltliner*	dry white	Austria	Grüner Veltliner
Haut-Médoc	dry red	Bordeaux	Cabernet Sauvignon, Cabernet Franc,
			Merlot, Malbec, Petit Verdot
Haut-Poitou	dry white	Loire	Sauvignon, Chardonnay, Pinot Blanc,
			Chenin Blanc
	dry rosé/red		Gamay, Pinot Noir, Merlot, Cabernet Franc
Hermitage*	dry red	N. Rhône	Syrah, Marsanne, Roussanne
	dry white		Roussanne, Marsanne
Heurige (new wine)	dry white	Austria	Grüner Veltliner
Inferno	dry red	Lombardy	Nebbiolo
Irancy	dry rosé/red	N. Burgundy	Pinot Noir, César, Tressot
Irouléguy	dry red	SW France	Cabernet Sauvignon, Cabernet Franc, Tannat
	dry white		Courbu, Marseng
Jasnières*	dry/off-dry white	Loire	Chenin Blanc
Juliénas*	dry red	Beaujolais	Gamay
Jura, Côtes du	dry red	E. Cent. France	Pinot Noir, Pinot Gris, Poulsard, Trousseau
	dry white		Chardonnay, Savignin
Jurançon	dry/sweet white*	SW France	Manseng, Courbu +
La Clape	red	Languedoc	Carignan, Grenache, Cinsault, Terret Noir
	dry white	Languedoc	Bourboulenc, Clairette, Grenache Blanc +
Lacryma Christi	dry white	Campania	Coda di Volpe
Ladoix*	dry red	Burgundy	Pinot Noir
Lagrein	dry rosé/red	NE Italy	Lagrein
Lalande-de-Pomerol	dry red	Bordeaux	Merlot, Cabernet Franc,
			Cabernet Sauvignon, Malbec
Lambrusco	dry red†	Emilia-Romagna	Lambrusco
Languedoc, Coteaux du	dry red	Midi	Carignan, Cinsault, Mourvèdre, Syrah,
			Grenache +
Latricières-Chambertin*	dry red	Burgundy	Pinot Noir
Lessona	dry red	Piedmont	Nebbiolo
Liebfraumilch	off-dry white	Rhine	Silvaner, Müller-Thurgau, Riesling
Lirac	dry rosé/red	S. Rhône	Grenache, Cinsault, Mourvèdre, Syrah

WINE NAME	STYLE	REGION	GRAPE VARIETY
Listrac	dry red	Bordeaux	*Cabernet Sauvignon*, Merlot, Cabernet Franc, Malbec, Petit Verdot
Locorotondo	dry white	Apulia	Verdeca, Bianco d'Alessano
Loupiac	sweet white	Bordeaux	Sémillon, Sauvignon, Muscadelle
Lussac-St-Émilion	dry red	Bordeaux	*Merlot*, Cabernets, Malbec
Mâcon	dry white	Burgundy	Chardonnay
	dry red		Pinot Noir
Madiran	dry red	SW France	*Tannat*, Cabernet Sauvignon, Cabernet Franc +
Malaga	sweet white	Spain	Pedro Ximenez, Lairen, Moscatel +
Maréchal Foch	dry red	Ontario/New York	Maréchal Foch
Margaux*	dry red	Bordeaux	*Cabernet Sauvignon*, Merlot, Cabernet Franc, Malbec, Petit Verdot
Marsannay	dry rosé*/**red**	Burgundy	Pinot Noir
Maury	sweet red	Midi	Grenache, Muscats, Maccabéo +
Mavrodaphne	sweet red	Greece	Mavrodaphne
Mavroud	dry red	Bulgaria	Mavroud
Mazis-Chambertin*	dry red	Burgundy	Pinot Noir
Médoc	dry red	Bordeaux	Cabernet Sauvignon, Merlot, Malbec, Petit Verdot
Menetou-Salon	dry white	Loire	Sauvignon
	dry red		Pinot Noir
Mercurey*	dry white	Burgundy	Chardonnay
	dry red		Pinot Noir
Meursault*	dry white	Burgundy	Chardonnay
	dry red		Pinot Noir
Minervois	dry red	Languedoc	*Carignan*, Grenache, Syrah, Cinsault, Mourvèdre
Monbazillac	sweet white	Bergerac	*Sémillon*, Sauvignon, Muscadelle
Mondeuse	dry rosé/red	Savoie	Mondeuse
Montagny	dry white	Burgundy	Chardonnay
Montefalco Rosso	dry red	Umbria	*Sangiovese*, Trebbiano, Malvasia
Montepulciano d'Abruzzo	dry red	Abruzzi	Montepulciano d'Abruzzo
Monthélie*	dry white	Burgundy	Chardonnay
	dry red		Pinot Noir
Montlouis	dry white/sparkling	Loire	Chenin Blanc
Montrachet*	dry white	Burgundy	Chardonnay
Montravel	dry/off-dry white	Bergerac	Sémillon, Sauvignon, Muscadelle
Morellino di Scansano	dry red	Tuscany	Sangiovese
Morey St-Denis*	dry red	Burgundy	Pinot Noir
Morgon*	dry red	Beaujolais	Gamay
Moscatel de Setúbal	sweet white	Portugal	Muscatel
Moulin-à-Vent*	dry red	Beaujolais	Gamay
Moulis	dry red	Bordeaux	*Cabernet Sauvignon*, Merlot, Cabernet Franc, Malbec, Petit Verdot
Musar (Château)*	dry red	Lebanon	*Cabernet Sauvignon*, Syrah, Cinsault

WINE NAME	STYLE	REGION	GRAPE VARIETY
Muscadet	dry white	Loire	Muscadet
Muscat of Samos	sweet white	Greece	Muscat of Samos
Musigny*	dry red	Burgundy	Pinot Noir
Naoussa*	dry red	Greece	Xinomavro
Nebbiolo	dry red	NW Italy	Nebbiolo
Nemea*	dry red	Greece	Agriorgitiko
Nuits, Côte de	dry red	Burgundy	Pinot Noir
Nuits St-Georges*	dry red	Burgundy	Pinot Noir
Orvieto	dry/off-dry white	Cent. Italy	Trebbiano, Malvasia, Grechetto
Pacherenc du Vic Bilh	dry white	SW France	Arrufiac, Courbu, Marsengs +
Palette	dry white†	Provence	Clairette, Ugni Blanc, Grenache Blanc, Muscats +
	dry rosé/red		Mourvèdre, Grenache, Cinsault +
Passe-Tout-Grains	dry red	Burgundy	Gamay, Pinot Noir
Patrimonio	dry rosé/**red**	Corsica	Niellucio, Sciacarello, Grenache, Vermentino, Ugni Blanc
Pauillac*	dry red	Bordeaux	Cabernet Sauvignon, Merlot, Cabernet Franc, Malbec, Petit Verdot
Pécharmant	dry red	Bergerac	Cabernet Sauvignon, Cabernet Franc, Merlot, Malbec
Periquita	dry red	Portugal	Periquita
Pernand-Vergelesses*	dry white	Burgundy	Chardonnay
	dry red		Pinot Noir
Petit Chablis	dry white	Burgundy	Chardonnay
Picolit	sweet white	Friuli-Venezia-Giulia	Picolit
Pierrevert, Coteaux de	dry white	S. Rhône	Clairette, Marsanne, Roussanne, Ugni Blanc
	dry red		Carignan, Cinsault, Grenache, Mourvèdre, Syrah
Piesporter	off-dry white	Mosel	Riesling
Pomerol*	dry red	Bordeaux	*Merlot*, Cabernet Sauvignon, Cabernet Franc, Malbec
Pomino*	dry red	Tuscany	Sangiovese, Cabernet, Pinot Noir
	dry white		Chardonnay, Pinot Bianco, Pinot Grigio
Pommard*	dry red	Burgundy	Pinot Noir
Pouilly-Fuissé* (**-Lorché, -Vinzelles**)	dry white	Burgundy	Chardonnay
Pouilly-Fumé*	dry white	Loire	Sauvignon
Pouilly-sur-Loire	dry white	Loire	*Chasselas*, Sauvignon
Primitivo di Manduria	dry red	Apulia	Primitivo di Manduria
Prosecco	dry/off-dry sparkling	Veneto	Prosecco
Provence, Côtes de	**dry red**	Provence	Carignan, Syrah, Cabernet Sauvignon, Mourvèdre +
	dry white		Clairette, Sémillon, Ugni Blanc +
Puligny-Montrachet*	dry white	Burgundy	Chardonnay
Quarts de Chaume*	sweet white	Loire	Chenin Blanc (or Pineau de la Loire)
Quincy	dry white†	Loire	Sauvignon

WINE NAME	STYLE	REGION	GRAPE VARIETY
Rasteau	sweet red	S. Rhône	Grenache Noir/Gris/Blanc
Ravat (Vignoles)	off-dry/sweet white	NE United States	Ravat (Vignoles)
Recioto della Valpolicella*	sweet red	Veneto	Corvino, Rondinella, Molinara +
Recioto di Soave*	sweet white	Veneto	Garganega, Trebbiano
Refosco	dry red	Friuli-Venezia-Giulia	Refosco
Regaleali	dry white	Sicily	Catarratto, Inzolia, Sauvignon
	dry red*		Perricone, Nero d'Avola
Retsina	dry white/rosé	Greece	Savatiano/Rhoditis
Reuilly	dry white	Loire	Sauvignon
	dry rosé/red		Pinot Noir, Pinot Gris
Riceys, Rosé de	dry rosé	Champagne	Pinot Noir
Richebourg*	dry red	Burgundy	Pinot Noir
Rioja*	dry red	NE Spain	*Tempranillo*, Garnacho, Graziano, Mazuelo +
	dry white		Viura, Malvasia
Rivesaltes, Muscat de	sweet white/red	S. Rhône	Muscats +/Grenache
Roero	dry red	Piedmont	Nebbiolo
Romanée, La*	dry red	Burgundy	Pinot Noir
Romanée-Conti			
(-St-Vivant)*	dry red	Burgundy	Pinot Noir
Rosé d'Anjou	dry rosé	Loire	Cabernets, Pineau d'Aunis, Gamay +
Rosso Conero	dry red	Marches	*Montepulciano*, Sangiovese
Rosso di Montalcino	dry red	Tuscany	Sangiovese Grosso
Rosso di Montepulciano	dry red	Tuscany	Sangiovese Grosso
Roussette	dry white	Savoie	Roussette
Rubesco*	dry red	Umbria	*Sangiovese*, Canaiolo
Ruchottes-Chambertin*	dry red	Burgundy	Pinot Noir
Rully	dry white	Burgundy	Chardonnay
	dry red	Burgundy	Pinot Noir
Ruster Ausbruch	sweet white	Austria	Welschriesling, Muscat-Ottonel
Sagrantino	dry red/off-dry	Umbria	Sagrantino
Saint-Amour	dry red	Beaujolais	Gamay
Saint-Aubin	dry white	Burgundy	Chardonnay
	dry red	Burgundy	Pinot Noir
Saint-Chinian	dry red	Midi	Carignan, Grenache, Lledoner, Mourvèdre, Syrah
Saint-Émilion*	dry red	Bordeaux	*Merlot*, Cabernets, Malbec
Saint-Estèphe*	dry red	Bordeaux	*Cabernet Sauvignon*, Merlot, Cabernet Franc, Malbec, Petit Verdot
Saint-Joseph*	dry red	N. Rhône	Syrah
Saint-Julien*	dry red	Bordeaux	*Cabernet Sauvignon*, Merlot, Cabernet Franc, Malbec Petit Verdot
Saint-Péray	dry white/sparkling	N. Rhône	Roussanne, Marsanne
Saint-Pourçain	dry red	Auvergne	*Gamay*, Pinot Noir
	dry white		*Tressalier*, Chardonnay, Sauvignon, Aligoté +
Saint-Romain	dry white	Burgundy	Chardonnay
	dry red		Pinot Noir

WINE NAME	STYLE	REGION	GRAPE VARIETY
Saint-Véran	dry white	Burgundy	Chardonnay
Sainte-Croix-du-Mont	sweet white	Bordeaux	Sémillon, Sauvignon, Muscadelle
Sainte-Foy	dry/off-dry white	Bordeaux	Sémillon, Sauvignon, Muscadelle
	dry red		Cabernets, Merlot, Malbec, Petit Verdot
Sake	dry/sweet white	Japan	rice wine
Sancerre	dry white	Loire	Sauvignon
	dry red		Pinot Noir
Santa Magdalener	dry red	Trentino-Alto Adige	Schiava, Lagrein, Pinot Noir
Santenay*	dry red	Burgundy	Pinot Noir
Santorini	dry/sweet white	Greece	Asyrtiko
Sarmento	dry red†	Tuscany	Sangiovese
Sassella	dry red	Lombardy	Nebbiolo
Sassicaia*	dry red	Tuscany	*Cabernet Sauvignon*, Cabernet Franc
Saumur	dry white	Loire	Chenin Blanc, Chardonnay, Sauvignon
	sparkling white/rosé		*Chenin Blanc*, Chardonnay, Sauvignon/
			Cabernets, Pinot Noir, Gamay +
	dry red		Cabernets, Pineau d'Aunis
Sauternes*	sweet white	Bordeaux	*Sémillon*, Sauvignon, Muscadelle
Savennières*	dry white	Loire	Chenin Blanc (or Pineau de la Loire)
Savigny-lis-Beaune*	dry red	Burgundy	Pinot Noir
	dry white		Chardonnay
Schiava	dry red	NE Italy	Schiava
Schloss Johannisberg*	dry white	Rheingau	Riesling
Seyssel	dry white†	Savoie	Roussette
	sparkling		Roussette, Chasselas, Molette
Seyval Blanc	dry white	Ontario/New York	Seyval Blanc
Sfurzàt	dry red	Lombardy	Chiavennasca (Nebbiolo)
Sizzano	dry red	Piedmont	Nebbiolo
Soave	dry white	Veneto	*Garganega*, Trebbiano
Spanna	dry red	Piedmont	Nebbiolo
Szekszárdi	dry red	Hungary	Kadarka
Tâche, La*	dry red	Burgundy	Pinot Noir
Taurasi*	dry red	Campania	Aglianico
Tavel	dry rosé	S. Rhône	*Grenache*, Cinsault, Carignan, Syrah,
			Mourvèdre
Teroldego Rotaliano	dry red	Trentino-Alto Adige	Teroldego Rotaliano
Tignanello*	dry red	Tuscany	*Sangiovese*, Cabernet Sauvignon
Tocai Friulano	dry white	Friuli-Venezia-Giulia	Tocai Friulano
Tokay (Tokaji)*	dry/sweet white	Hungary	Furmint, Hárslevelü
Tokay d'Alsace*	dry white	Alsace	Pinot Gris
Torbato di Alghero	dry white	Sardinia	Torbato
	dry red		Sangiovese, Canaiolo, Trebbiano
Torgiano	dry white	Umbria	Trebbiano, Grechetto
Toul, Côtes de	dry red/rosé†	NE France	Pinot Meunier, Pinot Noir, Gamay
	dry white†		Aligoté, Aubin, Auxerrois

WINE NAME	STYLE	REGION	GRAPE VARIETY
Touraine	dry white	Loire	Chenin Blanc, Arbois, Chardonnay
	dry red/rosé		Cabernets, Malbec, Gamay, Pinot Noir +
Tricastin, Coteaux du	**dry red**/rosé	S. Rhône	Grenache, Syrah, Cinsault, Mourvèdre, Carignan +
	dry white		Clairette, Grenache Blanc, Bourboulenc, Ugni Blanc, Picpoul
Tudia Bianco	dry white	Sicily	Inzolia, Trebbiano
Tursan	**dry red**/rosé	SW France	*Tannat*, Cabernets, Fer
Vacquéyras	dry red	S. Rhône	*Grenache, Syrah, Mourvèdre, Cinsault, Carignan*
Valdepeñas	dry red	La Mancha	*Airén*, Cencibel (Tempranillo), Garnacha
Valençay	dry red/rosé	Loire	Cabernets, Cot, Pinot Noir, Gamay +
	dry white		Sauvignon, Arbois, Chardonnay, Chenin Blanc +
Valgella	dry red	Lombardy	Nebbiolo
Valpolicella	dry red	Veneto	Corvina, Rondinella, Molinara +
Valtellina	dry red	Lombardy	Nebbiolo
Vega Sicilia*	dry red	NW Spain	Cabernet Sauvignon, Merlot, Malbec, Tinto Aragonés, Garnacha +
Verdicchio	dry white	Marches	Verdicchio, Trebbiano, Malvasia
Verduzzo	dry/sweet white	Veneto/Friuli	Verduzzo
Vermentino	dry white	Sardinia	Vermentino
Vernaccia di San Gimignano*	dry white	Tuscany	Vernaccia
Vespaiolo	dry white	Veneto	Vespaiolo
Vidal	dry/sweet white	Ontario/New York	Vidal
Vin Jaune*	dry white	Jura	Savagnin
Vin Santo*	sweet white	Cent./N. Italy	Grechetto, Malvasia, Trebbiano, (Trentino) Nosiola
Vinho Verde	dry white†	N. Portugal	Alvarhino, Loureiro
Vino Nobile di Montepulciano*	dry red	Tuscany	*Sangiovese*, Canaiolo, Trebbiano, Malvasia
Vivarais, Côtes du	dry red	S. Rhône	Grenache, Syrah, Mourvèdre, Cinsault, Carignan
Volnay*	dry red	Burgundy	Pinot Noir
Vosne-Romanée*	dry red	Burgundy	Pinot Noir
Vougeot, Clos de*	dry red	Burgundy	Pinot Noir
Vouvray*	dry/sweet white	Loire	Chenin Blanc
Yquem, Château d'	sweet white	Bordeaux	Sémillon, Sauvignon Blanc
Zinfandel	blush/rosé, **red***	California	Zinfandel

FOOD AND WINE

HOW TO TASTE WINE

Wine appeals to all five senses: sight, smell, taste, touch and hearing. It's mainly the first three you have to consider when judging the quality of a wine. In that order too, because the first sensory response you have is to colour, then smell as you lift the glass to your nose, and finally taste.

Step 1: Sight

Hold the glass against a white background. The wine should look clean and bright. Study the colour, tilting the glass so you can see the rim where the wine touches the glass. Young wines will hold their colour to the rim; older wines begin to fade. White wines start life water-white and gain colour with age. Reds start purple and lose colour. Browning edges are a warning sign that suggests age or oxidation.

Swirl the glass and watch the transparent wet residue on the sides form into tears ("legs") and slide down the glass. This is alcohol. The thicker and more slow-moving these tears, the higher the alcohol content.

Step 2: Smell

Swirl the wine in the glass. This action causes the esters that carry the wine's aromatics to evaporate and rise. You'll get a more concentrated bouquet by swirling. You can tell 75 percent about a wine with your nose. The bouquet will tell you what the wine will taste like; the only thing it won't tell you is how long the taste will linger on your palate.

Look for faults first. Are there any off-odours—the smell of vinegar (volatile acidity), prunes (oxidation) or damp basements (corkiness)? The wine, depending on the variety or blend, should smell of fruit, flowers, sometimes vegetables (especially Sauvignon Blanc), vanilla or coconut, or toast and smoke if aged in oak.

Step 3: Taste

Take a sip and let the wine wash over your entire palate. The first sensation you'll notice is the wine's sweetness (the taste buds that register sweetness are at the tip of the tongue). As the wine works its way to the back of the mouth you'll experience acidity (a lemon-like flavour) and, in red wines, a slight bitterness. This is tannin.

Feel the weight of the wine in your mouth. High-alcohol wines will be full-bodied. Ask yourself if the wine is in balance. A great wine will be seamless: the fruit, acidity, alcohol, oak and tannin will be perfectly in harmony.

Here's a wine taster's secret: suck in air when the wine is in your mouth. You'll extract more flavour, just as you get more of the wine's bouquet by swirling it in the glass.

HOW TO SERVE WINE

Glass Choice

Choose glasses that flatter the wine. Avoid coloured or heavily engraved glass—you want to see the wine's colour. A plump tulip shape is best for reds, and use a long-stemmed glass for whites so that your hand doesn't heat up the bowl.

Serving Temperature

Serving wine at the wrong temperature can spoil the taste. A red that reaches room temperature 22°C (72°F) will taste flabby, as the alcohol starts to evaporate. A white served too cold—frosting the glass—will lose its flavour.

Chilling a wine lowers perception of its sweetness and emphasizes the acidity, making the wine taste fresher. What then are the proper serving temperatures for wine? Well, it's a good idea to take stock of the weather. On a cool day your whites and reds can be slightly warmer. On a hot day serve whites well-chilled and reds at cellar temperature.

Red wines: optimum serving temperature is 16° to 20° Celsius (60° to 68° Fahrenheit). Serve fruity reds such as Beaujolais and Pinot Noir (red Burgundy) at cooler temperatures than Cabernet Sauvignon (red Bordeaux) or Rhône. Serve older wines on the cooler side.

White wines: optimum serving temperature is 7° to 10° Celsius (45° to 50° Fahrenheit). The sweeter the wine, the lower the temperature, but not so cold that the glasses frost up. The same holds true for sparkling wines and champagnes.

Rosé wines: optimum serving temperature is 7° to 10° Celsius (45° to 50° Fahrenheit). However, semi-sweet and sparkling rosés can be served at a cooler temperature.

Chilling Time

It doesn't take long for a wine to chill down to the required temperature. Twenty minutes in an ice bucket half-filled with water and a couple of trays of ice cubes (so that the level is neck-high on the bottle) is sufficient. An hour in the fridge will bring the wine down to 10° Celsius (50° Fahrenheit). For fruity red wines (Beaujolais, Valpolicella) that you want to chill lightly, ten minutes in an ice bucket or fifteen to twenty minutes in the fridge will suffice. Then remove the wine from the cold and let it stand on the table (on a mat or plate so that you don't mark the surface).

WINE IN THE KITCHEN

The cunning cook will always have a glass of wine at his or her elbow—to refresh, inspire and enjoy. And if some of that wine gets tipped into the frying pan or cooking pot, so much the better for the ultimate delight of the guests.

The uses of wine in food are manifold. You can employ wine to marinate meat, game and poultry. You can splash some into the sauce, beef up a soup, freshen up fruit and berries, whip up a sabayon, heat up a fondue or prepare a sherbet. Wine will also jazz up jams, jellies, chutneys and preserves. And you can use wine in salad dressing instead of vinegar, especially if you want to serve wine with the salad.

When you cook with wine, here are some pointers to keep in mind:

- Don't add to a dish any wine that you would not drink from a glass. A very human tendency is to want to save a wine that tastes a little off and use it for cooking. But why add a flavour to food that you've already decided you don't like in the wine? Ensure that your cooking wine is sound.
- Keep in mind you are not adding alcohol to a dish if the wine is heated for a few minutes in the cooking process. Most of the alcohol will evaporate, since it has a lower boiling point than water. Water boils at 100° Celsius (212° Fahrenheit) while alcohol boils at 77° Celsius (171° Fahrenheit). (Alcohol also has a lower freezing point than water.)
- Never boil wine by itself. It can burn and introduce harsh flavours into your dish. Simply allow it to simmer gently.

- When you substitute wine for vinegar in salad dressing, simmer the wine and reduce it by half. Then allow it to cool before you mix it with the oil and condiments. Heating wine concentrates its flavour and sweetness as well as its acidity, and gets rid of most of the alcohol.
- For best results choose cooking wines that have lots of flavour. Delicate, old or subtle wines get lost in rich dishes.
- If you add wine at the beginning of preparation you will cook away the flavour. Add the wine towards the end of the cooking process.

Red Wine Headaches

Some people react badly to red wine—one glass and they get a headache. What causes this headache is tannin. Tannin releases histamines in your system, and if you are allergic to them you will get a headache. For many red wine–headache sufferers an Aspirin taken half an hour before wine consumption will keep the headache at bay (but don't follow this advice if your doctor has prescribed a daily dose of Aspirin).

White wines don't have a high degree of tannin because the juice is pressed from the grapes, so usually there is no contact with the skins during fermentation (the pits, stalks and skins are the source of tannin). Beaujolais, because of its method of production, also has very little tannin. That's why you can drink Beaujolais Nouveau with pleasure (and no headache) when it's only a few weeks old.

- Don't add raw wine to a dish just prior to serving. It will not get a chance to meld with the other tastes, and the alcohol will be apparent.
- Don't add more than the recipe calls for. You want to be generous with your guests, but spiking a dish with too much wine will add acidity to the food.
- Don't use your best wines for cooking. If you want to keep the heel of a bottle for kitchen use, pour enough olive oil into the bottle to cover the surface and exclude air. The wine will keep for a week this way (the oil will separate from the wine when you pour it out slowly).
- You can also store wine for cooking by freezing it in an ice cube tray.
- If you are decanting an old wine for dinner, use a coffee filter so that the sediment is left in the bottle. Then use the wine to deglaze the pan.

Wine Cooking Hints

- The acidity in wine can cause milk, cream and eggs to curdle. To avoid this, add the wine—previously reduced and cooled—towards the end of preparation.
- Wines have their own flavours that can enhance those in a dish.

Beaujolais: cherry
Cabernet Sauvignon: cassis
Chardonnay: apple, pear
Oaky Californian and Australian Chardonnays: vanilla
Pinot Noir: raspberry
Riesling: lemon-lime
Sauvignon Blanc: vegetal flavours
Syrah/Shiraz: blackberry
Sherry: nuts

- Avoid adding wine directly to vegetables, as its acidity impedes the cooking process. Add it to the pot halfway through the cooking process.
- Poaching fruit in wine makes an excellent (and easy-to-prepare) dessert. It works particularly well with peeled pears (try poaching them in Amarone!), peaches, plums and cherries. If you use a dry wine, add a tablespoon of honey or sugar. Sweet dessert wines such as Sauternes, port, Marsala and Madeira don't need any sweetening.

How to Cook with Wine
Marinades
- Wine tenderizes and flavours meat and poultry, but be aware that red wine will stain chicken and other white meats.
- Most red-wine marinades need oil to help lock in the wine's flavour.
- For optimum results, in a pan, reduce the wine along with the other ingredients in the marinade; deglazing will concentrate the flavours.
- Allow the meat to marinate in the refrigerator overnight (use a plastic bag or zip-lock pouch so you can turn the meat easily and get uniform marination). The absorption process speeds up if you marinate at room temperature.
- Don't marinate fish in white wine for too long. The acidity will discolour the flesh and make it spongy.
- If you intend to use a marinade as the sauce for the dish, make sure that it is not overseasoned. You can always add condiments, herbs or spices later if required.

Sauces, Stocks, Soups and Stews

- Don't overdo the wine. The ratio should be one part wine to three or four parts liquid base; otherwise, the wine flavour will predominate.
- Red wine will colour the sauce or stock.
- The tannin and acidity of reds help to balance the flavours of hearty meat dishes.

Stuffings: Wine is perfect for ensuring that your stuffing does not go dry. White wine is preferable, since its acidity will complement the herbs and spices.

Cheeses: Wine and cheese is a natural pairing. When you make a cheese sauce, pour in a little white wine. Its acidity will cut the fattiness of the cheese.

Adding "Raw" Wine

- Add a dash of sherry to soup just before serving, but don't pour wine into stews, casseroles or sauces unless the wine has been heated to drive off the alcohol. The alcohol will spoil the taste of the dish.
- Splashing wine onto desserts does work, especially fruit and berry dishes. Choose a sweetish wine such as Asti Spumante or any Muscat-based dessert wine.

FOOD AND WINE MATCHING

In the movie *Sideways* the protagonist, Miles, despondent over his failed literary efforts and the loss of his lady love, opens a treasured bottle of 1961 Château Cheval Blanc in a fast-food joint. While eating a hamburger, he proceeds to drink it, all by himself, from a plastic cup. (W. Blake Gray of the *San Francisco Chronicle* writes that the movie's producers originally wanted to use a bottle of Pétrus, but when Christian Moueix, the proprietor of Château Pétrus, read the script, he wisely declined to donate a bottle.)

I have little sympathy for Miles. Drinking a cherished bottle is not going to lift your spirits when you're despondent. If you feel awful the wine is going to taste awful. In Miles's case it was sheer masochism to squander his best wine on a hamburger that he probably couldn't even taste.

Sixty percent of the enjoyment of wine is timing. It has everything to do with mood and ambiance. Let me give you an example: You are invited to dinner by your bank manager and he serves you a 1961 Pétrus. Just as you are lifting the glass to your lips, he tells you that the reason he's invited you is that he has to foreclose on your mortgage. That wine will taste like wormwood, and the memory of it will haunt you for the rest of your gustatory life. On the other hand, say you're at a picnic with someone you love. The sun is shining, you're happy and you've chilled a simple bottle of Beaujolais in a stream. You've got a baguette, a round of Camembert, some spicy Italian salami—a feast. Under those circumstances the wine will taste like the nectar of the gods.

Wine is not beer and it's not spirits. Wine belongs on the dinner table. A well-chosen wine can make a meal into an occasion. But how do you put the two together to enhance each other's flavour? The old adage of "white wine with fish and white meat, red wine with red meat" is okay as far as it goes, but it limits you in your range of options. This basic rule was developed because certain oily fish, such as salmon, sardines and anchovies, will make robust tannic reds taste tinny, and aesthetically, red wines look better with meat than white. If for some reason you do not drink red wine, it's no crime to have a glass of Chardonnay or champagne with your steak. Dionysus won't suddenly appear at your table and set about you with a vine stalk.

There are no rules for marrying food and wine, only certain principles that will help you in your choice. *Always match the wine to the strongest flavour on the plate.* Consider pairing a dish with a bottle of wine as you would two sparring partners. They have to be the same weight and strength; otherwise, one will easily overpower the other. The weight and power of a wine depend upon its alcohol content and fruit character. A wine weighing in at 13 percent alcohol by volume or more (look at the bottom of the label) will be full-bodied whether it's white, red or rosé. Wines from hot growing regions such as the Rhône, California and Australia will generally be high in alcohol and will exhibit lots of fruit character.

By contrast, the wines of northern Europe, especially the dry German whites, will be light and delicate and high in acidity. Acid is another component of wine that makes it marry well with most foods. Wines that you may find too dry for your taste when consumed as an aperitif will go well with salty dishes—try Muscadet with anchovies or fino sherry with olives, for example.

Food and Wine Affinity Chart (Reds)

GAME (Rich, full-bodied reds)	BEEF, LAMB, DUCK (Full-bodied to medium-bodied reds)	HAM, PORK, HAMBURGER (Medium-bodied to light-bodied reds)	CHICKEN, VEAL (Light-bodied reds)
Châteauneuf-du-Pape	Château-bottled Bordeaux	Young Bordeaux	Alsace/German Pinot Noir
Côte Rôtie	Red Burgundy	Loire reds	Beaujolais
Hermitage	Cabernet Sauvignon	Valpolicella	Corbières
Petite Sirah	Pinot Noir	Beaujolais Crus	Minervois
Shiraz	Barolo	Fronsac	Savoie
Amarone	Barbaresco	Grignolino	Bardolino
Brunello	Chianti Classico	Valais	Dolcetto
Zinfandel	Vino Nobile	Chelois	Santa Magdalener
Baco Noir	Rioja	Dornfelder	
Dão/Bairrada			
Maréchal Foch			

Food and Wine Affinity Chart (Whites)

SALMON, LOBSTER, CRAB (Full-bodied, oak-aged whites)	WHITE FISH (Medium-bodied whites)	SHRIMPS, SCALLOPS (Medium-bodied to light-bodied whites)	OYSTERS, MUSSELS (Light, crisp wines)
White Burgundy	Chablis	Entre-Deux-Mers	Muscadet
Château-bottled Graves	Pinot Blanc	Sauvignon Blanc	Loire Sauvignon
Pouilly-Fumé	Dry Vouvray	Dry Riesling	Petit Chablis
Sancerre	Riesling Kabinett	Aligoté	Coteaux Champenois
White Rhône	Orvieto	Auxerrois	Frascati
Viognier	Soave	Grüner Veltliner	Galestro
Pinot Gris/Grigio	Verdicchio	Tocai Friulano	Mosel Riesling
Old Rioja (W)	Rioja/Penedès whites		Vinho Verde
Chardonnay			Fendant
Dry rosé			

To give you a sense of the gradation of food and wine from rich and heavy to light and delicate, have a look at the Food and Wine Affinity Chart. It starts with game, the heaviest and most highly flavoured of meats, and works its way down through the red meats to the white. In the fish/seafood section the richest flavours are salmon, lobster and crab, working down through white fish and more delicate shellfish to oysters and mussels, which demand the driest of white wines.

Each category on the chart lists the generic style of wine that would best accompany the dish and suggests certain wine regions or grape varieties. However, what complicates the equation is the manner in which you prepare the dish in question. For instance, a plain grilled steak calls for a medium- to full-bodied red wine. But if you prepare it as a pepper steak or as steak tartare with Worcestershire sauce, onions and pepper, the additional condiments will require something a little more powerful to match up. So you would move up the ladder a notch and choose something from the heavy reds section. A simple steamed sole calls for a crisp, light white such as a Soave or a dry Riesling, but if you add a cream sauce to the dish the added sweetness of the cream will suggest a white wine one step up, with more body and fruit; for example, Californian or Australian Chardonnay, a white Beaune or a Riesling Spätlese.

These food categories and the complementary wine styles are offered only as a rough guide.

• If you like your hamburgers heavily spiced with garlic and pepper, choose a heavier wine style. The spicier the dish, the more powerfully flavoured the wine has to be to stand up to it.

- If you are using a tomato-based sauce, choose a wine with more acidity. Try a northern Italian red (Barbaresco, Chianti, Valpolicella) rather than a French red (Bordeaux or Burgundy) or a New World Cabernet Sauvignon.
- If you use a lot of butter or cream in a dish, you are introducing sweetness to it. This means you will require a wine with lots of fruit. If the choice would have been a white Burgundy, switch to a Chardonnay from California or Australia.
- The chicken and veal section is a crossover category between red and white. Your choice will depend on how you prepare the dish and what colour you want your sauce to be. If you're cooking coq au vin, the traditional recipe calls for a bottle of red Burgundy, and it would be sensible to have that wine on the table, but in Alsace they prepare the dish with Riesling.

Tips for Matching Food and Wine

- Salty foods require wines with high acidity. High-acid red and white wines come from northerly growing areas such as Germany, Alsace, Loire, Ontario and New York State.
- Fried or greasy foods need wines with good acidity and/or effervescence to clean the palate.
- Sweet wines with good acidity, such as Vouvray and Riesling, go well with sweet-and-sour dishes.
- Duck and goose will taste less fatty if consumed with young red wines with evident tannin; for example, young red Bordeaux, red Burgundy, Barbaresco or Chianti.
- If you like your meat rare, choose a red wine with good tannin (young Bordeaux, Burgundy, etc.). If you

like your meat well done, without a trace of blood, opt for a fruity red with as little tannin as possible, such as Beaujolais or any red made by carbonic maceration, or mature Spanish Rioja.

- When matching a sweet wine to a dessert, make sure that the wine is sweeter than the dish; otherwise, the food will bring out the wine's acidity.
- The best all-round wine for Chinese food is a dry Vouvray from the Loire. Try a lightly chilled Beaujolais-Villages with Peking duck.
- The best wine for Indian food is beer. If you must have a wine, choose a rosé from the Rhône or a German Riesling Spätlese.
- The most versatile wine for food is champagne—it's even good with breakfast.
- When in doubt about a food–wine match, choose a sharper, more acidic wine—bitter is better. Wines you may find tough to drink by themselves (too acidic, too full-bodied, too tannic) may go well with a particular food group; for example, Muscadet with oysters. Check the Food and Wine Affinity Chart for possible matches.
- If you are serving more than one wine with a meal, choose the main-course wine first. Serve lighter before heavier wines, and younger before older (immature wines suffer in comparison with older bottles).

Some Classic Foods and Wines to Match

There is, of course, no one wine that is perfect for a dish to the exclusion of all others. However, as a guide to felicitous match-ups, here are some suggestions for pairing up well-known recipes—up and down the scale—with an appropriate wine style. The recommendations are for grape variety and/or region.

Chicken

Chicken Cacciatore	Chianti
Chicken Kiev	white Burgundy
Cold chicken	Beaujolais
Coq au vin	red Burgundy
Curried chicken	Gewürztraminer
Tandoori chicken	Australian Shiraz

Duck

Canard à l'orange	Riesling Auslese
Duck pâté	Alsace Muscat
Peking duck	Beaujolais Crus

Turkey

Dark meat	Saint-Julien (Bordeaux)
White meat	Californian Chardonnay

Seafood/Fish

Coquilles St. Jacques	Pouilly-Fumé
Fish and chips	Soave
Fritto misto mare (deep-fried seafood)	dry Vouvray
Frog's legs	Sauvignon Blanc
Gefilte fish	Pinot Blanc (Alsace)
Gravlax	white Rhône
Lobster Newburg	Californian Chardonnay
Moules marinières	Muscadet
Oysters	Brut champagne, Chablis
Prawn/shrimp cocktail	white Graves
Quenelles	Chardonnay
Sardines	Vinho Verde
Smoked salmon	dry Gewürztraminer
Smoked trout	Sancerre

Beef and Veal

Beef Wellington	Côte de Beaune
Boeuf bourguignon	red Burgundy
Calf's liver	red Mâcon
Chili con carne	Amarone
Escalope of veal	Chablis
Goulash	red Zinfandel
Pepper steak	Barolo
Roast beef	Médoc
Shepherd's pie	Beaujolais
Spaghetti bolognese	Barbaresco
Steak tartare	Brunello di Montalcino
Veal cordon bleu	Puligny-Montrachet

Lamb

Couscous	Crozes-Hermitage
Irish stew	Entre-Deux-Mers
Leg of lamb	red Rioja
Rack of lamb	red Bordeaux
Shish kebab	red Zinfandel

Pork

Bacon and eggs	Beaujolais
BBQ spareribs	Shiraz
Frankfurters and beans	Barbera
Ham omelette	Cabernet d'Anjou
Hot dogs	Beaujolais
Prosciutto and melon	LBV port
Roast pork and apples	Vouvray
Salami	Barbaresco

Desserts

Apple pie	Late Harvest Riesling
Baked Alaska	sweet sparkling
Cake	Madeira (Malmsey)
Cheesecake	sweet Vouvray
Chocolate	LBV port
Christmas pudding	off-dry sparkling
Crème brûlée	Sauternes
Pumpkin pie	cream sherry, Tokaji Aszú
Strawberries and cream	extra-dry champagne

Cheeses

Asiago	Barolo, Barbaresco
Bel Paese	Valpolicella/Barbera
Bleu de Bresse	Beaujolais *crus*
Boursin	dry rosé, Beaujolais
Brick	Cabernet Sauvignon, Sancerre
Brie	red Bordeaux, Cabernet Sauvignon
Caerphilly	Mosel dry Riesling, Manzanilla sherry
Camembert	red Bordeaux, Burgundy
Cheddar	red Rhône, Barolo
Chèvre	Sancerre, Sauvignon Blanc
Colby	red Médoc, Barbaresco
Cottage cheese	Soave, sparkling Vouvray
Cream cheese	Verdicchio
Danish blue	red Burgundy, sweet white (Barsac)
Edam	Rhine Riesling, Dolcetto
Emmenthal	unoaked Chardonnay, Rheinpfalz Riesling

Feta	retsina, Chablis
Gorgonzola	red Rhône, red Zinfandel
Gouda	Beaujolais, Bourgueil
Gruyère	Pinot Noir, Australian Chardonnay
Havarti	Soave, Silvaner
Lancashire	tawny port, dry sherry
Liederkranz	Rioja red, Australian Cabernet
Limburger	red Rhône, Traminer
Livarot	red Burgundy, Bordeaux
Mascarpone	Monbazillac, Müller-Thurgau
Monterey Jack	Cabernet, Petite Sirah
Mozzarella	Chianti, Valpolicella
Muenster	Gewürztraminer, dry Muscat
Oka	white Rhône, Verdicchio
Parmesan	Chianti, Bonardo
Pecorino	red Zinfandel, red Rhône
Pont l'Evêque	red Bordeaux, Burgundy
Port Salut	Chardonnay, red Saint-Julien
Provolone	Gigondas, Pouilly-Fumé
Reblochon	Gamay, red Rioja
Romano	Chianti Classico, Barbaresco
Roquefort	Sauternes, red Zinfandel
Saint André	Pouilly-Fuissé, Orvieto
Saint Paulin	red Bordeaux, white Burgundy
Stilton	port, Sauternes, icewine
Tilsit	Silvaner, Beaujolais

Vacherin	Cabernet d'Anjou, Sancerre
Wensleydale	red Rhône, white Burgundy

Nuts

Almonds	Chianti Classico Riserva, Orvieto Aboccato
Brazil nuts	Pineau des Charentes, old Barolo
Cashews	Alsace Silvaner, German Müller-Thurgau
Chestnuts, puréed	Sauternes, sweet champagne
Chestnuts, roasted	Recioto della Valpolicella Amarone, Late Harvest Zinfandel
Hazelnuts	white Burgundy, vintage port, cider
Macadamia nuts	Tokaji Aszú, Setúbal
Mixed nuts	amontillado sherry, Bual
Nuts and raisins	Amarone/dry Muscat
Pecans	Madeira, port, Pineau des Charentes, sparkling Vouvray
Pistachios	Asti Spumante, Picolit
Smoked nuts	Traminer, red Rhône
Walnuts	chilled Beaujolais Nouveau, port, sweet sherry, Malmsey

Wines for Vegetarians

There is no need to give up wine with meals if you are a vegetarian. However, matching wines to vegetable dishes, hot or cold, requires a little more consideration because of the herbaceous flavours of most plants. Avoid oaky wines and go for fresh young reds and whites with good acidity. Probably the best single wine for vegetarian dishes is an unoaked Sauvignon Blanc (Sancerre or Pouilly-Fumé from the Loire or a simple Chilean Sauvignon).

- For reds choose fruity wines low in tannin and oak flavours, such as Beaujolais. Dry rosé is also a good option.
- With salads opt for white wines with good acidity, such as Muscadet, Soave, Chablis or dry Riesling.
- For spicy, hot or curried dishes select a white wine with some residual sugar, such as a Riesling Spätlese or an off-dry Riesling, Gewürztraminer, medium-sweet Vouvray or Californian Chenin Blanc.
- For rich vegetarian food such as grilled portobello mushrooms, more full-bodied red wines with oak are appropriate. For cheese dishes, see the Cheeses section on page 282.

WINE ALTERNATIVES

There are times when you cannot find the wine you like in your local store, or perhaps you're feeling adventuresome and would like to try something new, something in the same style and weight but from a region you've never explored before. Here are some alternatives to well-known wines within the same taste and weight range.

Whites

Dry Chablis (Chardonnay grape)
Alternatives:
Abymes (Savoie)
Coteaux Champenois (still champagne)
Muscadet (Loire)
Aligoté (Burgundy)
Cortese di Gavi (Italy)
Soave (Italy)
Northern Italian Chardonnay
Torgiano (Italy)
Verdicchio (Italy)
Grüner Veltliner (Austria)
White Rioja (Spain)
White Penedès (Spain)
Weissburgunder (Germany)
Fendant (Switzerland)
New York/Ontario Chardonnay

Dry, Medium-Bodied
Mâcon-Villages (Chardonnay)
Alternatives:
Pinot Blanc (Alsace)
Sancerre (Loire)
Dry Vouvray (Loire)

Pinot Grigio (Italy)

Central European Chardonnay

Oregon Chardonnay

Washington Chardonnay

White Côtes du Rhône

Soave (Italy)

Corvo (Sicily)

Sauvignon Blanc (Chile)

Apelia (Greece)

Dry, Full-Bodied
Puligny-Montrachet (Chardonnay)
Alternatives:

Californian Chardonnay

Californian Sauvignon Blanc (Fumé Blanc)

Australian Chardonnay

New Zealand Chardonnay

New Zealand Sauvignon Blanc

Pinot Gris (Alsace)

Pouilly-Fumé (Loire)

Condrieu (Rhône)

Viognier (California)

Medium-Dry, Medium-Bodied
Liebfraumilch (Müller-Thurgau, Silvaner, Riesling)
Alternatives:

Riesling (Germany, Austria)

Silvaner (Alsace)

Muscat (Alsace)

Müller-Thurgau (Germany)

Scheurebe (Germany)

Traminer (Northern Italy, Yugoslavia)

Gewürztraminer

Riesling (Australia)

Riesling (California)

Riesling (New Zealand)

Chenin Blanc (Australia)

Malvasia (Italy)

French Colombard (California)

Reds

Dry, Light-Bodied Beaujolais (Gamay)
Alternatives:

Valpolicella (Italy)

Bardolino (Italy)

Grignolino (Italy)

Sarmento (Italy)

Chinon/Bourgueil (Loire)

Pinot Noir (Alsace)

Clairette (Languedoc)

most German reds

Swiss reds

Savoie reds

Jura reds

Gamay Beaujolais (California, Ontario)

Dry, Medium-Bodied
Red Bordeaux (Cabernet Sauvignon, Cabernet Franc, Merlot)
Alternatives:

Bergerac

Californian Cabernet Sauvignon and Meritage blends

Australian Cabernet Sauvignon

New Zealand Cabernet Sauvignon

South African Cabernet Sauvignon

New York/Ontario Cabernets

Chilean Cabernet Sauvignon

Argentinian Cabernet Sauvignon

Spanish Cabernet Sauvignon

Camarate, Periquita (Portugal)

Italian Merlot

Argentinian Malbec

Dry, Medium-Bodied
Red Burgundy (Pinot Noir)
Alternatives:

Oregon Pinot Noir

Californian Pinot Noir

German Spätburgunder

Austrian Blauburgunder

Italian Pinot Nero

Hungarian Nagyburgundi

Chilean Pinot Noir

New Zealand Pinot Noir

South African Pinotage

Ontario Pinot Noir

Barbera (Italy, California)

Dry, Full-Bodied
Red Rhône (Syrah, Grenache)
Alternatives:

Zinfandel (California)

Petite Sirah (California)

Primitivo (Italy)

Barolo (Italy)

Amarone (Italy)

Castel del Monte (Italy)

Brunello di Montalcino (Italy)

Vino Nobile di Montepulciano (Italy)

Sicilian reds

Australian Shiraz

South African Pinotage

Bull's Blood (Hungary)

EPILOGUE:
BUILDING MY CONDO CELLAR

When Deborah and I decided to move into a condo, I had to decide what to do with the contents of my thousand-bottle cellar in the basement of our three-storey brick house. When we moved into the house, I had the cellar built, designed and constructed by the Wine Establishment. I went back to this company when I was thinking about creating a cellar in the condo. There was not enough room in the condo suite to replicate the cellar I was about to leave behind, but I thought that if I could buy extra locker space in the parking garage I could have it walled off and insulated to make a climate-controlled wine cellar.

After talking with one of the owners of the property—a wine enthusiast who empathized with my problem—I was offered a space to purchase a space that was not large enough to be sold as a parking bay but larger than a locker space. It measured nine feet by ten feet, with a ceiling of thirteen feet. I asked Laird Kay of the Wine Establishment to come up with a design.

When I approached Laird, he had just finished a big job in Bermuda that featured a large room with a tasting table for twelve, a reserve room with a dumb waiter and an elevator. My vision was more modest; I wasn't looking for a glamorous show cellar (after all, who wants to go down to a parking garage to see a stash of wine). But since Laird also designed small, closet-sized cellars, he was my man. When he had finished his initial drawings we sat down to have a chat about the process.

I asked him what had gone through his mind when I took him down to visit the site where the cellar would be built. Did he think I was nuts? Laird diplomatically explained that people typically prefer to stay close to their wines. And, given the unique location of my cellar, there were some mechanical issues we had to work through, such as rattling air shafts, as well as the issue of security. "Obviously, if it's a public access area," said Laird, "we don't want everyone to know that there is a very high-end wine collection behind this blank door." (Laird obviously hasn't seen my cellar contents!)

The primary concern was to create an envelope that would hold the climate; the cellar would need to be humidified to provide equilibrium with its temperature. A few engineering issues had to be dealt with. At the back of the space was a large air shaft that drew air down into the lower floors of the parking garage; that needed to be enclosed. "Even when you see an empty space," Laird advised me, "you have to understand that the room will shrink because it needs to be insulated and vapour-barriered. At thirteen feet the ceilings are quite high, which is very good for storage. Overall it's a good space, very clean and newly built, so there isn't going to be water seepage. In a lot of cellars we go through, the client has a space in the basement, so there's always an issue with potential water seepage."

Since the cellar would be at a different temperature than the parking garage, it would be more susceptible to cooling from outside, so we needed to build a double wall system. First we had to insulate the wall, then put up the vapour barrier. After that yet another layer of insulation would be added so there would be no condensation. "The extra insulation," Laird explained, "is so that we don't get ghosting of the studs [the studs showing through the wall]."

Then we got down to discussing the building materials. Laird advised using non-combustible materials because the building is a high-rise residence; instead of using wood studs we would use metal studs. And he recommended using Dow SM insulation, which is available in precut slabs of various widths to give various R-values between 10 and 30 (R-value is a measure of thermal resistance used in the building and construction industry; the higher the number, the more effective the insulation). This insulation would be placed between the studs.

We didn't want to insulate the floor, because that would mean more of a step-up when entering the cellar. But we needed to vapour-barrier it because, even though there wasn't any direct water seepage, a concrete floor slab is an air barrier but not a moisture barrier. When cars are parked in a garage in the winter, they're often covered with water and slush, so these areas tend to have high humidity. To stop any water from getting into the space, we would need to wrap the entire cellar in a vapour barrier. The walls would be wrapped with a six-millimetre polyethylene vapour barrier—a heavy-duty plastic—which would be Tuck-Taped at every joint so there would be no point where outside air could get in. On the floor we would use a Schluter membrane, a dimpled orange plastic material similar to the vapour barrier used in shower stalls. Then we would lay down a mortar bed and tile on top of it.

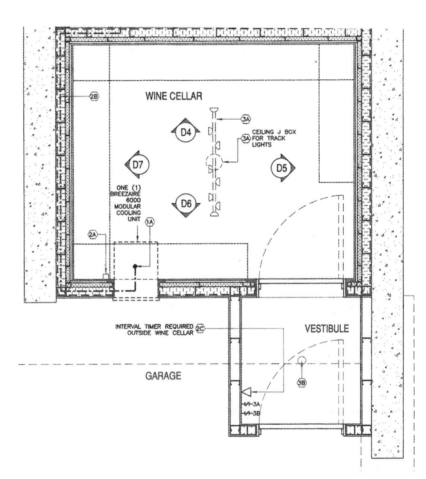

At this point in the discussion my wife, Deborah, wanted some input. As far as I'm concerned, tiles are tiles—something you walk on. I'd be happy with rubber, in case I dropped a bottle. But Deborah wanted to know about colours and textures. Laird took us through the options, advising us that because wine cellars have to be as organic as possible (to avoid off-gases that might taint the wine), it was preferable to use ceramic or porcelain tile. In high-end jobs Laird's clients have requested limestone tiles or even sheets of marble. The problem with marble, however, is that it tends to be very porous. If you break a wine bottle on marble, the floor is often ruined. We also needed the tile to be thick enough that if a bottle was dropped, the tile would not break. "You need something that's at least three-quarters to one-half inch thick to prevent any cracking," said Laird. "For larger jobs we do what is called a Bordeaux trench—a trench filled with pea gravel so that when a bottle is dropped close to the racking it falls on the gravel, and that force is dispersed and the bottle is saved."

For a previous cellar I had a beautiful wooden door with massive hinges that looked like the entrance to a rural French cathedral; it was adorned with porcelain plaques. The location of the new cellar made this option a non-starter (for security reasons), so we chose a double system. The entrance had to look as inconspicuous as possible—an industrial hollow-core metal slab door that would be unassuming. It would have a lock mechanism and there would be a vestibule before the second door; I would be able to close the first door so no one could see directly into the cellar. The second door could also be a metal door but it would have to be insulated so that it would not sweat and fitted with an automatic door bottom, which is similar to a windshield wiper blade. When you turn the door handle, the blade comes up, and when you close the door, the blade drops down. "We find it works better than a sweep because a sweep tends to degrade over time and you get more air leakage," said Laird.

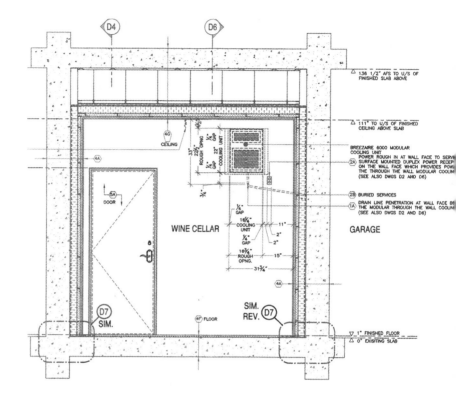

Next came the building of the walls. Laird proposed to cover the insulation with three-quarter-inch plywood so that when we were installing the racking we could screw it in anywhere and not worry about finding the studs. A bottle of wine weighs about three pounds—you don't want the racking to fall down on top of you if you lean or trip against it. Cement board, a heavy-duty drywall similar to what is used in bathrooms, would be placed on top of the plywood. That would then be taped and sanded, then painted with water-based paint.

Obviously the most important piece of equipment the cellar needed was a cooling unit, which would require its own electrical circuit—you don't want it tripping off when you turn on the lights. Such a unit doesn't use that much power, but when it powers up there's a spike in the amperage. Cooling units come in various sizes based on the cubic air volume of the room. We chose a Breezaire 6000; its parts are made of metal and therefore usually more durable. This particular unit can cool up to 900 cubic feet.

Of course, there would be water runoff from the unit. Cooling coils always need a drain; otherwise, excess moisture can build up within the room. It was difficult to find a main drain in the parking garage, so we decided to snake the drain hose through the wall structure. The condensation would drip down into the air shaft behind the wine cellar to a giant drain at the bottom of the shaft, two storeys down.

When we talked about lighting, I suggested pot lights, but Laird pointed out that they would have to be insulated because of the moist environment. He recommended the simpler option of track lighting with as many heads as I wanted, plus a dimmer switch.

With all the insulation, vapour barriers and tiles in place, what were the final dimensions of the cellar? Without the racking, Laird told me, it would be seven and a half by nine feet by eight feet high. I was concerned about the dramatic lowering of the ceiling: with an initial height of thirteen feet to play with, Laird had lowered it to eight. "I dropped down the ceiling because we wanted the air volume to be lessened," he explained. "I could have taken it up, but you would have been cooling space you would not be using. You only want racking up to eight feet. The logistics of trying to get wine up ten feet is very hard, especially when going up a ladder. We recommend nine feet maximum in terms of access and reach for the racking itself. When we install the racking we can put a grille over the cooling unit to match the racking and you won't see it."

The best racking allows maximum air circulation around the bottles. Laird recommended racking for single bottles at the top that allows each bottle to be cradled between cleats, with a gap behind the racking to allow air to circulate. The material we chose was California redwood, a non-aromatic softwood accustomed to high levels of humidity. According to Laird, California redwood does not warp, twist or swell as much as other woods and is the industry standard.

So what was the price estimate for all of this? Built to spec with the racking system I had chosen, the final bill would be about $25,000. You can buy a lot of wine for that—but I wanted my cellar. We had gone this far, so I commissioned Laird to do the architectural drawings (see pages 294 and 296). Then, disaster. The economy took a nosedive, and with it the investment money I had planned to use to pay for the project. By this time Deborah and I had moved into our condo and my wines were safely stored off-site at the Fine Wine Reserve. I felt bad about giving up on my dream cellar, but I still had to find somewhere to store my wines so that they would be easily accessible. I could have left them slumbering off-site, but this would entail a thirty-minute journey to pick up a few bottles whenever I needed them.

I contacted the owners of the condo building and asked them if they had another, less grandiose space that I could purchase to put in a couple of five-hundred-bottle wine cabinets rather than going to the expense of creating a climate-controlled room. There was such a space: eight feet wide, ten feet long and eight feet high, with a floor area of eighty square feet. If I were to create a proper cellar in this space there would be plenty of room for my thousand bottles—even with a tasting area—but it could also be loaded with double-deep racking to accommodate up to two thousand bottles.

However, after a chat with Gary Larose of Rosehill Wine Cellars, I learned that you can't just stick a wine cabinet in a room and plug it in. You need proper ventilation, and if the cabinet is in an unheated parking area, winter temperatures could require a heater on a thermostat to keep the bottles from freezing (for the consequences of fine wines being subjected to the rigours of winter, see page 76). Given that, I thought I might as well revert to the original plan and build a real cellar in the space I had purchased. The research I had done with Laird Kay and the Wine Establishment had given me solutions to the problems of situating a wine cellar in a condo basement—information I could put to good use.

I contacted an old friend of mine, Michael Drobot. In 1983 he had opened a business called Vintage Keeper, specializing in cooling units and wine cabinets. After I explained my predicament, Michael suggested that he could build a cellar with all the appropriate climate control and racking systems—if we could make a sort of reality-TV video simultaneously. It took me only a megasecond to agree, and his prices were the lowest I could find in the industry.

We arranged to meet at the building with Michael's engineer, designer and renovator, as well as the building's reps and lawyer. As luck would have it, Michael got stuck in China on business, so Adam Balogh, a professional engineer and Michael's VP, came to the meeting instead, armed with a camera to document the site so he could fill in the details for Michael later. Soon after, I received this e-mail:

Tony: I talked to Adam this morning about your project. It sounds like a lot of fun and we should be able to provide you with an environment where you might even spend some idle time. I asked Adam to contact the construction foreman and let him know not to change the door other than to provide a ½″ clearance at the bottom to allow for the tile or granite or whatever you prefer. There is no need to insulate concrete that is more than 10 feet underground. It stays 50 degrees year round. I would propose that we give you [a] 48″-high combination (individual bottle and bin style) all heart redwood racking placed on a 5″ approx. base faced with redwood base moulding, using standard corner units to turn the corners. We could include some ambient hidden lighting if you wish.

Adam will arrange to shoot the first stages. We will also document the construction of the inner drywall, bases, moulding, etc. By that time we could install and film the installation of the redwood. By the way, we will install two cooling systems one on each wall. If one should ever fail, the other will kick in. You will be able to monitor the temperatures from outside the room as you pass by each night. Regards, Michael

Michael also asked me to give him a sense of what kind of lighting, flooring, tables and other decorative touches I wanted. I suggested simple track lighting since the site wasn't intended to be a show cellar, but I really wanted a ledge or a small table to stand bottles on and also to be able to accommodate a few magnums and champagnes in the slots. We ended up choosing gunmetal-grey tiles for the floor and dramatic black for the walls, to show off the bottles when light is thrown behind them and spotted in front from the overhead track.

Michael convinced me that the space should be handsome, "even if it is only yourself who gets to see the show!"

A few days later I received a three-dimensional computer model of the proposed cellar from Adam, with some preliminary layouts of racking with a capacity of about 1,500 to 2,000 bottles. After I showed off the diorama of the cellar to one of the building engineers, he expressed some concern about keeping it warm during the winter. As always, Michael had the answer:

Tony: Of course we will be adding an automatic temperature-controlled heater that will turn on whenever the cellar goes below 50 degrees. It will warm the cellar to the set point. The temperature of the soil 10 feet below grade is a constant 10 degrees C throughout the planet including the Arctic. This is why we left your floor without insulation. For most of the year the soil will help to cool your cellar.

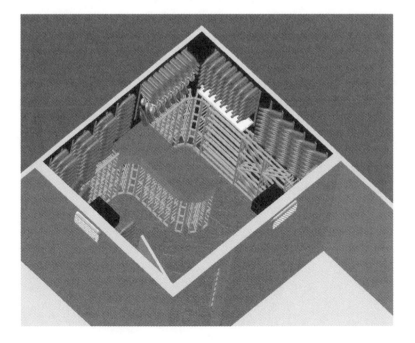

There should be an absolute minimum of power use for this cellar except from August through September when the soil heats to its peak above the 10 foot level and penetrates to a lower level. Regards, Michael

Michael Drobot's crew began work in February 2009, with Michael managing to keep on top of the project from Shanghai. His plant manager supervised the construction and arranged for installation of the drywall, tile, lighting, insulation (foil-backed urethane), a temperature-controlled heater for the winter, base and crown moulding and the table inset, as well as painting. Most of the materials were assembled at the shop and delivered to the cellar site on the day of installation. When the installation was finished in March, it took only a few hours to install the racking.

I finally have my cellar, and it looks spectacular! And it really is a show cellar after all with its black marble counter, two stools and a variety of display racking, from the conventional California redwood slots to innovative wall-mounted plastic cradles. There are slots for half-bottles (I have lots of icewine and Late Harvest Rieslings), slots for larger bottles and magnums and sections for wooden cases. Now the imperative is to fill it with wine—gaps in the racks look like a smile with teeth missing. I've also had a special lock fitted and an alarm system put in to scare off any unwanted visitors wielding corkscrews.

I now have my dream cellar and it's large enough for two to taste in. I am a happy man.

GLOSSARY: WINE VOCABULARY

Certain wine terms may be unfamiliar to those who have a casual interest in the subject. Some of these words are technical, others are wine descriptors. Together they form a language that is the shorthand of the winemaking industry. There is also a vocabulary that experts use among themselves to describe the bouquet, taste, style and health of a wine. You may come across some of these descriptions on wine lists, or they may crop up on "shelf-talkers" and other promotional blurbs at your local liquor store. Don't be put off by the jargon; it's really only a shorthand way of describing the wine.

TECHNICAL TERMS

ACETIC: describes evident acidity that gives the wine a sharp, sour taste.

AFTERTASTE: the flavour that remains on the palate after you have swallowed the wine. A gauge of quality is how long the flavour lasts. By the same token, the aftertaste of a wine can be poor if it is overly acidic or tannic.

ALCOHOLIC: an alcoholic wine is one that feels heavy in the mouth and hot as it goes down your throat. You can see a wine is high in alcohol by swirling the glass; the transparent film of liquid left on the sides of the glass will be thick and slow-moving as it falls back to the surface of the wine.

ALEMBIC: a pot still used for distilling wine into brandy. The term derives from the Arabic word *al-anbiq*, meaning "a still."

AMPELOGRAPHER: someone who studies grapevines.

BLEED: the French call it *saigner*: to bleed off juice from the fermenting vats to intensify the colour of red wines. The bled-off juice is usually bottled as a rosé.

BRETT: the short form for *Brettanomyces*, considered a flaw by New World vinters. Evident in European wines and agreeable at low levels, at higher levels this yeast can impart a barnyard note to the wine.

BRIX: the measure of the sugar content of grape juice. In Canada it usually varies between 19 and 25, depending on ripeness. Halving the Brix reading will give you a rough guide to the alcoholic strength of the fermented wine.

CANOPY MANAGEMENT: balancing the vines to produce more concentrated flavours in the grapes. Various pruning techniques are used, including debudding, shoot positioning and leaf removal.

CARBONIC MACERATION: a technique first used in Beaujolais to make light, fruity red wines that can be consumed young. Whole uncrushed grape clusters are placed in a closed stainless steel vat or an open wood fermenter. The weight of the top grapes presses down on those below, breaking their skins and starting fermentation. The fermentation jumps in a chain reaction to each of the berries and occurs inside the skins. Very little tannin is extracted this way, and when the grapes are lightly pressed after a few days, the wine can be consumed within a matter of weeks. This is how Beaujolais Nouveau is made.

CHAIS: the French term for a barrel cellar.

CLONAL SELECTION: selecting the best plants in a vineyard to propagate in order to improve the quality and yield of fruit from the vine.

COOPERAGE: the place where barrels are made; also the collective noun for barrels.

CRU: a French term that denotes where the wine was grown. In 1855 the Bordeaux wine merchants classified the region's best wine into five growths: First Growth, Second Growth, Third Growth, etc.

CUVERIE: the French term for where wine is made, usually underground in Europe, or in a temperature-controlled building in contemporary facilities.

GRAVITY FEED (or FLOW): a winery uses the force of gravity to transport its grapes and wine from one process to the next instead of subjecting them to the pressure of pumping, which can compromise flavour. This means that the grapes are received at the top of the winery and fed by their own weight into the crusher; the juice flows into fermentation tanks below; and the wine for aging in barrels or in tanks is fed by pipes to the lowest level for aging and bottling.

LAGAR: a rectangular stone vat with metre-high walls used for foot-treading grapes in Portugal's Douro region.

MENISCUS: the surface of wine in the neck of the bottle.

MERITAGE: rhyming with *heritage*, a term coined in California in 1981 (by the winner of a competition in the *Los Angeles Times*) to denote a Bordeaux-style blend. For reds, it's a blend of Cabernet Sauvignon, Merlot and Cabernet Franc; for whites, a blend of Sauvignon Blanc and Sémillon, sometimes also with Muscadelle.

M.W.: Master of Wine—the highest academic degree you can get in the wine trade, and more difficult to obtain than a Ph.D. At the time of writing there were only 277 M.W.'s in the world.

NÉGOCIANT: a French term for a company that buys grapes, must or wine and assembles it for sale.

PHYLLOXERA: a louse that feeds on the roots of vines and ultimately kills them. Phylloxera destroyed the vineyards of Europe from the 1860s to the end of the nineteenth century. The only remedy was to graft European varieties onto resistant North American rootstock.

QWPSR: a European Union designation meaning "Quality Wines Produced in Specific Regions"—a level up from simple table wines.

REVERSE OSMOSIS: an electronic process for removal of alcohol or acetic acid from wine to bring it down to regulatory levels.

ROTARY FERMENTATION: the use of horizontal fermentation tanks that rotate slowly to ensure maximum skin contact with juice to extract more colour for red wines, especially Pinot Noir.

TENTING: a technique developed in cold growing regions during the winter and early spring to protect the vines, which are covered with sheets of plastic secured over the lowest trellising wire.

VIN DE PAILLE: "straw wine," a concentrated sweet dessert wine made from dried grapes. Originally they were left to dry on straw mats, hence the name.

WINE-TASTING TERMS

AROMA: basically the smell of the grapes in freshly made wine; in other words, the recognizable perfume of a specific grape variety. **BOUQUET**, on the other hand, is the smell of wine that has aged in the bottle and become more complex.

AROMATIC: think of a rich, spicy perfume that pervades the taste of the wine as well as its bouquet. Good examples are Gewürztraminer and Muscat.

ASTRINGENT: This descriptor has more to do with tactile sensation than taste. A wine that is high in tannin and acidity will leave a dry, scratchy feeling on the roof and insides of your mouth. Red Bordeaux and Barolo can be very astringent.

AUSTERE: a polite term for a wine that's really hard to drink because it lacks fruit or other pleasurable qualities. It is usually applied to expensive wine that should taste better, but because you paid a bundle for it you don't want to admit you've bought a dog. The opposite is **GENEROUS**.

BACKWARD: a wine that should have developed but hasn't; slow to mature; needs more time in the cellar.

BAKED: grapes grown in hot climates can get sunburned, especially if there is little rainfall. This can give the wines a baked character: you can taste a roasted, earthy flavour.

BALANCE: a wine is in balance when all of its components—fruit, alcohol, acidity, tannin and oak—are harmonious. If one or more of these parts predominates, the wine will be out of balance.

BARNYARD: a bouquet most characteristic of some red and white Burgundies (and Pinot Noirs and Chardonnays grown in other regions). If you have ever mucked out a stable you will know this smell—slightly rotting hay with an overtone of manure. This sounds revolting, but in a wine it has an attractive quality and is a term of praise (wine people are weird).

BARREL AGING: a winemaker can age wine in either stainless steel vats or oak barrels. Stainless steel is inert and retains the freshness of the fruit; oak, because of the presence of air, matures the wine and imparts flavours of vanilla, coconut and toast. It is more expensive to age a wine in oak than in stainless steel, and this will be reflected in the price.

BEAUJOLAIS NOUVEAU: a wine to drink young, lightly chilled. The new wine is released on the third Thursday of November (see also **CARBONIC MACERATION**).

BITTER: a taste that can result from tannin (bite into a grape pit and see how bitter it is) or from underripe grapes or grapes from young vines.

BLUSH: a style of wine made usually from Zinfandel in California. The wine has a faint tinge of pink and a perceptible sweetness. Produced in the same way as rosé, with a few hours of skin contact with the juice to extract a little colour (see also **ROSÉ**).

BODY: a wine is either light-bodied, medium-bodied or full-bodied. This is a direct result of the amount of acid in the wine and the extract from the grape. Body expresses itself as weight in the mouth.

BOTRYTIS: a fungus (official name *Botrytis cinerea*) that attacks the skins of ripened grapes in warm, humid conditions. This growth pierces the skins and allows water to evaporate from the fruit, thus concentrating the sugars and acids. The dried-out grapes look disgusting on the vine (rather like dead bats) but they make wonderfully honeyed wines such as Sauternes and Beerenauslese. Botrytis has a characteristic smell of **PETROL** (gasoline).

BOTTLE AGE: wines, unlike spirits, mature in glass bottles. They change over the years, whereas Scotch and gin remain the same. Bottle age gives wine mellowness and a more intense bouquet. Eventually a wine that has matured will begin to decline.

BOTTLE SICKNESS: there is a great difference in taste between a wine in the cask and one that has been newly bottled. The act of bottling introduces large quantities of oxygen into the wine, which initially gives off-flavours before the wine settles down after a few weeks.

BOUQUET: the smell of a wine after you pull the cork and pour some into a glass. With practice you can tell the condition of the wine as well as its taste from this smell. That's why wine waiters give you a sample in your glass before pouring for the whole table. A mature wine (one that has aged for fifteen years or more) may give off a bouquet that has nothing to do with fruits, flowers or vegetables; it can be a mixture of more organic smells such as leather, chocolate or coffee beans.

BUTTERY: a smell and a taste usually associated with oak-aged Chardonnay grown in warm climates such as California and Australia.

CAT'S PEE: a smell associated with Sauvignon Blanc wines, usually when the grapes get overripe.

CEDAR: a smell of fine red Bordeaux wines associated with the Cabernet Sauvignon grape; sometimes called "cigar box."

CHOCOLATE: a smell you can find in rich red wines, especially from the Rhône.

CLEAN: devoid of flaws, off-odours and unpleasant tastes.

COMPLEX: describes a wine that has many levels of perfume and taste sensations; in other words, an interesting and very good wine.

CORKED: describes a wine that has turned, usually because of oxidation, and smells and tastes of vinegar. Both whites and reds may have a brown hue. This has nothing to do with the cork (see also **CORKY**).

CORKY: describes a smell in the wine caused by a bad cork. A cork that is infected can change the taste of the wine, or traces of the bleaching agent used to lighten it can add a chemical flavour.

CREAMY: a sensation of wine on the palate—an unctuous fruitiness and softness found in Chardonnays grown in warm conditions.

CRISP: describes white wines with perceptible acidity, wines that refresh the palate.

DEPTH: a wine that has depth offers different levels of enjoyment, a richness of bouquet and flavour that changes in the glass.

DRY: describes a wine whose sugars have been fully fermented. There will be some residual sweetness from the fruit, but the acidity will give it a dry finish.

DUMB: a wine that has nothing to say; an undeveloped, immature wine whose bouquet and flavours are locked in. This is the oenological equivalent of a sullen adolescent.

DUSTY: describes the aftertaste and mouth feel of maturing tannins in red wines.

EARTHY: tasting of the soil, a quality found in reds from hot growing regions.

ELEGANT: describes a well-balanced wine of high quality, used mainly for lighter wines. Rich, full-bodied wines would be termed robust, meaty or some other graphic term.

EUCALYPTUS: certain Californian and Australian Cabernet Sauvignons have a bouquet of eucalyptus because the grapes were overripe. This can also manifest as a bell pepper smell.

EXTRACT: when the water in wine is removed by centrifuge, the remaining solids are the dry extract. The concentration of flavour depends on how much dry extract there is.

FAT: describes a weight-challenged wine, full of alcohol and extract, heavy on the palate, overly rich. This can be a compliment or a criticism, depending on context.

FINESSE: a synonym for elegance, describing a wine whose elements are perfectly in harmony.

FINISH: the final taste of the wine; the sensory impression left in the mouth once you have swallowed it.

FIRM: describes a wine that has structure, thanks to its acidity; the opposite of **FLABBY**.

FIRST GROWTH: this does not refer to anything that happens in the vineyard. It is a designation of quality for Bordeaux wines. In 1855 the wines of Médoc and Graves were divided according to price and quality into five growths (*crus*); First Growths are the top wines.

FLABBY: describes a wine that lacks acidity to give it structure and length of finish. Such a wine will taste sweet and soft on the palate and then go nowhere.

FLAT: describes a wine that simply lies there on the palate and bores you to death, with no flavour, no life in it. Also refers to a sparkling wine that has been left too long in the glass and all the bubbles have disappeared.

FLINTY: certain wines, such as Sauvignon Blanc grown in cool climates, can have a bouquet reminiscent of struck flint—slightly smoky.

FLORAL: smelling of flowers. You find flower smells in Riesling (spring flowers), Gewürztraminer (roses) and some reds (lilac, iris).

FORWARD: describes a young wine that shows more maturity than its age would suggest; an overachiever.

FOXY: describes the smell of wines made from Labrusca grapes (the native North American varieties such as Concord and Niagara), an unpleasant aroma that puts you in mind of a dog that's been out in the rain. The term derives from wild or "fox" grapes.

FRESH: describes a wine whose bouquet starts your mouth watering and whose taste enlivens and cleanses the palate because of its crisp acidity.

FRUITY: describes a wine with good extract that tastes of fruit—cherry, plum, gooseberry, melon, blackberry, blackcurrant, etc.

FULL-BODIED: describes a high-alcohol wine that feels rich and weighty in the mouth.

GENEROUS: richly extracted fruit, a mouth-filling wine experience.

GERANIUM: one flower you do not want to smell in a wine. Its unpleasant odour indicates a microbiological fault in the wine, induced during fermentation.

GRAPEY: certain wines taste exactly like the fresh grapes they were made from—Muscat and Muscadelle are prime examples.

GREEN: describes wines that taste immature either because the grapes were not ripe enough at harvest or the vines were still young.

GRIP: a wine with grip has a real presence that asserts itself on the palate, especially tannic wines such as young Cabernet Sauvignon.

HARD: describes a wine with excessive tannin that will take several years' bottle age to soften up, such as Barolo and red Bordeaux.

HERBACEOUS: smelling of freshly cut grass and flowers; used of young white wines, particularly Sauvignon Blanc.

HONEYED: sweet wines take on a honey-like bouquet with age. You can smell honey in Sauternes, old Late Harvest Rieslings and icewines.

LEGS: when a glass is swirled, the liquid alcohol clings to the sides of the glass and eventually falls back to the surface of the wine in tears or "legs." The Germans call this phenomenon *Kirchfenster*, or "church windows," which they resemble. The thickness of the legs and the speed at which they move give you an indication of the wine's alcoholic strength. The slower the legs, the higher the alcohol.

LENGTH: the staying power of a wine's aftertaste. The longer you can taste it, the better the wine.

LIGHT: lacking body (alcohol) but not necessarily flavour. The wines of the Mosel in Germany are light but have wonderfully rich Riesling flavours.

LUSCIOUS: a term used to describe dessert wines when the sweetness, creaminess and softness are balanced with enough acidity to keep the wine from cloying on the palate.

MADERIZED: comes from the *Madeira*. When white wines get too old, they begin to turn brown and taste like Madeira—slightly oxidized, flat and tinny.

MEDIUM DRY: describes a wine that has perceptible sweetness but finishes dry. Examples include some Vouvray, Chenin Blanc and Riesling Spätlese.

MEDIUM SWEET: one level above medium dry on the sweetness scale. Examples include Riesling Auslese and Picolit.

MUST: the juice of white grapes or the juice and skins of black grapes before fermentation.

MUSTY: describes the smell of a dank cellar, usually associated with a bad cork or a dirty barrel.

NOBLE ROT: an easier name for the benign disease *Botrytis cinerea* (see **BOTRYTIS**).

NOSE: the smell of a wine; its bouquet or aroma.

OAKY: describes the smell and taste of oak in a wine, which is especially apparent when the oak is new. The smells and flavours can range from vanilla and coconut to spices such as nutmeg and cloves.

OFF-DRY: describes a wine that has some residual sweetness but finishes dry. Examples include German Rieslings and most white house blends.

OXIDIZED: describes a wine that has been exposed to air, rendering it flat and prune-like in taste.

PÉTILLANT: French for slightly sparkling but not visibly so; a sensation of bubbles on the tongue from dissolved carbon dioxide gas; for example, in young Riesling.

PETROL: yes, this means the smell of gasoline. It's the characteristic smell of aging Riesling, and very appealing too.

PLONK: a humorous name for a simple, everyday quaffing wine.

RACY: describes a fresh, light white wine with stimulating acidity; for example, Mosel Riesling.

ROSÉ: a pink wine, either dry or semi-sweet, made from red grapes. The newly pressed grape juice is left in contact with the skins for a matter of hours to extract the colour desired by the winemaker.

SHORT: describes a wine whose flavour suddenly drops out, a wine with no discernible finish, usually as a result of rain during the harvest, which swells the grapes and dilutes the fruit and sugars.

SOFT: describes a wine that has mellowed with age. Sweet wines also have a softness because the sugar masks their acidity.

SPICY: describes an exotic spiciness like cardamom, found particularly in Gewürztraminer.

SPRITZIG: a German term describing the prickling on the tongue from wines that have bound-in carbon dioxide (see also PÉTILLANT).

STEMMY: describes the green, bitter taste of grape stems that cause excess tannin in the wine.

SULPHUR: Sulphur and sulphur compounds are used to prevent oxidation and to kill off any bacteria in wine. In France barrels are cleaned by burning sulphur sticks inside them.

SULPHURY: describes the smell of sulphur in wine that has been overly treated with sulphur products. Up to thirty parts per million of sulphur is barely detectable on the nose; more than that and you get a burnt matchhead smell.

TANNIN: an astringent, bitter-tasting compound that occurs naturally in the skins, stalks and pits of grapes. Wood tannins are present in oak barrels too. Tannin acts as a preservative, allowing a red wine to age gracefully. Eventually the tannin will precipitate out and fall to the bottom of the bottle as fine sediment.

TART: describes a wine that is high in acidity, usually because of unripe grapes.

ULLAGE: the head space between the business end of the cork and the meniscus of the wine. Any more than an inch of ullage is a signal that the wine may be oxidized.

VANILLA: the smell and taste of new oak, especially evident in Australian wines.

VARIETAL: a single grape type whose name will appear on the label in New World wines. Examples include Chardonnay, Merlot and Pinot Gris.

VINEGAR: if a wine smells of vinegar, send it back. It's over the hill.

VOLATILE ACIDITY: too much and the wine begins to smell and taste like balsamic vinegar. All wines contain some volatile acidity, but excessive amounts indicate that the wine is starting to turn to vinegar.

WEIGHT: how the wine feels in the mouth—the heavier on the palate, the more alcohol. Weightier wines come from the hotter growing regions, where sunshine can build up grape sugars.

WOODY: describes a wine that has been kept too long in oak, imparting a woody flavour.

BIBLIOGRAPHY

Aspler, Tony. *The Wine Atlas of Canada*. Toronto: Random House Canada, 2006.

Beckett, Neil, ed. *1001 Wines You Must Taste Before You Die*. New York: Universe, 2008.

Brook, Stephen. *Liquid Gold: Dessert Wines of the World*. London: Constable, 1987.

Cooper, Michael. *Wine Atlas of New Zealand*. Auckland: Hodder Moa, 2008.

Cox, Jeff. *Cellaring Wine*. North Adams, MA: Storey Publishing, 2003.

D'Agata, Ian. *The Ecco Guide to the Best Wines of Italy*. New York: HarperCollins, 2008.

Gold, Richard M. *How and Why to Build a Wine Cellar*, 4th ed. San Francisco: Wine Appreciation Guild, 2007.

Goldberg, Howard G. *All About Wine Cellars*. Philadelphia: Running Press, 2003.

Halliday, James. *Australian Wine Companion*. Prahan, Victoria: Hardie Grant Books, 2008.

The Internet Movie Database. "Trivia for *Sideways*." http://www.imdb.com/title/tt0375063/trivia

Kumar, Mahesh. *Wine Investment for Portfolio Diversification*. San Francisco: Wine Appreciation Guild, 2005.

Meltzer, Peter D. *Keys to the Cellar: Strategies and Secrets of Wine Collecting*. Hoboken, NJ: John Wiley, 2006.

Metcalfe, Charles, and Kathryn McWhirter. *The Wine and Food Lover's Guide to Portugal*. London: Inn House Publishing, 2008.

Sims, Perry. *The Home Wine Cellar: A Complete Guide to Design and Construction*. Philadelphia: Running Press, 2004.

Smith, Jeff. *The Best Cellar*. Los Angeles: Volt Press, 2006.

Sokolin, David, and Alexandra Bruce. *Investing in Liquid Assets: Uncorking Profits in Today's Global Wine Market*. New York: Simon & Schuster, 2008.

Stevenson, Tom. *Wine Report 2004–2009*. London: Dorling Kindersley,

Stewart-Wilson, Mary. *Queen Mary's Dolls' House*. London: Ebury Press, 1955.

Taber, George M. *To Cork or Not to Cork: Tradition, Romance, Science and the Battle for the Wine Bottle*. New York: Scribner, 2007.

van Zyl, Philip, ed. *Platter's South African Wines 2009*. Cape Town: Newsome McDowall, 2009.

Wallace, Benjamin. *The Billionaire's Vinegar*. New York: Crown Publishers, 2008.

Woodmorappe, John. *Noah's Ark: A Feasibility Study*. Dallas: Institute for Creation Research, 1996.

Younger, William. *Gods, Men and Wine*. London: Wine & Food Society, 1966.

Image Credits

INDEX

TONY ASPLER has been writing about wine for more than thirty years and today he is the most widely respected wine writer in Canada. He was the wine columnist for the *Toronto Star* for over twenty years and has authored fourteen books on wine and food. He writes for a number of international wine magazines and co-founded the charitable foundation Grapes for Humanity. In December 2007 he was awarded the Order of Canada. Tony lives in Toronto. Visit his website at www.tonyaspler.com.